Cambridge Studies in Management

10

Debating coal closures

Cambridge Studies in Management

Formerly Management and Industrial Relations series

Editors
WILLIAM BROWN, *University of Cambridge*
ANTHONY HOPWOOD, *London School of Economics*
and PAUL WILLMAN, *London Business School*

The series focuses on the human and organisational aspects of management. It covers the areas of organisation theory and behaviour, strategy and business policy, the organisational and social aspects of accounting, personnel and human resource management, industrial relations and industrial sociology.

The series aims for high standards of scholarship and seeks to publish the best among original theoretical and empirical research; innovative contributions to advancing understanding in the area; books which synthesize and/or review the best of current research, and aim to make the work published in specialist journals more widely accessible; and texts for upper-level undergraduates, for graduates and for vocational courses such as MBA programmes. Edited collections may be accepted where they maintain a high and consistent standard and are on a coherent, clearly-defined, and relevant theme."

The books are intended for an international audience among specialists in universities and business schools, undergraduate, graduate and MBA students, and also for a wider readership among business practitioners and trade unionists.

Other books in the series:

Debating coal closures

Economic calculation in the coal dispute 1984–5

Edited by

DAVID COOPER

Price Waterhouse Professor of Accounting and Finance, University of Manchester Institute of Science and Technology

and

TREVOR HOPPER

*Lecturer in Accounting,
University of Manchester*

*The right of the
University of Cambridge
to print and sell
all manner of books
was granted by
Henry VIII in 1534.
The University has printed
and published continuously
since 1584.*

CAMBRIDGE UNIVERSITY PRESS

Cambridge

New York   New Rochelle   Melbourne   Sydney

CAMBRIDGE UNIVERSITY PRESS
Cambridge, New York, Melbourne, Madrid, Cape Town, Singapore,
São Paulo, Delhi, Dubai, Tokyo

Cambridge University Press
The Edinburgh Building, Cambridge CB2 8RU, UK

Published in the United States of America by Cambridge University Press, New York

www.cambridge.org
Information on this title: www.cambridge.org/9780521125970

First published 1988
This digitally printed version 2009

A catalogue record for this publication is available from the British Library

Library of Congress Cataloguing in Publication data
Debating coal closures: economic calculation in the coal dispute
1984–85 / edited by David Cooper and Trevor Hopper.
      p.   cm. – (Cambridge studies in management: 10)
Includes index.
ISBN 0 521 32861 6
1. Coal trade – Great Britian – Accounting. 2. Coal trade – Great
Britain – Cost effectiveness. 3. Coal Strike. Great Britian,
1984–1985.
I. Cooper, David (David J.). II. Hopper, Trevor, 1946–   .
III. Series.
HD9551.5.D39 1988
338.2'3–dc19   87-24634 CIP

ISBN 978-0-521-32861-6 Hardback
ISBN 978-0-521-12597-0 Paperback

Contents

Contents

1

Introduction: Financial calculation in industrial and political debate

D. J. COOPER and T. M. HOPPER

This collection of articles addresses the issue of the role of accounting and economic calculation in industrial conflict. All the articles contributed to a debate during one of the most intense industrial conflicts in the UK in recent times. This book is concerned to explore the manner and effect of interventions by economists and accountants in such conflict. The articles and reports, reproduced here (together with postscripts) for the first time, all focus on one such dispute – the 1984/5 coal strike in the UK.[1]

This specific focus has certain advantages. It is possible to compare and contrast the commentaries and thereby identify alternative perspectives to the underlying economic and accounting issues raised in them. Thus one purpose of this introduction is to provide a guide to these individual contributions, highlighting three underlying issues, namely accountancy calculations, economic calculations and management and energy policies. These three issues are general to all firms and industries in relation to the identification and measurement of enterprise performance. The contributions in this book raise questions about, for example, the adequacy of accounting reports in reflecting economic conditions, the assessment of managerial strategies to invest in new technologies and to rely on economies of scale, the differences between short- and long-term strategies and the conflict between national and enterprise interests (and how these interests are constructed). A focus on the NCB (now renamed British Coal) enables these issues to be addressed in the context of a detailed understanding of one industry. The first section of this introduction highlights the contrasting positions regarding these issues.

A second advantage of the focus on one dispute is that it is thereby possible to consider the effects of these contributions in general to the progress and outcome of the dispute. It is possible to consider the impact (if any) of these interventions in the conflict. This raises issues concerning the interrelationships between politics, industrial muscle and calculative logics in industrial relations. What were the effects of these contributions – which offered various financial calculations or challenged the calculations of others – in terms of the outcome of the industrial relations conflict? In short, using the insights of Foucault (1980), a study of the contributions in this book, taken together, provides an illuminating example of the relationship between knowledge and power. The second section of this introduction explores these themes.

Themes in the contributions

A prominent theme in modern industry concerns closures, rationalisations and change in activity. These rearrangements may be more difficult to implement in recessionary conditions and it is in these conditions that increased concern is placed on the purposes and calculations that both underlie and legitimise proposed changes. The miners' strike of 1984/5, based as it was on proposed plant (or colliery) closures, is the most prominent example of this stimulus to discussions and calculations. In this section we explore accounting, economic and strategic issues raised in various reports and studies written by academic accountants and economists, and which gained the most prominence by that conflict.

The significance of the reports

These reports are of an enduring interest for at least three reasons. Most immediately the arguments contained in the papers included in this book were used sometimes explicitly, sometimes implicitly, by the participants in the dispute – the government, the National Coal Board and the National Union of Mineworkers, and on occasion were discussed in the press and in the media. After all, the strike was triggered off by the NCB's announcement of the closure of five allegedly 'uneconomic' pits and the protracted negotiations between the NUM and the NCB during the dispute centred on the extent to which 'economic' criteria should be brought into decisions about pit closure, and what should be the parameters of 'economic'. While the debate about precisely how accounting and economic analysis should be brought to bear on the issue of pit closure took several months to start, it played some role in the public discussion especially in the later months of the dispute and in the coal producing areas most likely to face closures. Moreover, the issue did not end with the dispute. The argument about pit closures and the reorganisation of the industry, both in the UK and in the EEC more generally, has continued.

Financial calculation

The second respect in which the analyses presented here are of more than ephemeral interest concerns the relationship between profitability and economic value. This issue is relevant to a much wider arena than the coal industry. The extent to which, and the circumstances in which, the market criterion of profit is a reliable measure of economic benefit is a fundamental issue in economic management. Clarification of it is of the greatest importance if adequate responses are to be developed to the problem of mass unemployment, sensible investment strategies and the crisis of the economy in the UK and elsewhere. On the one side it is argued that it is necessary to purge the economy of all unprofitable activities if growth and fuller employment are to be restored. On the other it is argued that the economy benefits from the contribution of all available resources, whether or not these activities are deemed profitable by the market.

Such divergent positions are based on entirely different views as to how the economy works. They illustrate in a sharp way the diametrically opposed conclusions about an apparently down-to-earth and practical matter, to which different theoretical positions lead. The major differences between the studies in Part I do not rest on mistakes of logic made by one or other participant. Economics or accounting is not simply a matter of applying a self-evident set of theoretical propositions to the case at hand. The relationship between enterprise profit and economic value depends on assumptions about the workings of the economy.

The relationship between economic and accounting calculations of profit is also crucial, particularly when accounting reports are treated as objective and truthful. The truth is constructed according to a set of accounting conventions, many of which have little connection with economic concepts of profit. Whilst this may be well known to accountants and those economists who have occasion to use accounting statements (Inflation Accounting Committee, 1975; Whittington, 1983), what is less well appreciated is that accounting reports help to constitute the legal boundaries of the enterprise. This may be illustrated by the debates which have taken place concerning the European Commission's 7th Directive on Company Law (1983). In effect, this directive sought to achieve standardised practice in the EEC concerning the boundary of an enterprise and required that the activities of subsidiary companies be consolidated (or incorporated) into those of the parent. Such legal and accounting regulations highlight the contrived, and essentially contestable, nature of what is external and what is internal to the enterprise. This debate about the boundaries of an enterprise – what should or should not be treated as external costs – had resonances in the debates on the NCB's finances.

3

Introduction

The third enduring contribution of this book is its analysis of management policy. The NCB is an example of a large organisation that has invested heavily in planning (Smith, 1984) and this concern with planning and policy is no doubt related to its size, geographical dispersion and interrelationship with other industries. Indeed it was partly because of the clear failure of private enterprise to consider such issues that led to the nationalisation of coal in 1947. As the contributions in Parts II and III of this book indicate, issues of coal closures were debated in the context of energy, regional and investment policy. Crudely put, the issues were about coal versus nuclear power, the role of Scottish, Welsh and other 'peripheral' regions and whether investment in new technology should be used to control labour and save jobs or to create safe employment. It is likely that the investment and product appraisal and marketing strategy of the coal industry will remain a part of public discussion whatever the focus of control. Thus it is illuminating that recent calls to privatise the coal industry (Robinson and Marshall, 1985; Boyfield, 1985) fail to address issues of the interdependence of industries, regional policy and investment strategies and energy policy except for a faith in the rationality of free markets and a silence about the distributional effects of free market solutions. Thus this book should contribute to debates about the role of planning and managerial strategies in a modern interconnected economy. These debates extend well beyond the coal industry and whilst they are currently most pronounced in the public sector, especially the nationalised industries, there is little reason not to expect the advocates of free markets and the anti-planners to extend their attack on large enterprises such as Hanson Trust, ICI and Shell.

These three reasons why the reports in this book are of enduring interest – a concern for history, exploring the relationship between economic and accounting calculations and the role of strategic considerations – structure the rest of this section of the introduction. The presentation of the history of the debates is not explicitly covered partly because the mere act of collecting the reports together may be sufficient. Further, these debates continue (most recently the First Report from the Energy Committee, 1986–7) and it does not seem opportune to produce a separate history of their writing (although for one such attempt see Berry *et al.*, 1986).

In outlining the contents of this book, this section is divided into three parts. The first two deal with accounting and economic calculations as discussed in Part I of this book and the third with issues of strategy and policy, as presented in Parts II and III of this book. More specifically the first deals with what we term 'accounting' problems, whether the NCB's accounts both at national and pit level provide a satisfactory basis for assessing the financial position of the industry and the returns from particular pits. Next we deal with the broader 'economic' issues of the extent to which profit to the NCB (correctly assessed) is an indicator of economic benefit to society. Lastly we deal with the 'industry' or 'energy policy' issues relating to the development of the coal industry in a broader context.

The accounting issues

The government frequently justified the need to do something about 'uneconomic pits' by the overall operating loss of the NCB (£358 million in 1983/4) and in particular the size of total government subsidies (£1.34 billion) to the industry.[2] It was pointed out by Glyn during the strike, and Woolf after it, that the figure for operating loss was misleading due to the inclusion of costs, such as pensions to retired miners and payments by the NCB in respect of subsidence, which were not actually part of the current costs of producing coal. A further reason why the total government subsidy was so high was because the capital structure of the NCB meant that interest payments represented a disproportionate burden as compared to other industries (the NCB having no share capital and associated dividends, where the latter are not considered a cost but an appropriation from profits). Finally, the remaining portion of the government subsidy, representing the social costs of pit closure, again should not be seen as part of the current costs of production of coal; nor was there any reason why they necessarily should be financed by the industry. It was pointed out in reply that part of subsidence payments which represented prudent provision for future payments as a result of the current year's mining (rather than the sudden rush of claims which was reflected in the enormous figure of £245 million in 1983/4) should indeed be regarded as an operating cost. Apart from this, the reservations expressed about an over-simplistic interpretation of 'operating loss' or 'government subsidy' did not meet with much disagreement, although confusion still arose. Thus even the prime minister regarded the subsidy as a 'matter of fact', rather than the product of legal and accounting conventions and price negotiations between the NCB and the Central Electricity Generating Board (CEGB).

Accounting for the costs of production, the profitability of individual pits and the issue of individual pit closure was discussed by Berry *et al.* (published in *Accountancy* in January 1985, but widely discussed in draft form for several weeks before that). This criticised the NCB's use of cost and profit figures for individual collieries as a basis for deciding whether individual pits were 'economic' or not. The theme of this paper is the arbitrary, and indeed manipulable, nature of both the proceeds and costs side of the pit accounting statements. The price received by the NCB for most of its coal is a transfer price negotiated with another nationalised industry; an individual pit's proceeds depends heavily on its production budget and on the mixing of coal types. On the cost side, important items are arbitrarily allocated between pits; historic cost depreciation and other overheads which would not be saved by pit closure are irrelevant to decisions about whether pits should be kept open. Finally, the paper emphasises that decisions should be based, not on past results, but on predications about the future, when mining conditions may be entirely different.

Subsequent contributions, produced after the coal dispute and not included in this book, have elaborated the analysis in relation to costs (Custis *et al.*, 1985) and to revenues (Kerevan *et al.*, 1985). The report by Custis *et al.*, commissioned by the NCB in the light of the article by Berry *et al.*, whilst not surprisingly critical of Berry *et al.*, nevertheless indicates that only those cost items which are variable should be taken into account when assessing pit closures. In appendixes 4 and 5 of their report they provide a considerable volume of material about the variability of overhead costs, both in the colliery and at area and national head-quarters. The report by Kerevan *et al.*, commissioned by the British Labour Group in the European parliament in response to the EEC Coal Directorate's close and import plan of 1985, demonstrates the fragility of the so-called 'world price' for coal. Most of the coal available at that time appeared to be being dumped below long-run cost or was from South Africa. Further, the price for such coal depends critically on currency exchange rates and international shipping rates. Accounting statements typically do not distinguish fixed from variable costs and incorporate revenue figures based on administered, negotiated prices related to this notional world price for coal.

These accounting commentaries, found in Berry *et al.* and in parts of Glyn, threw doubt on uninformed use of accounting statements of profit or loss and, in effect, challenged the way NCB management justified their assessments of pit profitability. It is unfortunate that the shift in the NCB's planning criteria – based on production costs per gigagoule (a measure of heat output) – do not seem to acknowledge the force of the accounting arguments about full costing and the irrelevance of historic costs. Of course, the accounting arguments were two-sided and while they called for wider public discussion of the NCB Annual Report and Accounts and the role of accounting statements in investment (and divestment) decisions, they did not in general seem to imply that pits should not be closed. For example it could be that more refined consideration of what price should be put on coal would argue for a lower rather than a higher price (making colliery losses worse). Fuller consideration of how output allocations were carried out might show that Area managers were protecting weaker pits. The distinction between operating costs and avoidable costs, however, emphasises that pit accounts were giving a systematically misleading picture by suggesting much greater savings from pit closure than would actually eventuate since depreciation, Area and HQ expenses and so forth, allocated to individual pits, would still have to be borne elsewhere.

In general, then, the discussion over accounting questions took the financial position of the NCB as its frame of reference and argued about whether the information used to justify pit closures gave a reliable indication of the impact of closure on the NCB's financial position (or indeed on the financial position of the nationalised industries in total, if the important point about transfer pricing of coal within the public sector is borne in mind). Accounting statements are of considerable significance in that they help constitute the terms and nature of the debate about pit profitability. These issues will be returned to in the second section of this introduction when we consider the general effects and significance of the discourse in industrial relations.

The economic issues

The economic debate – notably between Davies and Metcalf, Minford and Kung, Glyn and Robinson (in order of their availability, if not publication) – raised the fundamental question of the extent to which financial calculation about profit to the NCB did represent the correct way to calculate whether the pit was making an economic contribution to society as a whole.

It is worth recalling at the outset the basic argument in favour of regarding the profit which an enterprise makes from the use of resources as a true indicator of the net benefit to society from that activity. Under what conditions is the equation of 'profitable' with 'economic', which was taken as axiomatic in government and NCB statements about 'uneconomic' pits, actually valid?

The matter hinges entirely on the question of opportunity cost. The opportunity cost of using resources in one enterprise is the value of production which is foregone by society by those resources being so used. If the costs which the enterprise actually incurs correctly measure the opportunity cost to society, then any excess of the enterprise's proceeds over these costs represents the market value of the extra benefit to society from that use. Since this excess is the enterprise's profit there is a one-to-one equation between profit and net benefit to society.

A simple example may help to clarify the point. Suppose a miner is paid £150 per week and that miners' pay represents the only cost to the pit. If he produces £100 of coal then the pit will make a £50 loss. If it was the case that pit closure would lead to that miner being employed elsewhere and producing goods and services to the value of £150, then society would clearly be better off if the pit closed and he moved to the other job, assuming that the 'multiplier' effect of the coal industry on the rest of the economy was not substantially different from the multiplier effect in the new job. The gain to society would be the extra £50 worth of production, precisely equal to the loss involved in his employment in the pit. Implicit therefore in the identification of 'profitable' and 'economic' is the assumption that money costs represent opportunity costs, and that money proceeds are a correct measure of the value of production.

But how could this not be the case? Economics textbooks are conscientious in pointing out instances of 'market failure', where costs or benefits may not be taken into account in market prices. A relevant one would be the 'externality' of coal-mining which causes subsidence and therefore costs to people living in the area. Such costs are a real cost of getting the coal and should (as argued earlier) be taken into account in calculations of profit. But the crucial 'market failure' at issue in the debate about 'uneconomic' pits is not a case of externalities at all. Rather it concerns the much more basic assumption of whether there is any opportunity cost at all from resources being used in the coal industry in a situation where the market fails to ensure that resources released from one industry are absorbed into another.

Assume in the above example that if the pit was closed the miner would become unemployed. Then instead of the opportunity cost of his employment in mining being £150 per week it is actually zero. Society would not benefit by £50 more production if the miner transferred to another industry. On the contrary the £100 worth of coal would be foregone and nothing received in exchange, not to mention the knock-on effect on suppliers, the economy more generally and the balance of payments. Even though the pit was making £50 per week loss, its continuation represented a net social benefit of £100 per week. Its closure on the basis that it was making a loss would be quite unjustified. Subsidising it would be beneficial to society as a whole.

Beneficial to whom, however? In the simple case considered above the miner is better off by £150 per week. But the extra production he contributes is only £100 per week. So the rest of society is in effect subsidising his income to the tune of £50 (precisely the subsidy the government has to pay to the mine). This could well be regarded as justifiable on grounds of income distribution, but the fact of subsidy would be an important consideration. The tax and benefit position may transform the situation, however.

Assume that the miner pays £50 per week in taxes and national insurance contributions. Suppose also that if he loses his job in the pit he received unemployment benefit of £50 per week. In that case he is only £50 per week better off at work (his take-home pay of £100 less £50 unemployment benefit). Since he contributes £100 of production, then the rest of society actually gains from the pit being kept open. This is reflected in a very clear way in government finances. Pit closures mean the loss to the government of £50 per week tax revenue and additional unemployment benefit of £50 per week. This means a deterioration in government finances of £100; as compared to this the subsidy required to keep the pit open is only £50 per week. The government (that is the taxpayers) are £50 per week better off by keeping the pit open. This is of course not necessarily the case. If the subsidy required to keep the pit open was more than £100 per week then taxpayers would suffer.

Clearly, this example of why calculations of private profitability may diverge from public benefit depends on the recognition of idle resources with zero opportunity costs. It is not an analysis that is specific to the coal industry and indeed 'many would consider the argument to be more concerned with the case for selective (regional) employment subsidies' (O'Donnell, 1985, p. 110). The argument does, however, collapse in times of full employment.

However, the example highlights the differences between the four main contributors on the economic issues concerning coal closures. The calculations of the economic viability of loss-making pits depend upon two absolutely crucial assumptions. First is the question of whether the resources used in high-cost pits do in fact have an opportunity cost. Will miners find alternative employment if the pit is closed? The studies contained in this book make very different assumptions about this, and as a result come to very different conclusions. The second question is whether the proceeds attributed to the coal produced do in fact represent its value. This latter point has already been mentioned earlier in connection with transfer pricing between nationalised industries. The point is a more general one, however, because the NCB was stockpiling coal, with little prospect of finding a market for some of its production.

The view that there was no opportunity cost in employing miners was first stated by Glyn (*Guardian*, 28 May 1984), who claimed that under the prevailing circumstances 'unemployed miners would either not find a job, or if they moved to another pit or found work in another industry, this would mean that someone else would remain in the dole queue so no additional output would result to make up for the loss of coal production'. This is the assumption underlying the more detailed analysis in his paper. At the other end of the spectrum of assumptions, Minford and Kung assume not only that miners will be re-employed, but the transfer of the government subsidy to other uses will actually lead to a net increase in employment.

This issue is discussed in the Davies and Metcalf paper, which sets out in detail the real resources and opportunity costs argument. This paper also emphasises that some mechanisms have to be suggested whereby the reduction of jobs in the coal industry (and industries producing inputs for the coal industry, as Glyn points out) itself leads to the creation of extra jobs elsewhere. They suggest that miners may set up in business for themselves or that their unemployment may depress wages and lead to more jobs being created. Minford and Kung believe that the government could spend the saving in subsidy to the NCB which would create more jobs than were lost in the NCB (Robinson makes a similar point). It has also been argued that if the government operates its macroeconomic policy with a target for unemployment, then the loss of jobs in mining will be offset by other (by implication more productive) jobs elsewhere.

The conclusion is that such calculations about the resource benefits or losses for pit closure depend entirely on macroeconomic assumptions about how the economy works (or about government macroeconomic targets). Thus Minford and Kung, believing that the economy is perfectly self-equilibrating, argue for the closure of all unprofitable pits. Glyn, arguing that the economy will produce no employment gains to offset pit closures, argues that pits should be kept open to exhaustion (and that in fact in every case keeping them open will benefit government revenue as well as the miners concerned). Davies and Metcalf, believing in slow and partial self-equilibration, suggest that a staggered programme of pit closures is justified on economic grounds. These wildly different conclusions do not mean that the whole approach is somehow wrong; it rather emphasises that real attention should be focussed on the underlying assumptions.

Robinson, in relying on the 'rough justice of the market place', is in effect adopting a similar position to Minford and Kung. That is, he believes that market prices not only are reflected in the proceeds of the NCB, but he also believes that these prices are correct. We have already referred to the issue of the value to be placed on coal (see Davies and Metcalf, especially). In a situation where the NCB was overproducing coal and stockpiling at considerable expense, was it in fact right to credit 'marginal' pits, which would be closed if capacity was reduced, with average proceeds from coal? It was argued for example that the correct valuation was the 'world price', which was the price at which such coal could be sold overseas, or indeed at which marginal supplies could be imported if capacity was cut back. Use of such an elusive variable as the world price, subject to many fluctuations in a notoriously thin market, has its drawbacks. Added to which it was argued that expansionary policies by the government would provide an adequate market. But still, any reduction in the proceeds credited to such marginal pits would increase their losses, and make it less likely that resource considerations would justify their being kept open. These debates draw attention to the crucial effects of the choice of the 'counterfactual' against which to assess the impact of pit closure. The appropriate counterfactual (such as marginal coal being exported cheap or being beneficially used in an expanding economy) is open to serious argument.

Two other economic considerations were raised in the discussion. Davies and Metcalf pointed out that closing pits would imply that some miners' families moved homes, with consequent waste of social capital (houses lying idle, public facilities underused etc.). This was an additional cost of closure, at any rate unless alternative jobs were provided. An important point to note here is that despite the issue being 'social capital' it is an entirely 'economic' question. The tendency to treat anything other than narrow profit and loss as 'social' (and thus implicitly non-economic and carrying implications of special pleading) bedevilled much discussion. Of course many social considerations connected with destruction of communities were raised in the dispute. But the issues discussed in this section, over real resource costs and waste, are thoroughly economic.

The other point concerns the special feature of coal as a non-renewable resource. Schumacher's objection to closing pits before the mine-able reserves were exhausted, because this would sterilise reserves of coal, was often quoted, but not developed. It was merely pointed out that it was treating subsequent generations doubly shabbily if not only were all the best coal seams exploited, but less good reserves were rendered prohibitively expensive to recover due to premature pit closure. This leads us beyond general economic considerations as they were applied in the dispute, and on to more specific debates about the history of the coal industry – how and why it had reached the position it faced in 1984. Indeed this is a weakness of all the articles which focus on economic and accounting calculations. Apart from Robinson's more general contribution to energy policy in Part III of this book, the authors did not address the issue of why there were, in 1984, so many high-cost and, by conventional calculations, unprofitable collieries.

Introduction

The context of the debates: regional, energy and management policy

As the strike progressed, greater attention began to be paid to the relation between 'economic pits', past policies of the NCB management, and then energy policy more generally. These issues were, explicitly and implicitly, examined in the Monopolies and Mergers Commission Report (1983), and the proceedings of evidence to the Sizewell B Inquiry (1987). A feature of this research has been how the available evidence, plus reports and articles in coal journals, has been pieced together by analysts to construct a broader picture of implicit strategies, sometimes at odds with those officially proclaimed.

Five sets of broader issues, concerned with the context of the financial debates, predominated. First, there is the issue of the economic strategies of NCB management which are discussed in Part II of this book. As noted by Cutler *et al.* and Kerevan and Saville, there is a history of past over-optimism about the coal market, embodied in the 1974 *Plan for Coal*. This is also summarised in the second article by Robinson on the economic background to the coal dispute. These reports are important in indicating that the problems of the industry were not solely due to high-cost segments, but were rather a problem of coping with over-capacity due to major planning errors. Moreover, as Robinson and Fothergill examine, future projections of coal demand may similarly err on the optimistic side, giving rise to even greater concern for the future of the industry.

Secondly, related to this, was the important issue raised especially by Cutler *et al.*, of whether the NCB's past policy of investing in super pits was (and is) justified. They argue that, taking the net present value (NPV) calculations for the appraisal of the proposed investment in the Selby coalfield, as outlined in the Monopolies and Mergers Commission (1983) report, the benefits of the new pits are not at all obvious, but rather rest on 'knife-edge' economics. Small changes in assumptions (such as a different discount rate) soon render that investment 'uneconomic'. Also they argue that the fact that the NCB calculated pit costs without including the cost of capital invested (and indeed reckoning depreciation at historic cost) systematically distorted the results in favour of newer capital-intensive pits as opposed to the older, usually smaller, labour-intensive ones. This may have contributed to the relative starving of the 'peripheral coalfields' of investment resources with the effect that they could not increase productivity rapidly, leading to higher costs and thereby losses (a point documented for the Scottish coalfield by Kerevan and Saville).

The net result of over-optimistic market forecasts and the massive investment in new capacity was that when demand proved to be static (at best), the pressure was on to close marginal pits. However, the question remains whether the strategy of concentrating investment in new super pits, as opposed to older existing ones, is the most valid in management's own terms, notwithstanding the issues of regional policies, net losses and gains to the Exchequer, and social costs and benefits.

Thirdly, the issue of technology is further dealt with in detail by Burns *et al.*, who provide a fascinating case study of the development and implications of radical changes in how coal is mined. Pre-publication reports of this work, commissioned by the NUM, may have contributed to miners' fears for future employment, a major concern expressed throughout the strike. Flowing from their work was the implication that not only were many thousands of jobs put at risk by the new super pits, but that even the partial introduction of such technology in established pits would cost many thousands more jobs. In addition, the new automatic controls present a threat and challenge to the underground workers' ability to control much of the operations themselves. Thus it is suggested that the new technologies are not just related to cost-savings, but rather are attempts by management to increase their control at the expense of miners (for further comment on this argument, see Hopper *et al.*, 1986).

Fourthly, as the strike progressed greater attention began to be paid to the position of coal within energy policy more generally. Given the aforementioned interdependencies this is perhaps unsurprising. However, as Fothergill, and Cutler *et al.* note, analysing data surrounding the Sizewell B Inquiry, the longer-term future of coal as a major source of electricity supply is dubious, given the evidence presented by the CEGB and the Department of Energy. Official sources explicitly point to a preference for an increasingly nuclear future. But both Fothergill and Cutler *et al.* question whether this is the most economic route on conventional methods of cost analysis, as well as raising the importance and significance of other factors such as safety, health and defence. Significantly, when energy data other than that for coal are subject to scrutiny, similar uncertainties and deficiencies in the data are revealed.

Summary

The themes of the papers in this book have been grouped into three issues. First, the contribution and limitations of accounting and economic analyses are demonstrated in Part I. In this part fairly conventional analyses from accounting thought (notably contribution analysis) and economic thought (notably cost benefit analyses of employment and output) are applied to pit closure decisions both for individual collieries and for the NCB as a whole. In Part II, such analyses are developed in greater detail, emphasising the role of management strategies, calculations and, in retrospect, miscalculations in increasing or decreasing the investment and involvement in coal-mining. Finally, Part III explores the context of the coal dispute with each contribution implicitly or explicitly asking about the broad factors that lead to the industrial conflict. These contributions focus on energy supply and demand and technical change in the coal industry. Together with papers found in the earlier sections, they show how an understanding of the nature and contribution of financial calculations in industrial and political debate requires an appreciation not only of the specific industry, but also its history and position in the economy, regionally, nationally and internationally (in this case in relation to employment and energy policy).

The impact of the contributions

The relationship between financial calculation and industrial struggle has never been a clear one. There have been analyses of what the role of information should be in collective bargaining (e.g. Foley and Maunders, 1977; Cooper, 1984), but these prescriptions have not found direct parallels in studies of the actual use of information in conditions of normal conflict (Owen and Lloyd, 1985), let alone the intense struggle surrounding the NCB in 1984/5.

It is difficult to assess the impact of the contributions in this book on the strike, and in subsequent debates about the coal industry. Arguments are produced, disseminated and used in a variety of ways, often after considerable delays and in an unintended manner. Several of the contributions were written for specific parties involved in the dispute – Glyn, Fothergill and Burns *et al.* worked in association with the National Union of Mineworkers, and Kerevan and Saville with Scottish local government, concerned about the impact of pit closures on their locality. These contributions were certainly discussed both in the build-up to the strike and during it. Subsequently, many of the contributions have informed debates elsewhere – in public inquiries about specific pit closures (Horden, Polkemmet and St John's collieries, *inter alia*), in debates in the House of Commons and European Parliament about the management and nature of the UK and European coal industry and in the confidential reports following appeals by the mining unions to the joint consultative arrangements in the industry.

Financial calculation

Despite the use of the arguments and knowledge presented in this book in public and private debate, the impact of these arguments is difficult to assess. Believers in the power of rational argument may take heart from the way in which the NCB's own report (Custis *et al.*, 1985) agreed with the demand in Berry *et al.* that there is a need for improved accounting reports (stressing contributions) and more managerial care in justifying closure decisions. The Select Committee on Energy report of the coal industry (1987) endorsed this view and recognises the value of social cost-benefit analyses, as illustrated by the contributions in Part I of this book. However, the effect of these debates does not seem to have yet affected practices within British Coal or government policies. Investment and closure decisions are being taken on the basis of full cost calculations, British Coal have been encouraged to consider only internal effects in their commercial decisions (leaving external effects to a government which itself is hostile to explicit regional, energy or information technology policies).

So why have the contributions had little impact on practice, especially when the veracity of their mode of argument has rarely been disputed? This question prompts a consideration of what is the role of financial calculations in industrial disputes. Three broad issues arise, namely the variety of roles of information in organisational and social life, the tactics of the academics who produced the calculations, and the interaction of economic and financial arguments with the political domain.

Roles of calculation

It is frequently assumed that information and calculation are produced in order to be useful in decision-making, acting as an input to the process of specifying outcomes and assessing proposed policies. From this decision-orientated perspective failure to use financial calculations and the use of 'imperfect' or 'misleading' calculations in industrial relations may be due to lags in learning or incompetence. Although there may be grounds to question the competence of participants in the coal dispute, it is quite clear that both the NCB, through their own economists and managerial strategists, and the unions, through their own research officers and sympathetic academics, had access to most of the arguments presented in this book. However, they do not seem to have used the information as the decision-orientated perspective would suggest. If this line of argument is pursued it leads to a questioning of the connection between calculations and decisions. The decision-making process may not be the orderly and rational process depicted in textbooks.

Financial calculations and arguments may be produced to structure, condition or otherwise influence the decision-making process. Information may be used not to aid decision-making but to produce the boundaries of legitimate debate. During the strike the NCB and the government appealed to commonsense notions of the market place and the impartiality of market prices. Financial information, and particularly that produced by professional accountants employed by the NCB, was seen to be neutral, objective and to identify the economic 'facts of life' (and for many pits and mining communities, of death). The debate was structured around definitions of profitability which reflected, and indeed helped to reproduce, particular concepts of cost and benefit. These concepts distinguish private from social costs and benefits and consequently any appeal to social costs and benefits appears as special pleading. Debates about the appropriate objectives of a nationalised industry, or indeed any organisation in a strategic sector of the economy, are avoided if the assumptions inherent in financial calculations are ignored. In this case the unexplicated assumptions, favourable to NCB policies, included the belief that industries should run according to commercial criteria, with no concern for the consequences of action outside their legal boundaries.

This is not to imply that the terms of debate are necessarily consciously or deliberately structured by cunning people concerned to dupe their enemy. Rather it points to the unexamined basis of commonsense definitions of economic categories and the mechanisms by which such definitions get reproduced and reinforced by everyday discourse. Even within industrial conflict, the very engagement in debate about 'uneconomic pits', 'loss-making industry' and so on reinforces the categories and the terrain of debate. Thus, in the coal dispute, the NUM appeared to be engaging in intellectual arguments which seemed to be on the margins of the terrain of debate. The NCB relied on a bluff, honest person who lent credibility to their slogans by repeating the argument without ever examining it. In this, they exploited the media's concern with instant entertainment and personalities and its bias against elaborate discussions and understanding.

Thus, information and financial calculation may help to structure debate. Arguments and calculations may also be produced not as an input to the decision-making process but as justifications for decisions which have been taken on other grounds (Burchell *et al.*, 1980). Certainly this was the argument in Berry *et al.* – that one form of calculation of profits (from the many alternative methods available) was being used by the government and NCB management to justify the closure of pits when these decisions had been taken on other criteria which were not being made explicit. One of the surprising characteristics of financial calculations is that whilst the final figure appears objective and hard, the process of its production is extraordinarily malleable. The production of financial statistics involves estimates of the future (for example about demand and the life of equipment), alternative methods of measurement and contested conceptions of the planning horizon. These estimates, assumptions, methods and conceptions can produce financial statistics which may, at one extreme, be deliberately designed to obfuscate issues or provide rationales for proposed decisions. In less extreme ways they may have the effect of rationalising actions or plans. A conception of information as being used after a decision is made, with its role as an input to decision-making being less central, is one that is not yet widely appreciated in the literature on the role of information in industrial relations, although it seems to be recognised by participants in disputes.

The tactics of the academics

A second issue which arises in an analysis of the impact of financial calculations in industrial disputes is the role of the producers of these calculations. Many of the contributors in this book had no direct connection with either party in the coal dispute and this image of impartiality may be thought to increase the likely impact of their interventions. Yet it could be argued that the contributors who have had a serious and long-lasting impact were those whose interventions were part of a political strategy; they had worked out a role for financial discourse not as an academic exercise of topical relevance but as an engaged political activity.

Together, it was never easy for the academics to find a point of intervention. They did not help themselves because in their usual undisciplined and individualist way they disagreed amongst themselves and came up with proposals which were hardly 'practical politics'. These issues arose most obviously in the economists' debate about the social costs of closure. All the economists agreed that coal closure should be decided within a framework of calculation about social cost. But they came up with very different answers about the social costs of closure, mainly because they disagreed about the re-employment prospects of redundant mineworkers. On the left Glyn argued redundant miners would never be re-employed, on the right Minford and Kung assumed they would be instantly re-employed, while Davies and Metcalf argued the miners would be re-employed at standard wages over ten years. It was easy to dismiss such contributions when their answers about social cost appeared to depend on political positions which determined their assumptions. More fundamentally, there was the problem that Glyn and others on the left appeared to be demanding that coal-miners be treated as a special case. More than three million manufacturing jobs have been lost in Britain through de-industrialisation over the past decade. Journalists, such as Christopher Huhne of the *Guardian*, argued that if coal mines were kept open on social cost grounds then, in all logic, the practice of subsidy should be extended to manufacturing industry. But this extension of the practice would run into obvious problems about the overall cost of the strategy. In addition it might have the unacceptable consequence of freezing process and product technology. Centrist opinion accepted that unemployment was an evil which should be resisted but doubted whether it could or should be resisted wherever the social costs were high.

Less obviously, the effectiveness of academic intervention was compromised because many contributions emphasised the importance of different issues. This disparateness was more or less inevitable when the reports were being produced independently by small teams working in different parts of the country. The Manchester team of accountants raised the issue of whether and how accounting information was and should be used in closure decisions. The Bradford team on technology questioned the Coal Board's choice of expensive advanced automation in the super pits. The Aberystwyth team of economic historians argued that the crisis in coal was caused by the NCB's past investment strategy, which had produced over-capacity. They doubted whether super pits would produce low-cost coal and pointed out, together with Fothergill, that if the government chose a nuclear energy policy then this would undermine the demand for coal in the long run. The Scottish team highlighted the technical characteristics of coal in 'peripheral' areas and the artificial nature of market prices. In retrospect, all these interventions were constructive attempts to define different aspects of the crisis in coal. But, during the strike, the academics' constant redefinition of the issues weakened their intervention. More fundamentally, it was never easy to get any of the non-economic issues onto the agenda of public debate. All of them in one way or another challenged management's right to manage, a right which is sacrosanct in Britain. Before or after the coal strike, outsiders who query the rationality of the forms of calculation undertaken by management have never persuaded them to reformulate enterprise strategy.

After the strike there has been little political will to resist pit closures as and when proposed by management. Public inquiries have been ad hoc, inevitably focussing as much on local issues, and have been ignored by the NCB. For all the fuss about independent colliery review procedures, the defeat of the miners ensures that the NCB does not have to carefully justify closure, only to assert that it is necessary. Even the most elaborate and rationalistic calculations by 'outsiders' are marginalised because these commentators are not in full possession of the 'facts', as defined by the management of British Coal.

Summary

In this section of our introduction, we have argued that financial calculations are enmeshed in industrial relations and conflict. We have pointed out that information may be used to support preconceived positions and decisions – its roles of providing ammunition and rationalisations to support arguments for either side in an industrial conflict (Earl and Hopwood, 1981). In a capitalist society it is not surprising that accounting and economic information have been harnessed most effectively by management and the agents of capital in support of their arguments (Ogden and Bougen, 1985). Our discussion, however, has also sought to emphasise the less obvious ways in which financial calculations become intertwined with economic, social and managerial issues such as the nature of good management and the role of markets and planning. Interventions which fail to deal with these wider issues are likely to be marginalised, especially if they are themselves disjointed and idiosyncratic.

The French social theorist, Foucault, has argued that knowledge, both in its silence and its articulation, produces power. For example, the ability to produce knowledge of a specific pit, perhaps in terms of its profitability or productivity, enables power to be exercised in ways which might otherwise not be imagined or legitimate. In debating coal closures, legitimate knowledge seems to have been the almost exclusive province of the NCB and government. Although some of the contributions in this book helped to articulate and extend this legitimate knowledge, most of the contributors produced what was seen as illegitimate knowledge. By bringing together many of these contributions, suitably brought up to date, and by producing this introductory essay, it is hoped that this book will help to provide a critical mass to both sides of the debate and thereby to improve the management of the industry.

It may not, at present, be politically feasible for a major union, such as the NUM, to be directly involved in the management and governance of its industry. On the other hand without such action the union may face emasculation. If the NUM were to be more positively involved in the forward planning and management of the industry, notwithstanding political problems, the question arises of whether it has the expertise, arguments or resources to be effective. The signs from the Colliery Review Procedures, albeit under difficult and exceptional circumstances, are not promising. Rather than offering an informed challenge to management, union involvement carries the danger, due to lack of expertise and information, of legitimating managerial ends. However, as the Polkemmet and St John's public inquiries suggest (albeit without NCB involvement) counter arguments do exist. This book cannot deal with the problem of management's disclosure of information, but it can indicate the debate which can be articulated.

Indeed, in the years of the hegemony of consent, the management of the coal industry was dominated by engineers, with finance and economics held firmly in the background. Such was also the orientation of the coal workers' unions. In a period where the state adopts a policy of coercion and popular authoritarianism and where the market 'demands' are strengthened through increasing financial stringency, finance has become more central in management (Hopper *et al.*, 1986). The mining unions may need to parallel this development. Given the long-term and unpredictable nature of the industry and the inevitably contestable nature of financial calculations, debate needs to be stimulated. An optimist might argue that different sets of data and assumptions should be fed into analysis and agreement achieved by consensus. However, in times of strain and conflict the pressure is to withhold contentious data, deny it is used, or pour scorn on sceptics. Also the very malleability of the accounting data lends itself to retrospective justification of the status quo. So long as financial information and argument is the monopoly of the managers of the industry and/or there is a belief in the unproblematic definition of unprofitable, then the more likely it will be that financial calculations will be partisan and be implicated in disputes and one-sided debates within the coal industry and elsewhere. If the coupling of knowledge and power in our society is often oppressive, the uncoupling of knowledge and power is worse because it produces results which are irrational and wasteful. What kind of society do we live in when we have massive unemployment and underutilisation of resources and cannot find the time to debate whether such redundancy is economically and socially desirable or necessary?

Finally, a word of thanks. This collection could not have been produced without the encouragement of the series editors, especially Anthony Hopwood, and the patience and vision of the publishers, in the form of Francis Brooke. We also relied on the co-operation and patience of all the contributors, who kindly also supplied postscripts, where appropriate. This introduction has been developed by the editors from notes prepared by Andrew Glyn, Richard Saville and Karel Williams. If there is merit in this volume, much of the praise should go to the people listed above. If there are errors, the reader might feel inclined to blame them. Unfortunately, as this is not practical, we accept, as is conventional, the responsibility for this introduction, the choice of contributions and the structuring of the book.

NOTES

1 The authors would like to thank Andrew Glyn, Richard Saville and Karel Williams for their extensive comments and help in drafting this introduction. However, neither they, nor the other contributors to this book, can be held responsible for the views expressed.
2 Comparable figures for 1984/5 (which was affected by the strike) were a loss of £1,642 million and government grants of £2,414 million. In 1985/6 operating profit was £535 million and grant was £563 million (mainly due to redeployment of miners, pension payments to redundant miners and pit closures).

REFERENCES

Berry, A., T. Capps, D. J. Cooper and E. A. Lowe (1986), 'The Ethics of Research in a Public Enterprise' in F. Heller (ed.), *The Uses and Abuses of Social Science*, London: Sage.
Boyfield, K. (1985), *Put Pits Into Profit*, London: Centre for Policy Studies.
Burchell, S., C. Clubb, A. G. Hopwood, J. Hughes and J. Nahapiet (1980), 'The Roles of Accounting in Organizations and Society', *Accounting Organizations and Society*, pp. 5–27.
Cooper, D. J. (1984), 'Information for Labour', in B. Carsberg and T. Hope (eds.), *Current Issues in Accounting*, Oxford: Philip Allan.
Council of the European Communities (1978), Seventh Directive on Company Law, *Official Journal of the European Community*, no. L193.
Custis, P. J., D. Morpeth, E. Stamp and D. P. Tweedie (1985), *Report of an Independent Committee of Enquiry on Certain Matters Relating to the Affairs of the National Coal Board*, London: NCB.
Earl, M. and A. G. Hopwood (1981), 'From Management Information to Information Management', in H.C. Lucas (ed.), *The Information Systems Environment*, London: North Holland.
Foley, B. and K. Maunders (1977), *Accounting Information Disclosure and Collective Bargaining*, London: Macmillan.
Foucault, M. (1980), *Power/Knowledge*, edited by M. Gordon, Brighton: Harvester.

Introduction

Habermas, J. (1976), *Legitimation Crisis*, translated by T. McCarthy, London: Heinemann.

Hall, S., C. Critcher, J. Jefferson, J. Clarke and B. Roberts (1978), *Policing the Crisis*, London: Macmillan.

Hopper, T., D. J. Cooper, E. A. Lowe, T. Capps and J. Mouritsen (1986), 'Management Control and Worker Resistance in the National Coal Board', in H. Willmott and D. Knights (eds.), *Managing the Labour Process*, London: Gower.

House of Commons (1987), *First Report from the Energy Committee Session 1986–87: The Coal Industry*, London: HMSO.

Inflation Accounting: Report of the Inflation Accounting Committee (1975), London: HMSO.

Kerevan, G. and R. Saville with D. Percival (1985), *The Case for Retaining a European Coal Industry*, Brussels: British Labour Group in the European Parliament.

Monopolies and Mergers Commission (1983), *National Coal Board: A Report on Efficiency and Costs in the Development, Production and Supply of Coal by the NCB*, 2 vols, Cmnd. 8920, London: HMSO.

O'Donnell, K. (1985), 'Brought to Accounting: The NCB and the Case for Coal', *Capital and Class*, 26, pp. 105–23.

Offe, C. (1975), 'The Theory of the Capitalist State and the Problem of Policy Formulation', in L. Lindberg, R. R. Alford, C. Crouch and C. Offe (eds.), *Stress and Contradiction in Modern Capitalism*, Lexington, Mass.: Lexington Books.

Ogden, S. and P. Bougen (1985), 'A Radical Perspective on the Disclosure of Accounting Information to Trade Unions', *Accounting Organizations and Society*, pp. 211–24.

Owen, D. and A. Lloyd (1985), 'The Use of Financial Information by Trade Unions Negotiators in Plant Level Collective Bargaining', *Accounting Organizations and Society*, pp. 329–50.

Robinson, C. and E. Marshall (1985), *Can Coal be Saved?* London: Institute of Economic Affairs.

Sizewell B Public Inquiry Report (1987), London: HMSO.

Smith, J. G. (1984), *Strategies Planning in Nationalised Industries*, London: Macmillan.

Whittington, G. (1983), *Inflation Accounting: An Introduction to the Debate*, Cambridge: Cambridge University Press.

PART I

The economics and accounting of the National Coal Board

2

Pit closures: some economics

G. DAVIES and D. METCALF

Introduction

The miners' strike dragged on with an apparently unbridgeable gap between the two sides. The National Coal Board (NCB) based its case for pit closures largely on the ground of finance – loss-making pits need to be closed in order to move the industry closer to break-even. The National Union of Mineworkers (NUM) on the other hand, based its case on geology – maximising coal production at almost any price. No closures, they said, can be contemplated until pits are exhausted, or are unsafe to mine. Since the criteria of finance and exhaustion are entirely separate, it seemed impossible to find a compromise between them. One possible way round this problem would have been to get both sides to talk about a third criterion – economics and real resources. This would involve agreeing that pits should be closed when their *real value to the whole economy* in net output and social terms was no longer positive. In general, this criterion would point to closure for most pits at a date somewhere between the loss of financial viability and the point of exhaustion.

But, apart from the potential attractions of this approach as a compromise formula, we argue that the real resource criterion is, on analytic grounds, highly relevant to the question which started the dispute: 'When is a pit uneconomic?' It is insufficient to answer this question simply by reference to the Coal Board's finance and accounting conventions (which do not take note of the social costs of pit closure, or of the true cost of labour in an underemployed economy). It is impossible to answer the question by reference to the NUM's criterion of exhaustion, which has no grounding whatsoever in economics or welfare theory. By contrast, we argue that the real resource criterion is capable of putting the 'economic' back into the issue of 'uneconomic' pits.

In its original form, this chapter was commissioned by 'Weekend World', London Weekend Television in September 1984, and was published in *The Economics Analyst*, Simon and Coates, September 1985.

25

The idea is simple. Even in loss-making pits, miners are generally contributing positively to national output. If these miners were put out of work and were unable to find alternative employment, they would produce nothing. National output would decline, and social costs would be incurred. On resource grounds, there may therefore be a case for leaving open, or phasing out more slowly, loss-making pits. This case is not open-ended. Financial costs (subsidies) are incurred in keeping loss-making pits open. Furthermore, as time passes the real value of the coal produced may begin to fall short of the real costs of producing it. After this point the pits should be closed on virtually any criterion;[1] before this point, it is for the government to decide whether to make available the finance to enable resource gains to take place.

All recent governments have subsidised loss-making pits, implicitly recognising that resource gains are worth paying for. The present government has, so far, been no exception. But now there are suspicions that a push is on towards a target of eventual financial break-even for the industry, a target which would mean substantial closures on top of the 4m tonnes of capacity which was the immediate trigger for the current dispute. This, perhaps, is what is really at issue. In this chapter, we look at the possibility of closing the 12 per cent of capacity (40,000 jobs and perhaps 50–60 pits) which might be needed to halve the Board's normal losses. We conclude that:

1. On narrow NCB/Department of Energy financial grounds, there is a strong case for early closure. The financial 'rate of return' on an 'investment' in redundancy payments is around 17 per cent p.a. on our central assumptions. However, the financial rate of return to the Treasury as a whole is much less, at around 3–5 per cent p.a.
2. Anyway, financial criteria are, we argue, much less clear-cut than may appear at first sight, since implicit political judgements are necessarily involved, and accounting conventions raise problems.
3. On our suggested criterion of real resources (and taking into account social costs), our methodology suggests that the 50–60 pits should perhaps be closed *on average* after five years. Immediate closure of the entire group for financial reasons would involve significant resource losses in the early years. However, there are almost certainly some pits on the margin of the industry which ought to be closed immediately, even taking full account of the social and real resource arguments.
4. This might imply a resource optimum involving some 5–6 closures a year, not dissimilar from the average achieved in the *Plan for Coal* years 1974–83. However, this would be much less than required for

financial break-even by the NCB, and much more than required on an exhaustion principle.

All of these conclusions are subject to the imperfect data we have been working on, and on assumptions which can be legitimately disputed. Only the industry itself has access to the information needed to decide when any individual pit should be closed to ensure a real resource optimum. But the methodology in this chapter could certainly be used in practice to help the NCB/NUM to answer the question: how long, in the interests of the community as a whole, should loss-making pits be left open?

The financial case

The question of the 'economics' of pit closures is frequently addressed solely in terms of finance – how much the NCB or the public sector would save by switching from high-cost to low-cost pits compared with the financial costs of redundancy payments and additional unemployment benefits. The resolution of this issue should be comparatively simple. The first-year costs of pit closures almost always outweigh the first-year financial benefits, since redundancy payments are incurred immediately while reduced NCB losses accrue over a much longer period of time. On these narrow financial grounds, the decision is therefore exactly analogous to any other commercial decision on new investment: does the eventual rate of return make the capital outlay worthwhile (that is, does the 'investment' in redundancy payments earn a return which exceeds the public sector's test rate of discount)? Opinions differ even on this narrow question (see for example the NUM/Department of Energy interchange in the House of Lords Select Committee Report, 1983/4), but on our analysis the rate of return to the NCB and Department of Energy on closure far exceeds the test discount rate. Hence, on narrow financial grounds it can be argued that there is a case for early closure of many pits. However, on wider financial grounds, when unemployment benefit and lost tax revenue are brought into the picture, the case is far weaker.

To make the case for or against closures on narrow financial grounds, three pieces of evidence are needed: the cost of redundancies to the NCB or to central government; the annual financial costs of keeping loss-making pits. On the cost of redundancy the Department of Energy has stated (*ibid.*, p. 303) that 'the total cost of redundancy payments of all kinds to those now entering the Redundant Mineworkers Payments Scheme (RMPS) is likely to be about £30,000 to £35,000 at present-day prices over a ten year period'.[2] This figure comprises lump-sum and weekly payments under the RMPS and statutory redundancy payments under the Employment Protection (Consolidation) Act. The RMPS is administered by the NCB on behalf of the Department of Energy, but the NCB does not incur the spending under the RMPS. When calculating a financial rate of return we initially focus on the return to the NCB and Department of Energy. The only cost the NCB incurs is its share (59 per cent) of the statutory redundancy payments. But the NCB would not reap all the financial benefits from closure (i.e. lower losses) because central government would reduce its subsidy to the NCB as the losses decline.

Turning to the financial cost of keeping pits open, the Department of Energy says that the highest-cost 12 per cent of NCB capacity incurs losses of £275m a year (1983/4 prices) and employs 40,000 people on colliery books. This implies a financial cost per miner of £6,875 a year, but again there are slight complications. First, the annual loss would certainly mount over time, since pits will produce less output and require more (non-labour) inputs as they approach exhaustion. This factor again implies that the rate of return estimates below are underestimates. On the other hand, some of the costs could possibly be imputed to non-miners, and this is a factor which could lead to some overestimate on the rates of return.

Finally, there is the question of how long the loss-making pits are assumed to be left open; the longer they are open, the larger the (present value of) losses and the stronger the financial case for closure. We assume five-year and ten-year life-spans for these pits. (In the Monopoly and Mergers Commission Report on the NCB in 1983, it is estimated that of the 70 collieries which made losses of over £10 per tonne in 1981/2, 33 had reserves which would last for more than ten years at the existing rate of working.) What, then, would be the rate of return to the public sector from 'investing' in the closure of the highest-cost 12 per cent of capacity, which costs £6,875 per miner per year to keep open? On the assumption that the cost to the public sector of a single redundancy is £32,500, all incurred in the first year (see above), then the real rate of return would be 2 per cent p.a. on the (unrealistic) assumption that the average pit-life is five years, or 17 per cent p.a. on the much more realistic assumption that the average life is ten years. This latter figure comfortably exceeds any conceivable test discount rate for the public sector.

If instead we estimate the financial rate of return to the public sector as a whole the picture is very different. In this case we must add to the costs side of the equation the unemployment benefits and lost tax revenue. The House of Lords Select Committee on Unemployment (1982) put these costs at £5,000 per unemployed person in 1981/2, equivalent to around £5,500 in 1983/4 prices. We assume (see below) that the prob-

Pit closures: some economics

ability that the redundant miner's job will get replaced elsewhere in the economy is 0 on redundancy, rising to 1 in year 10. So these Exchequer costs of unemployment are initially £5,500 per redundant miner, falling to zero in ten years' time. When these costs are added in, the financial rate of return to closure falls to 3 to 5 per cent depending on assumptions about the profile of benefits (see appendix). This is probably below the test discount rate for public investment, so on these wider financial grounds there is only a slim case for closure *on average* among the worst 12 per cent of pit capacity. This is not to deny that the very worst pits will have higher losses than the average and that, therefore, a financial case could probably be made for closing such pits. But equally, the wider financial case for closing the intra-marginal pits among the worst 12 per cent is probably very weak.

We therefore conclude that in many, or probably most, of the highest-cost pits there is a good case on narrow NCB/Department of Energy financial grounds for early closure. However, the signal to the Treasury should be different from the signal to the NCB or Department of Energy, because when unemployment benefits and lost tax revenue are included in the picture the real financial rate of return to closure of many of the worst 50–60 pits is below the test discount rate. Therefore, even on financial grounds, society should pursue a slower closure programme than that which is optimal for the NCB. However, we shall argue below that these financial considerations are not the only criteria which can be taken into account when discussing the issue of pit closures.

The finance constraint

In an economy where the government is operating under tight financial constraints on its budgetary operations, the above considerations are particularly significant. If total public expenditure is cash-limited, then public sector subsidies to keep pits open need to be judged against the opportunity cost of switching these subsidies to alternative areas of public sector activity, such as subsidising other industries, or spending equivalent sums on job creation schemes. The case for closing high-cost pits relies (at minimum) on the proposition that the public funds so released could be used more effectively in alternative areas such as these; and in our view this proposition can probably be defended in some cases. But it should be noted that the case for closure relies also on a more complicated implicit assumption: that there are no areas elsewhere in the public sector where the government's *current* activities are even less financially 'viable' than keeping open the highest-cost pits. In some cases, this issue can be tackled straightforward: for example, it should be possible to compare subsidies to coal mines with subsidies to steel mills on financial grounds. However, there are many far more complicated questions which do not lend themselves to financial comparison. It is impossible on financial grounds to compare spending £100m on the health service (or on pensions, or on a new defence system) with spending the same amount in subsidies to the coal industry, especially if a value is attached to the existence of mining communities and to the social infrastructure which has been built up to service them. Questions such as these are inherently political in nature, and can only be settled by political criteria. The apparent purity of a financial rate of return calculation is simply insufficient.

The government, whether it would admit as much or not, already recognises that narrow financial criteria are not always and everywhere paramount (or simple), since loss-making pits are already subsidised, and have been continuously since 1979. There have even been occasions where ministers have taken credit for spending more on subsidies and investment in the pits than their immediate Labour predecessors. Furthermore, the question of whether or not individual pits are loss-makers is to some extent arbitrary, depending on other decisions taken by the Cabinet. The most obvious of these is whether or not to build new nuclear power stations, a decision which must be based on environmental and political considerations as well as on strict financial grounds. Even more important, comparisons between the financial positions of different nationalised corporations can be heavily distorted by the widely different treatment of capital charges between industries. Most of the NCB's financial losses in recent years have been made up of interest charges to the central government, and it seems likely that the NCB has benefited from far fewer interest waivers than other industries, notably steel. If the treatment of coal had recently been as generous as that of steel, it is possible that many pits would be immediately removed from the loss-making category (though possibly not those which are on the NCB's current list for immediate closure).[3]   None of these arguments suggests that narrow financial considerations are irrelevant in deciding whether or not to close pits, which is what the NUM's 'exhaustion' principle would seem to imply. It is certainly hard to find convincing arguments in favour of this principle, which appears unrelated to financial, economic or social welfare considerations.[4] However, it can equally be argued that strict financial criteria for closure are far from clear-cut, since (1) they inevitably raise implicit political questions which are often not directly attacked by the government or the Board in arguing for their closure programme; (2) figures which relate simply to the NCB/Department of Energy ignore knock-on effects elsewhere in the public accounts; and (3) the question of financial viability is anyway something of a moving feast, depending on financing conventions which differ between nationalised industries, and on government decisions in other areas which have large political contents.

Economics and resources

However, the debate on closures should not stop there. It is quite possible for pit closures to be financially desirable for the NCB while being economically undesirable for the community as a whole. The more difficult, but arguably more important, issue of what we shall term 'economic' desirability depends on resources and output. Even in the highest-cost pits, miners are usually contributing positively to national output. If these miners' jobs were lost, and the people displaced were unable to find employment elsewhere, productive jobs would be lost. Output would therefore fall to levels which would be still further below most definitions of full capacity. On resource grounds, there may consequently be a case for leaving open, or phasing out very slowly, the loss-making pits.

How strong is this case? It depends mainly on a comparison between the real value (shadow price) of the coal produced in high-cost pits, compared with the real value of output which could be produced by miners in alternative jobs. In addition, it depends on the social costs which would be incurred in closing down mining communities. All of these elements involve measurement problems.

The real value of coal produced

It is difficult to value the coal produced simply at the price paid by the Central Electricity Generating Board (CEGB) to the NCB for coal (£46 per tonne). This is because (1) resource costs apart from labour are incurred in mining and transporting the coal (notably the use of fuel – most of the mining capital stock probably has a real value in alternative uses close to zero) and (2) not all of present UK coal output is purchased by the electricity industry or other final users, since supply already exceeds demand and a proportion of output is stocked. The real value of the coal is therefore somewhere between nil (on the assumption that it could never be sold at any price) and £46 per tonne.

It has been suggested to us that the value attached to the output of marginal pits should in fact be nil or negative, since the coal goes to stock while resource costs are incurred in production and storage. While we recognise this argument, we find it unconvincing for several reasons: (1)

even if the coal were going permanently to stock it would have *some* insurance value against the possibility of future supply disruption; (2) one reason why coal stocks were rising up to the autumn of 1983 was the fact that UK Gross Domestic Product (GDP) had fallen far below trend, and this may not be a permanent state of affairs; (3) there is surely some price at which the coal could be exported to a European market which is forecast to become increasingly reliant on imported coal over the next 20 years; (4) again, there is surely some price, now or in the future, at which coal would be unequivocally superior on financial grounds to either oil or nuclear fuel as an input to power stations (and other industries for that matter). To value the coal at nil would be to deny all these possibilities.[5] On the other hand, to value it at £46 per tonne would be to ignore the plain fact that the full output of existing capacity cannot be sold on a free market. Hence, some compromise solution is necessary.

The obvious way round this problem is to value the coal at a world price (less those production costs which are incurred in resource terms). However, the world market in coal is very narrow, and the NCB certainly cannot be viewed as a price-taker in this market. Two alternatives present themselves. The coal could be valued at £30 per tonne, the figure which seems to be used in the NCB accounts to value coal going to stocks. Alternatively, it could be valued at the price currently realised by the industry on coal exports, which in the first seven months of this year seems to have varied between £28 and £30 per tonne. In the examples below, we have used a price of £29 per tonne (less the resource costs incurred in production). It will no doubt be argued by some economists that this price is higher than can be justified for the last few million tonnes of output of the coal industry at present. This case is arguable for the most marginal pits at present, but in our example below we consider the case of the highest-cost 14½m tonnes of output as our 'marginal slice' of the industry for analysis. Since by no means all of this output goes to stock or exports, there is a case for valuing it at considerably above £30 per tonne. We therefore feel that our figure is a reasonable compromise.

The alternative uses for labour

The simplest approach here can be defended – it is to argue that, in an underemployed economy, redundant miners would produce zero extra net resources in alternative employment. This proposition hinges on the belief that at present the level of employment is determined by aggregate demand, and that within a fixed level of demand any new jobs found by redundant mineworkers[6] would simply displace workers from jobs elsewhere. On the other hand, it could be argued that redundant mineworkers would *eventually* create extra net jobs in the economy, either through entrepreneurial skills and/or through depressing the general level of the real wage.[7] In this latter case, the alternative labour should be valued at the marginal net product of the workers in these jobs (proxied by the wage level).

It is perfectly plausible to argue that the marginal net product of miners in alternative jobs is in fact zero in the short run, since it is hard to believe that any net job gains would rapidly follow pit closures. In that case, there is a good short-term argument on resource grounds for leaving most pits open – the real value of the coal produced can surely not in general be classed as zero. However, in the longer run, say five or ten years, some of the redundant miners are presumably going to find alternative jobs without displacing other workers by one of the above routes, especially if the economy ever returns to full employment. At this stage, there would again be a resource loss from keeping open the high-cost pits.

Social costs

When a pit closes, two kinds of social costs are incurred. First, the situation derived from living in a thriving, homogeneous community is lost. Second, as miners and their families move elsewhere, they require new social capital – housing, schools, health care and so forth – and this must be scored as a social cost. In our example we do not impute any value to the first cost. In the case of social costs for new houses and so on we proceed as follows: (1) we take the replacement value of the capital stock of housing, health and education; (2) we multiply that figure by a real rate of return to get an annual value; (3) we see what proportion of that annual value is attributable to 40,000 miners and their families; (4) we adjust the resulting figure downwards for (a) any excess capacity in education and health care, (b) depreciation, (c) the fact that the social costs might in any case have to be incurred at some future stage (for example, if the mine is exhausted without the provision of alternative employment in pit localities), so all that the closure does is hasten its provision. The social-cost figure should, on the other hand, be adjusted upwards to allow for the provision of private capital. All these social gains from keeping the pits open should be added to the real value of the coal produced, or subtracted from the value of labour in alternative use. In the example below, we adopt the former alternative.

The decision on whether to close pits on resource grounds therefore depends on comparing the flow of real output and social gains over a relevant time horizon on two assumptions:

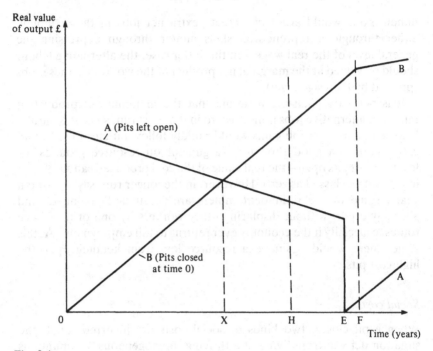

Fig. 2.1

A that the pits are left open;
B that the pits are closed, allowing mining labour gradually to 'shuffle'
   into alternative uses.

Since future output is worth less to the community than present output,
the flows of production under both of these options need to be discounted back to a *net present value*, using a suitable discount rate (which
represents the social rate of time preference). If the net present value of
production under option A exceeds that under option B over the relevant
time horizon, resource considerations suggest that the pits should be left
open. If not, they should be closed.

The analytics can best be understood by means of a diagram (see fig.
2.1). Assume that a pit (or group of pits) ceases to make a commercial
profit at time 0. A strict commercial enterprise would close it down at
that date. However, for the reasons explained above, this need not be a
decision which is optimal on real resource grounds. If the pit is left open,
the real value of net output might follow a path as outlined in line A. It
declines slowly for a period, reflecting the tendency for the non-labour

34

Pit closures: some economics

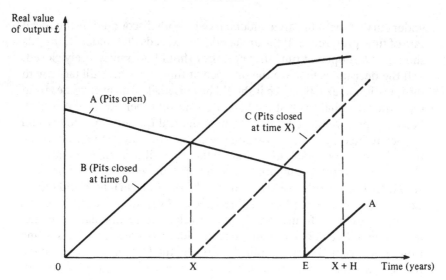

Fig. 2.2

costs of production to rise as the pit approaches absolute exhaustion. The net value of output drops to zero when the pit is exhausted at time E. (After that the line begins to rise again as the workers concerned find other jobs.) On the other hand, if the pit is closed at time 0, the output produced by the miners in alternative occupations is traced by line B. It rises gradually at first to reflect the fact that unemployed miners gradually find their way into alternative employment. At time F, all the workers have found alternative employment, after which the line rises only at the rate of underlying productivity growth in the industries concerned. In an economy where there is a binding long-term constraint on employment because of permanent demand deficiency, line B may not rise at all, implying that the pits should probably be left open to exhaustion.

The decision on whether or not to close at time 0 is still not simple. Net output would be higher with the pits left open (option A) until time X, after which it would be higher under option B. Does this mean that the pits should be left open until time X, and then closed? Unfortunately not. Output would only rise as shown in line B if the pits were closed at time 0. If, instead, the pits are closed at time X, output in alternative uses rises as shown in line C of fig. 2.2, rather than as shown in line B.

In order to decide whether to close at time 0, we need to compare the value of output produced up to a given time horizon (H in fig. 2.1), suitably discounted, under option A and B. This means comparing the area

35

under curve A with the area under curve B, both discounted by the social rate of time preference. If the area under A exceeds that under B, the pits should be left open at time 0; if not, they should be immediately closed.

If the decision is to leave the pit open at time 0, we are still faced with the question of exactly when it should be closed. The answer comes from repeating the analysis just explained for all time periods in the future. For example, we can consider the hypothetical question of what would happen if the pit were closed at some hypothetical date in the future – say time X. The area under curve C up to the same time horizon ahead of X (X+H) needs to be compared with the area under curve A from X to X+H. In other words, we simply move the origin from 0 to X and repeat exactly the same procedure outlined above. We do this for all possible closing dates in the future, and we plan to close at the first date when the area under curve A is less than the area under a curve such as C, starting from some point X in the future. Obviously, the further we look into the future, and the nearer to exhaustion we move, the more likely this criterion is to be fulfilled.[8]

Analytical conclusion

In the context of the present dispute, this type of resource argument fails to support either the miners' argument that all pits should be left open to exhaustion, or the NCB/government's tendency to argue that financial considerations should be all that matters. Instead, it suggests that economic/resource considerations should also be taken into account, and these generally would point to closure somewhere between the date of losing strict financial viability and the date of exhaustion. Therefore:

1. It is insufficient (and anyway not clear-cut) to examine pit closures from the standpoint only of financial considerations, as is often done by NCB and government;
2. Nor is it possible to argue even on economic or resource grounds for leaving open all pits to exhaustion, as the NUM appears to do;
3. To maximise UK real output, pits should be closed only when the resource gains from alternative employment outweigh the resource losses from lost coal output. This may involve quite long time-spans (depends on the precise numbers), but not infinite ones;
4. There will be financial losses to be incurred by the government in order to reap the economic gains involved in leaving high-cost pits open until criterion (3) is met;
5. The time-span in which these financial losses need to be incurred can be shortened by the active promotion of alternative employment by the NCB in areas threatened by pit closures. But the alternative

employment should probably, on resource grounds, come before the pit closures.

Example

The analysis in this chapter can only be properly applied to actual cases by the NCB itself, since only the Board has access to all the required information on a pit-by-pit basis. The example below should not, therefore, be taken as definitive, but only as an attempt to illustrate the analytical arguments with some real-life estimates. The estimates themselves are necessarily fairly rough.

In the example, we consider the question: should the NCB eliminate half its financial losses by immediately closing the 12 per cent of its output which currently has the highest operating costs? Or should it leave these pits open for a further period on national resource grounds? The pits in question produce 14½m tonnes of output per year and employ 40,000 miners.[9] They incurred losses of £275m in 1982/3, or about £300m in 1984/5 prices (in which all the following figures are calculated). We make the further assumption that all the relevant pits are left open, or closed, together. The calculation proceeds as follows:

Real value of coal produced

The annual value of coal produced, valued at £29 per tonne shadow price, is £420m. However, in order to work out the real resource value, we need to net out the costs of raw materials, fuels, transport etc. used in production. (We make no allowance for labour or for most capital costs.) Assuming that the pits in question have roughly the same cost relationships as the rest of the industry (that is, that the *ratio* between labour and material costs is roughly constant throughout the industry – see the cost breakdowns in the Monopolies and Mergers Commission Report (1983)), we calculate that around £261m of non-labour resource costs are incurred in producing the coal.[10] Therefore, the real resource value of the coal in year 1 is £420m less £261m equals £159m (or £11 per tonne, and £3,975 per worker). To allow for rising costs as pits approach exhaustion, we make the further (fairly arbitrary) assumption that the real net output of these pits drops by 25 per cent every ten years. This gives us a flow of real output for case A – leaving the pits open.

Real value of labour in alternative uses

If all the pits were to be closed immediately, 40,000 miners would be out of work. (This does nòt mean that 40,000 individual miners would be made redundant, just that 40,000 less people overall would be employed in mining.) For the reasons outlined above, these jobs would eventually be replaced elsewhere. We assume that it takes ten years for the economy to 'equilibrate', with all the displaced jobs being replaced. We value the potential alternative output produced by these workers by assuming that the 1984/5 estimated average earnings for male workers are maintained as total employment increases. This gives a value of £9,547 per new job created, or £382m per annum for 40,000 jobs created over ten years.

Social costs

When mining families move to other areas they require social capital and they abandon capital assets which would otherwise have a continuing value. The value of the stock of social capital in the UK for housing, health and education is £712bn (Blue Book, table 11.8, adjusted to 1984/5 prices). If we assume a real rate of return on these assets of 3 per cent, this implies the annual value of this social capital is £21.4bn. Assume the 40,000 miners in the worst 12 per cent of pit capacity have a total family size of 120,000. Therefore the 'miners' share' of the social capital is:

$$£21.4bn \times (120,000/56m) = £46m$$

It is worth noting in passing that this is equivalent to an annual value of only about £1,200 per family.

Two sets of adjustments should be made to this £46m figure. First, it should be adjusted upwards to allow also for the provision of private capital in the receiving areas (or, put differently, to allow for the losses made by shopkeepers and input suppliers in the mining areas). It seems probable that the private capital required would be at least as large as the £46m for social capital. Second, on the other hand, it should be adjusted downwards to take account of (1) any excess capacity which exists in education and, possibly, health in other geographical areas; (2) depreciation of the housing stock; (3) the fact that this new social capital will probably have to be provided at some time in the future, so keeping the mines open only postpones the provision of this capital, it does not eliminate its provision at some unspecified date in the future. In our calculations we have assumed that the two sets of adjustments cancel each other out, so we have taken the £46m calculated above as a rough estimate of the annual social value of the capital stock in the pit areas under consideration. We have added this amount to the real value of the coal produced in order to reflect the social gains from keeping mining communities in being. (This incidentally assumes that all the social losses would be incurred immediately on closure. In fact, they may build up

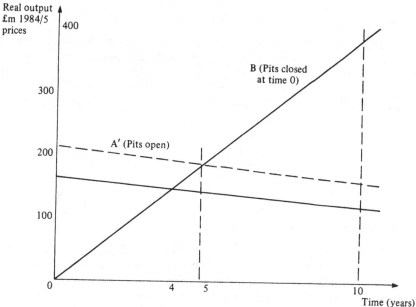

Pit closures: some economics

Fig. 2.3

more slowly than this, in which case the calculations below would be biased in favour of keeping the pits open for longer than a true optimum would suggest. However, we again feel that this factor is offset by the potentially large omission of any valuation of the private-sector capital stock in our figures.)

The relevant diagram at year 0 is shown in fig. 2.3. Line A represents the real value of coal produced; line A^1 adds to this the social gains; and line B shows the value of labour in alternative uses. The curves cross over between years 4 and 5. The economy is therefore better off with the pits open for 4–5 years, and worse off thereafter. Given this information, should the pits be closed? This depends on (a) the time horizon used and (b) the social rate of time-preference used. In the first instance we use a time horizon of ten years and a discount rate of 5 per cent per annum. Under these assumptions, the net present value (NPV) of output (including social gains) under the two options over ten years is:

		NPV of output £m
Case A	(Pits open)	1,455
Case B	(Pits closed)	1,336

Since A is greater than B, the pits should not be closed immediately.

39

Table 2.1

	NPV of output (£m)	
Year	A. Pits open	B. Pits closed
1	1,455	1,336
2	1,424	1,336
3	1,394	1,336
4	1,365	1,336
5	1,336	1,336
6	1,309	1,336

Nor, however, should they be left open to exhaustion. Given the present state of knowledge, we can compute the area under curves A and B with 10-year horizons, as they will appear 1 year hence, 2 years hence, 3 years hence etc. The relevant figures are shown in table 2.1.

Since B exceeds A for the first time in year 5, our present state of knowledge suggests that on average the pits should be closed in that year. However, unexpected changes in coal prices, costs, technology, general employment conditions and so on could lead to this conclusion being changed as and when these calculations are actually repeated at years 1, 2, 3 etc.

As can be seen from table 2.1, the NPV of output under the two options (pits open and closed) is fairly similar, which means that the actual decision on when to close is highly sensitive to small changes in underlying assumptions, and to changes in the time horizon and the social rate of time-preference used. The decision is particularly affected by changes in estimates of the following:
1. The shadow price of the coal produced;
2. The resource costs incurred in producing it;
3. The social value imputed to the capital stock in mining areas;
4. The build-up of alternative employment.

As one example of the sensitivity involved, we re-computed the figures on the assumption that the annual rate of return on the social capital stock is 4 per cent rather than 3 per cent. On this assumption, the crucial date for closure is postponed from five years to ten years into the future. However, if we instead make the (fairly extreme) assumption that the social gains are nil, the NPV of keeping pits open in year 1 is actually less than that of closing them. This would suggest on average that the pits should be closed now, though if we were actually able to apply the analysis on a pit-by-pit basis there would probably be many *individual* pits which should still be left open for a period.

Other examples could easily be computed showing the sensitivity of the closure decision to changes in assumptions. Some may feel that this sensitivity limits the applicability of the method discussed. However, we believe that the sensitivity is probably a consequence of using an average of many pits for our example: its proper application to individual pits would almost certainly produce much more clear-cut answers.[11]

Conclusion

In this chapter, we have considered two distinct alternatives: (a) leaving pits open on resource and social grounds, even if financial losses are incurred in the meantime; and (b) closing the pits at some future date and then allowing normal economic forces to re-deploy the displaced manpower over a further period of years. We have not considered a third alternative, which would be to close the pits, but actively to promote alternative employment by government action in the existing mining communities themselves. This would have different financial and resource consequences from both alternatives (a) and (b), and in some cases might be superior on all criteria to either (a) or (b). It would certainly avoid incurring the social costs which are inherent in the straightforward closure option. We have not considered this third possibility partly because of the extra complexities involved, but mainly because the direct promotion of employment in mining communities appears to have been ruled off the government's agenda for the present. If the government were willing to consider this option, it might represent an attractive third alternative to the choices presented here.

Until then, the above analysis stands. Although we would reiterate that the precise figures in our numerical example are subject to uncertainty, and although the analysis has not been applied to individual pits, the conclusions are nevertheless instructive. If the NCB wished to halve its financial losses by closing the highest-cost 12 per cent of its capacity immediately, we calculate that real resource losses would be incurred by so doing. On average, our figures suggest that the 50-60 pits[12] involved should be closed after five years. This would suggest that some pits should be closed immediately, even allowing in full for social real resource arguments. Other pits in this group should probably be left open for ten years or more, despite the financial losses. If the pits were closed evenly over ten years, there might be some 5–6 closures a year, roughly the same as in the 1974–83 *Plan for Coal*

(1974) period.[13] The NUM's 'exhaustion' criterion would almost certainly result in a much slower rate of closure. On the other hand, if the NCB wished to move directly to financial break-even, the closure rate would be much faster.[14]

Pits should in our view be closed when real resource and social considerations warrant. These considerations usually point to closure somewhere between the date of losing financial viability and the date of exhaustion. Although the 'real resource' methodology in this chapter is admittedly complicated, it could be used in practice to help the NCB/NUM answer the question: how long, in the interests of the community as a whole, should loss-making pits be left open?

Postscript

This paper was produced at speed in September 1985 as a contribution to the debate on pit closures. Even though the definition of 'uneconomic' was central to the dispute, by September other industrial relations issues were dominant. Nevertheless, we remain convinced that the problems outlined – particularly the valuation of labour, coal and social capital – are central to any debate about the size and structure of the British coal industry.

Since the end of the strike the pit closure programme has gone ahead at a rapid pace. This reflects the tight financial constraints imposed on the NCB by the government. If the concepts addressed in this chapter were to be employed the closures would have been slower. It is open to the parties to use ideas such as resource cost (rather than financial cost) in the Revised Colliery Review Procedures. In particular, emphasis on the low shadow value of labour in some areas and on the lost capital would, if accepted, reduce the speed of closure.

Appendix 1
Financial costs and benefits to the Treasury from closing the worst 12 per cent of capacity (£ per miner, 1983/4 prices)

| Year | Costs | | | | Benefits, i.e. | Benefits |
| | RMPS lump sum | RMPS continuing payments | Unemployment benefit/lost tax revenue | Total | subsidy savings from closure | assuming 25% rise over 10-year period |
	1	2	3	4	5	6
1	30,000	500	5,500	36,000	6,875	6,875
2	0	500	4,950	5,450	6,875	7,066
3	0	500	4,400	4,900	6,875	7,257
4	0	500	3,850	4,350	6,875	7,448
5	0	500	3,300	3,800	6,875	7,639
6	0	0	2,750	2,750	6,875	7,830
7	0	0	2,200	2,200	6,875	8,021
8	0	0	1,650	1,650	6,875	8,212
9	0	0	1,100	1,100	6,875	8,403
10	0	0	550	550	6,875	8,594

Sources: Department of Energy in House of Lords (1983/4); House of Lords (1982/3); MMC (1983)

Method

Ask the question what discount rate causes the ten-year present value of the costs (row 4) to equal the ten-year present value of the benefits (row 5). For illustration:

Discount rate	2%	4%
Benefits (£)	61,755	55,762
Costs (£)	59,721	57,030

Economics and accounting of the NCB

At a discount rate of 2 per cent the present value of the benefits of closure is greater than that of costs. At 4 per cent the reverse is true. We can conclude therefore that the internal rate of return to investing in closure, on the above figures, is 3 per cent. *Note*: if we assume that the benefits of closure rise by 25 per cent over the ten-year period (row 6) the rate of return is 5 per cent.

NOTES

1 Although not on the NUM 'exhaustion' principle.
2 One complication is that we have assumed that all the redundancy costs are incurred in the first year. In fact some of them are spread over several years. This implies that our calculations underestimate the rate of return to the NCB and Department of Energy.
3 On the question of interest charges, the House of Lords Select Committee concluded:
> There appears to be no uniformity of treatment of nationalised industries in this respect. This is illogical. There is no reason why the government should not treat the financial structure of the coal industry as it has treated the steel industry ... To write off part of the outstanding debt would improve the financial position at once, whereas closures of uneconomic pits take several years to have their full financial impact. In conjunction with closures it would help to give the industry a new start (House of Lords, 1983/4, para. 107).
4 The NUM's exhaustion principle appears akin to arguing that the iron industry should have continued using charcoal instead of coal for smelting until all the trees in Britain had been chopped down.
5 Note also that coal stocks increased by 5m tonnes in 1983. In order even to halve the NCB's losses, 14–15m tonnes of capacity would need to be closed, and much more if losses were to be eliminated altogether. Only a small proportion of this output currently goes to stock.
6 Or by people who would have found employment in the pits if colliery manpower were left at present levels.
7 It should be noted that, in the process of the economy 'equilibrating', the real wage for workers who were completely unconnected with mining will be depressed below the levels which otherwise would have been attained.
8 We have made no attempt to make any lump-sum adjustment for any real resource gains or losses outside our time horizon.
9 We have not attempted to make any allowance for any reduction in administrative employment if the pits are closed. Nor have we allowed for jobs and output which might disappear outside the coal industry.
10 This is a very rough estimate with a high degree of uncertainty attached to it.

Pit closures: some economics

Since some of the raw material and other bought-in costs have a high labour content in the supplying industries, it can be argued that the opportunity cost to the economy is much lower than the price paid by the NCB for these supplies. We have not allowed for this in our calculations. Potentially, this could be a major bias leading us to conclude in favour of earlier closures than should be the case.

11 Another reason for sensitivity is that we have probably chosen a group of pits which are genuinely on the margin of the industry, even on real resource grounds. Any attempt to move inside this marginal group to consider the much larger number of pits which would need to be closed for financial break-even would undoubtedly meet with much more clear-cut answers. Large resource losses would be made if such a programme were implemented.

12 An approximate figure based on the pattern of pit losses in 1981/2.

13 However, if this analysis were done on a pit-by-pit basis, the results would be most unlikely to provide an even rate of closure neatly spaced over ten years.

14 In order to move rapidly to break-even, many more pits than the number considered in our example would need to be closed. The resource arguments for keeping these pits open are much stronger than in the marginal cases we have analysed above.

In considering various break-even/closure/production combinations, it is obviously relevant to consider the NCB's entire programme for investment in expanding capacity. A slow-down in this programme would increase the likelihood that coal produced by the high-cost pits could be sold on a free market, but the Board's operating costs would be increased for any given level of output in theory, the real resource arguments on closure should take into account an infinite number of possible investment profiles for the Board. In our analysis, we have taken the investment programme as a given constant.

REFERENCES

House of Lords Select Committee on Energy Policy (1983/4), HL80, London: HMSO.

House of Lords Select Committee on Unemployment (1982/3), HL142, London: HMSO.

Monopolies and Mergers Commission (1983), *National Coal Board: A Report on Efficiency and Costs in the Development, Production and Supply of Coal by the NCB*, 2 vols, Cmnd. 8920, London: HMSO.

Plan for Coal (1974), London: Department of Energy.

3

The costs and benefits of coal pit closures

P. MINFORD and P. KUNG

Introduction

This chapter considers the costs and benefits of a pit closure programme, such as was under discussion in the recent coal-mining dispute. Section A considers the 'narrow financial calculation' of effects on public finances referred to by the Chancellor of the Exchequer in Parliament in July 1984. Section B then proceeds to look at wider calculations. The overall conclusion is that closing high-cost pits offers a substantial return to the nation, and that it is likely to *reduce* national unemployment.

Section A: The narrow PSBR calculation

Our estimates suggest that the public sector borrowing requirement (PSBR) cost of the miners' strike after 34 weeks was as high as £1.2bn. This includes:
1. Cost to the Central Electricity Generating Board (CEGB).
2. Cost to the National Coal Board (NCB).
3. Cost to British Rail (BR).
4. Loss of miners' tax and National Insurance (NI) contributions and addition in supplementary benefits paid to the miners' families.
5. Policing cost.
6. Savings in capital expenditure that would have been incurred had there been no strike.
7. Other costs.

1. *Cost to the CEGB*

The average consumption of electricity during the striking weeks under review (March–November 1984) is set at 60 per cent of that in January

This chapter is a slightly modified version of that which appeared in *Public Sector Review*.

Costs and benefits of closures

Table 3.1 *Cost to the CEGB*

	Tonnes	Price per tonne	£m
Extra oil used per week	294,525	133	39.17
Savings in coal per week	535,500	43	23.03
Net cost to CEGB per week			16.14

Assumptions: (a) Consumption of electricity during the striking weeks under review is 60% of that in a January week. (b) On average, 45% of the fuel used is coal during the striking weeks as opposed to the normal proportion of 80%. (c) Standard energy conversion factor between coal and oil is 0.55.

1984, that is, at 1.53m tonnes per week. Normally, coal represents 80 per cent of the fuel used by the CEGB. But during the striking weeks, on average, the proportion dropped to 45 per cent. Therefore, the amount of coal saved per week was $1.53 \times (80 - 45\%) = 0.5355$m tonnes, which at £43 per tonne is worth £23.03m.

On the other hand, more oil was burned as a substitute for coal. Given the standard energy conversion factor of 0.55 (that is, 0.55 tonne of oil produces the same amount of electricity as 1 tonne of coal), the amount of extra oil used is set at $0.5355 \times 0.55 = 0.294525$m tonnes per week, which at the average price of heavy fuel oil in the spot market of £133 per tonne cost some £39.17m per week. The net cost of burning more oil in place of coal is thus set at £16.14m per week.

2. Cost to the NCB

Loss of production from 12 March to 27 July 1984 (20 weeks) amounted to 29.467m tonnes (NCB estimates). The average loss is therefore 1.47335m tonnes per week. Assume that this production could have been sold at £43 per tonne, then the loss of revenue to the NCB is:

$$29.467 \times 43 \times 1/20 = £63.35\text{m per week}$$

But, on the other hand, some expenses were saved because of the cut in production during the strike. These include:

(a) Wages and wage charges
There are altogether 180,000 miners employed by the NCB. During the strike, the average attendance was around 30 per cent. As a result, the savings in wages and wage charges amounted to £21.9m per week (NCB estimates).

47

Table 3.2 *Net weekly cost of the dispute to the NCB*

	£m	£m
Loss of revenue due to the loss of production		63.35
Less savings:		
from wages and wage charges	21.90	
other variable operating expenses	20.93	
transportation	4.00	
storage	0.50	47.33
Total		16.02

(b) Variable operating costs such as mining expenses, lighting, heating and power, material and repairs

In a normal year, these expenses contribute 31 per cent to the total expenditure of the NCB. Based on the NCB's record, its weekly expenditure in a normal year is around £90m per week. Since most of the pits on strike were high-cost ones (for example, those in South Wales, Scotland and part of Yorkshire), it is estimated that around 0.75 of these variable costs could have been saved during the striking weeks, with weekly savings of:

$$£90m \times 31\% \times 0.75 = £20.93m$$

(c) Payment to British Rail for coal transportation

That was about £4m per week (BR estimates).

(d) Storage costs

According to the NCB, 4m tonnes of coal would have become excess stock had there been no strike. In this case, this would mean that the strike saved the NCB the cost of storing 4m tonnes of coal. The average cost of stocking coal in the first year was some £5 per tonne and the additional cost of putting stock down on the ground was about £1.50 per tonne. Therefore, the savings from not storing that 4m tonnes of excess production were:

$$£(4 \times 6.5 \times 1/52)m = £0.5m \text{ per week}$$

Therefore, the net weekly cost to the NCB is as shown in table 3.2.

3. *Cost to BR*

This was about £4m per week (BR estimates). This offset the saving in transportation cost to the NCB which is included above.

Costs and benefits of closures

Table 3.3 *Total cost of strike from 12 March to 2 November 1984 (34 weeks)*

	Cost per week £m	Total cost £m
1. Cost to the CEGB	16.14	549
2. Cost to the NCB	16.02	545
3. Cost to BR	4.00	136
4. Tax loss and increase in benefits	8.06	274
5. Policing cost	1.50	51
6. Savings in capital expenditure		− 400
7. Other costs		35
Total		1,190

Note: The effect of the strike on the PSBR of the 1984 financial year from 1 April to 2 November 1984 (31 weeks altogether) is estimated at £1.1bn.

4. *Loss of miners' tax and NI contribution and the increase in supplementary benefits paid to the miners' families*

The loss of miners' tax and NI contribution in the first 20 weeks of the strike averaged £5.56m per week (NCB estimate), whereas the increase in supplementary benefits paid out by the government to the miners' families was some £2.5m per week. The total would therefore be:

£5.56m + 2.50m = £8.06m per week

5. *Policing cost*

This was about £1.5m per week from the start of the strike (Phillips and Drew estimate). The sum is mainly for the overtime work done by the police force.

6. *Capital expenditure by NCB*

The planned level of capital expenditure for the financial year 1984/5 was £800m. The money would have been spent to maintain or increase the net revenue of coal pits, to meet safety needs, to undertake geological exploration and to provide new mines, and so on. But most of these projects were not carried out as a result of the strike. Consequently, it is estimated that some £400m in terms of cash flow was saved. But of that £400m, around £300m would have had to be spent following the strike.

Table 3.4 *The 24 most uneconomic collieries 1981–2*

Site	Saleable output ('000 tonnes)	Operating cost per tonne (£)	Operating loss per tonne (£)	Loss (£'000)
Cardowan	267	69.9	38.3	10,226.1
Sorn	57	58.1	21.5	1,225.5
Herrington	254	65.8	21.2	5,384.8
Sacriston	76	64.9	26.4	2,006.4
Bullcliffe Wood	191	48.4	19.4	3,705.4
Kilnhurst	138	66.6	25.6	3,532.8
Cortonwood	281	50.5	6.2	1,742.2
Snowdown	129	112.2	68.6	8,849.4
Tilmanstone	240	70.1	27.0	6,480.0
Treforgan	62	153.0	104.8	6,497.6
Abertillery	110	114.3	71.0	7,810.0
Nantgarw	165	87.3	42.5	7,012.5
Tower	134	87.0	33.2	4,448.8
Cynheidre	245	81.5	24.1	5,904.5
Bedwas	149	81.3	39.4	5,870.6
Penrikyber	140	79.6	33.8	4,732.0
Aberpergum	74	77.5	24.4	1,805.6
Mardy	189	76.6	24.6	4,649.4
Abernant	189	74.5	20.8	3,931.2
Oakdale	237	74.3	30.7	7,275.9
Garw	198	72.7	31.0	6,138.0
Blaenserchan	116	70.8	28.0	3,248.0
Markham	164	69.9	26.2	4,296.8
Celynen South	132	66.3	22.5	2,970.0
Total	3,937			119,743.5

Source: MMC (1983)

7. *Other costs*

Loss of equipment. The NCB announced that £20m worth of equipment was lost during the strike.

British Steel. The premiums and transportation paid to the international spot coal market for around 2m tonnes of coal that should have been supplied by the NCB amounted to some £15m in the period under review.

The sum of the two would be: £20m+£15m = £35m

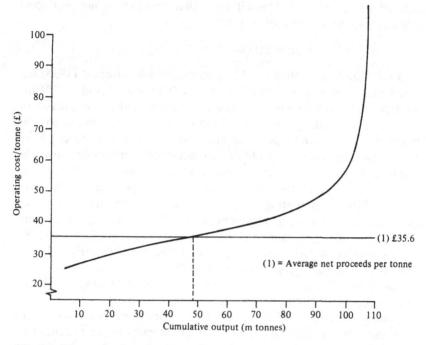

Fig. 3.1 Deep-mined production: unit operating costs against cumulative output, 1981/2 (MMC from NCB information).

The cost of the coal strike was high. But, as the Chancellor suggested, it has to be seen against the loss incurred by uneconomic pits. Table 3.4, which shows the operating results of the 24 most uneconomic collieries in this country in 1981–2, may provide us with some idea.

Table 3.4 shows that the cost of producing around 4m tonnes of output from the 24 most uneconomic pits in 1981–2 was nearly £120m. The average cost per tonne was as high as £74.58 and the average loss for one tonne of production was over £30. Figure 3.1 also shows that the marginal cost of producing more coal from uneconomic collieries is very high. Besides, the NCB also suggested that the present demand for coal is less than its intended supply by some 4m tonnes a year. This excess production can only be disposed of at a low export rate in the future. By cutting down the production by 4m tonnes, the Coal Board saves not only the operating loss (averaged at £30 per tonne) but also the difference between the average coal price and the low export rate. That difference is around £15. This will mean that savings from not producing that extra 4m tonnes of coal may be:

$$£[4\times(30+15)]m = £180m$$

In fact, the Monopolies and Mergers Commission Report (1983) has noted that most of the capital investment (planned at around £700m–800m per annum) has gone into collieries which are either unprofitable or of doubtful potential profitability. In this case, one can imagine that by restructuring the coal operation and diverting more resources from uneconomic collieries to profitable or potentially profitable ones, the nation can save still further resources. £180m is then probably a conservative estimate of the savings from cutting 4 per cent of the production. When discounting it as a perpetuity by the current rate for long-term index-linked government bonds (3.5 per cent), the present value of the savings is as high as £5.15bn. After allowing for the £200m capital investment that had to be spent after the end of the strike, the net present value of savings still stands at £4.95bn.

The narrow financial calculation referred to by the Chancellor is the comparison of the public sector costs of the strike with the net revenue gains from pit closures; after a strike of 50 weeks' duration its cost would be of the order of £2bn, while the discounted gains are of the order of £5bn, substantially greater. This, however, takes no account of the wider issues to which we now turn.

Section B. Wider calculations

National resources

This calculation is 'the narrow financial' one of the effects on the public finances referred to by the Chancellor. In practice, this is the most important calculation for a government which is aiming to reduce taxation. But it is not the only relevant calculation. One may also look at the effect on national resources (that is, the flow of net output). In this case, one asks what is the loss of output during this dispute and the gain to output after it when pits are closed. This is, on the face of it, easily computed:

Loss of net output as a result of the dispute = (extra cost of burning oil instead of coal) + (loss of coal output valued at world prices × the real rate of interest for one year).[1]

Gain to net output after dispute = reduction of high-cost coal output × excess of marginal cost of production over world price.

52

Costs and benefits of closures

Table 3.5 *Gains from colliery closure plans*

| | £ billion (present value) | |
	Gross gain from pit closure	Net gain
Public finance basis	16½	15½
National resource basis	16½	16

The former loss based on our figures is about £550m. The latter gain is £180m per annum, worth £5bn at present value, giving a net resource gain of £4½bn. It can be clearly seen that it gives the same picture as the financial calculation; the gain of pit closure is massive. Of course this gain on resources implies a further gain on overall jobs because these extra resources can be spent in the economy generally and will partly be spent on new jobs; the extra jobs from this source are estimated at about 3,000.[2]

One may go further and suppose that *all* uneconomic pits are closed (representing about half of NCB's current tonnage). The losses from the strike are the same, of course. The gain now becomes as in table 3.5. If all uneconomic pits were closed the national gain would be roughly treble that from the presently announced closure plan.

Other considerations

The unemployment aspect

It has been argued (by Davies and Metcalf, 1984; Glyn, 1984; see chapters 2 and 4 respectively) that payment of unemployment and supplementary benefits to miners unemployed as a result of pit closures, plus the loss of tax revenue they or their employers would have paid, should be included in the calculations. On this argument, public finances could be reduced by as much as £7,000 p.a. per man laid off by pit closures; and the gain to national resources would be only the reduction of high-cost output × excess (over world price) of marginal cost of production *excluding* manpower cost (this is excluded now as the manpower involved would not work elsewhere, so has zero value). The manpower cost is a large part of the marginal cost of production, so that the resources gain would also be dramatically reduced or even be negative. In other words, it might be better to have these coal miners producing *something* if it has a worth over and above the co-operating resources used up.

Economics and accounting of the NCB

This argument is based on a simple fallacy. It assumes that the *national* unemployment rate rises by the amount by which *mining* employment falls. Yet the fall in mining employment results from reduced public expenditure which is diverted into private or other public expenditure. Aggregate expenditure is not reduced nor consequently is aggregate demand for labour. Employment is displaced from the mines into other sectors. (Aggregate supply of labour is of course not affected by the switch in expenditure.)

Many people have pointed out that, if this argument were true, it would imply that little or no change in the structure of the economy would ever be worthwhile: a ludicrous conclusion which amounts to a disproof by *reductio ab absurdum*. However, it is as well to recognise the fallacy by which the absurdity arises. What its proponents may have implicitly in mind is one of the *indirect effects considered below*.

Indirect effects on the economy

There are indirect effects on national unemployment and output which must also be considered. We noted earlier that because resources are increased by closing high-cost pits this in fact *decreases* national unemployment; the reason is that by restructuring demand towards more efficient industries overall productivity rises and demand for labour is thereby increased; closing 4m tonnes of high-cost capacity would create about 3,000 jobs.

Secondly, there is the effect on the structure of taxation of high-cost pits. Strictly speaking, tax structure is separate from the total tax burden; but in practice there is a close link. There are two main ways in which high-cost pits are being paid for; first, by higher coal prices made possible by a quota on CEGB coal imports, and secondly by higher income tax (specifically at the present time reduced income tax thresholds). Both of these have particularly damaging incentive effects. The former is a tax on industrial energy, operating like a sales tax on manufacturing but one that is not rebatable on exports; it therefore reduces competitiveness (as say compared with an export rebatable VAT), and raises unemployment. The second falls heavily on low-paid employees, increasing the supply price of unskilled labour and so increasing unemployment. Hence in this discussion an indirect effect of high-cost pits remaining open is to increase unemployment. The effects of a £180m tax cut, split equally between these two forms, would take an additional 15,000 off the unemployment register according to the Liverpool Model.

Another aspect is the regional one. It may be argued that closing pits reduces jobs in high-unemployment areas while increasing them in low-unemployment areas; if this was so, some net increase in unemploy-

54

ment might result. However, the NCB offer included (1) transferring workers to other pits, (2) redundancy payments which in themselves make it possible to set up as self-employed, (3) a special job-trust to help initiate businesses in areas heavily affected. These measures are well designed to eliminate this particular problem. There is no evidence that on balance the new jobs in high-unemployment areas will not match up with the job losses.

The last aspect is that of labour-intensity. It might be argued that high-cost pits are more labour-intensive than the industries where new jobs will be created; if so, closing them would raise unemployment. But this is unlikely since new jobs are tending to be created in services, which are typically more labour-intensive than manufacturing.

Conclusion on other considerations

These other considerations clearly indicate lower national unemployment from closing high-cost pits; the rise in productive efficiency and the improvement in tax structure from closing just 4m tonnes of capacity would alone create 18,000 more jobs in total at a national level (i.e. over and above the job gains that offset the job losses in mining). This figure would be roughly trebled if *all* uneconomic pits were to be closed. The net effect of the regional and labour-intensity arguments would seem to be insignificant. Hence, it seems likely that on balance national unemployment would be reduced, as commonsense would indicate, by the closure of inefficient pits. What is absolutely clear is that the popular argument which adds the benefit and tax cost of the employment contraction in coal to the overall cost of closure is quite fallacious.

Overall conclusions

In these circumstances it is right to treat as a *minimum* estimate the net benefits conventionally calculated using market prices as a guide. And these indicate that the gain from pit closures both to public finances and to national resources would in any case be massive. What is more, the gain to continuing now with resistance to the NUM is even greater, because the cost of the strike is now a sunk cost; we have to weigh up the gain from making the closure programme stick against the loss from further strike action. This is without taking account of wider and equally significant issues such as the respect for the civil law on employment (and especially unions' compliance with the new union laws), the rule of law generally in the face of the recent violence, and the government's overall credibility; all of these wider issues point in the same direction that any final agreement must be one in which pit closures go ahead and any illegal tactics on the part of the NUM to avoid them be frustrated in a highly visible manner, *pour encourager les autres*.

NOTES

1 This output is only lost temporarily because it was made up after the dispute was over, so the cost is simply its deferral (for one year to allow for delays in re-starting and catching up of production).

2 This effect can be understood as follows. The excess of the value of the resources now used in high-cost pits over the value of their *product* is £180m per year. If these resources are diverted to other uses therefore the national product will be £180m higher; in the absence of additional demand, this will be sold abroad. This additional output and exports allow additional spending to take place until the current account of the balance of payments is in balance again; this additional spending draws additional labour resources into production (by raising real wages) because not all the addition is spent directly on imports, a proportion goes on home goods. This effect is calculated at about 3,000 jobs using the Liverpool Model (see Minford *et al.*, 1984).

REFERENCES

Davies, G. and D. Metcalf (1984), 'Pit Closures: Some Economics', 'Weekend World', September, London Weekend Television (reproduced in chapter 2).

Glyn, A. (1984), 'Economic Aspects of the Coal Industry Dispute', prepared for the NUM, October, mimeo Corpus Christi College, Oxford; see chapter 4.

Minford, A. P. L., S. Marwaha, K. Matthews and A. Sprague (1984), 'The Liverpool Macroeconomic Model of the United Kingdom', *Economic Modelling*, pp. 24–61.

Monopolies and Mergers Commission (1983), *National Coal Board: A Report on Efficiency and Costs in the Development, Production and Supply of Coal by the NCB*, 2 vols., Cmnd. 8920, London: HMSO.

4

The economic case against pit closures

ANDREW GLYN

Introduction

In setting out the economic case against pit closures, the wider social effects, not captured in the economic calculations, are not considered. This is because they have received ample coverage elsewhere. Section 1 shows that, contrary to government allegations that the coal industry was 'insolvent' before the dispute, the production of coal in 1983/4 more or less covered its underlying costs of production and financed the industry's investment. Next (section 2), the basic case against closure of the so-called 'uneconomic pits' is set out, showing that far from benefiting the rest of society this leads to higher taxation and lower living standards as a result of the loss of production involved. The costs of closure are then analysed in some detail (section 3) and used in calculations which show that there is not one single pit whose closure would benefit government revenue (section 4). The crucial assumption that the impact of closure on unemployment is a permanent one under current conditions is then justified (section 5). It is further shown that in these circumstances investment to develop reserves at existing pits is extremely beneficial (section 6). Pit closure can be justified neither by reference to the availability of cheaper imports (section 7) nor to lack of demand (section 8), nor to the coming on stream of new capacity (section 9). Finally, the extreme selfishness of pit closure in relation to future generations is explained (section 10). The conclusion is that under present circumstances there is no economic case whatsoever for pit closure before exhaustion of mineable reserves.

Appendix 1 sets out in detail how the calculations for the costs of

Sections 1 and 2 of this paper draw on articles by the author published in the *Guardian* (Glyn, 1984a, b). With the addition of sections 4, 7–10 and Appendix 1 this paper is a revision of *Economic Aspects of the Coal Industry Dispute* written for the NUM at the end of September. Information and criticism from many people from the NUM and from elsewhere is gratefully acknowledged.

closure of the individual pits were constructed and presents detailed tables showing the results for individual pits and for the pits as a whole ranked by the extent of their operating losses. Appendix 2 sets out calculations made for the cost of the dispute in terms of lost production. They show that these costs ran at £100m or more per week. By the end of 1984 they would have reached over £4½bn, probably £5bn, taking into account the increased cost of burning oil.

1. The NCB's finances

In support of the NCB's pit closure programme, the government has repeatedly referred to the NCB's losses and the consequent need for government subsidies.

After the publication of the National Coal Board's *Report and Accounts* for 1983/4 at the end of July, Peter Walker, the Energy Secretary, said that the taxpayer subsidised the industry to the tune of £1.3bn, or nearly £130 per week for each miner. He claimed that 'the 1983/4 loss, 18 per cent of turnover, showed that the Coal Board was insolvent' with an 'underlying imbalance' between costs and revenues. But the figures given by the NCB itself, in the detailed tables and notes to their accounts, show how misleading is this picture of an industry forced to rely on government subsidy to cover the costs of production.[1]

The government 'subsidy' covers the NCB's operating losses (£358m), its interest payments (£467m), and its 'social costs' (£344m) with an additional £150m or so direct government payments to redundant miners included in Walker's £1.3bn total. Each of these items will be considered in turn.

'Operating losses' in fact include a number of items which manifestly are not costs of production. The biggest of these is £245m of provision for payments of 'surface damage', the costs of meeting claims for subsidence in mining areas. The near doubling of this item in 1983/4 reflects a rush of claims, especially in the Mansfield area. But it does not reflect the estimated costs arising from this year's mining (a much lower figure). Rather it is the historical legacy of past coal-mining operations.

Another item under the heading 'other external charges' is £130m of 'charges in respect of past employees' (mainly pensions to retired miners). Quite correctly the item 'wage charges' includes pension contributions for existing employees. But pensions paid to retired miners, like compensation to people whose houses have suffered subsidence damage as a result of past mining, cannot be regarded as costs of getting out coal now.

Yet these two items (and there are other smaller ones of a similar nature) more than account for the NCB's operating loss. If they are left out then the NCB made an operating profit in 1983/4. And, but for the £200m or so effect of the strike and the overtime ban, the NCB would even have financed practically all of its £698m gross investment in fixed assets out of its own revenue.

Certainly claims for subsidence, pensions, etc. have to be met, but they would have to be met even if the NCB closed down. They are 'transfer payments' which result from past history, not payments in respect of current production. There is no reason why they should be met (via high prices or lower wages) by those who now use coal or produce it. It is perfectly equitable for the taxpayer (via government grants) to cover these payments; in no sense does this make them a subsidy to the production of coal.

The next chunk of 'subsidy' has to cover so-called 'social costs'. These are 'costs in respect of the closure of uneconomic capacity or redundancy of employees which are wholly or partly met by government grants'. Again, they are not a cost of producing this year's coal; indeed, they are a cost of not producing coal. They too are transfer payments which have to be made as a result of the contraction of the industry. But they would have to be made even if no coal was produced at all.

Exactly the same goes for the direct government payments to redundant miners. The costs of maintaining workers who are unemployed constitutes an economic argument for not closing pits in the first place. They do not, as the NCB's account suggests, represent an additional charge making the existing pits less economic.

The final item which has to be 'subsidised' by the government is the £467m of interest payments (£400m of which go straight back to the government). This huge figure directly reflects both the high interest-rate policy of the government and the fact that so much of the NCB's investment has been financed by fixed-interest loans.

It actually represented a pay-out of 6.3 per cent on the (replacement) value of the NCB's capital employed. It represents half as much again as is paid out in dividends and interest by private industrial and commercial companies, and more than twice the pay-out by nationalised industries as a whole.[2] So much of this part of the subsidy is paid by the government to itself to give itself an inflated return.

Rearranging the accounts to take due account of the economic categories involved yields the picture (table 4.1) that practically all of the government subsidies were used to cover historical and exceptional items. But for the cost of the dispute almost all of the industry's investment, which was hardly above current cost depreciation, would have been financed from its resources.

Economics and accounting of the NCB

Table 4.1 *NCB accounts 1983/4*

	Actual NCB accounts	Adjusted to economic categories
(1) PROFIT AND LOSS ACCOUNT		
	£m	£m
Turnover	4660	4660
− **Operating costs**	5018	4968
Raw materials and stores	947	947
Employee costs	2430	2430
Other costs (net)	1283	958[1]
Depreciation	(historic cost) 358	(replacement cost) 633
= **Operating profit**	− 358	− 308
+ Costs of dispute	n.a.	212
= **Underlying net profit**	n.a.	− 96
+ Depreciation	n.a.	633
= **Underlying gross profit**	n.a.	537
(2) APPROPRIATION OF PROFIT		
Underlying gross profit		537
+ Social grants and deficit grants from government		1145
= **Total receipts**		1682
− **Payments**		1136
Provisions for additional subsidence costs		195[1]
Pensions to past employees, etc.		130[1]
Social costs (redundancy, etc.)		344
Interest payments (net)		467
= **Underlying gross savings**		546
(3) CAPITAL ACCOUNT		
Investment in fixed assets		698
+ Additions to stocks		−92
= **Total investment**		606
− Underlying gross savings		546
− Profits on sale of assets		22
= **Underlying borrowing requirement**		38
+ Costs of dispute		212
= **Actual net borrowing**		240

[1] The figure for other net costs is adjusted from the NCB accounts to exclude all but £50m of the £245m provision for subsidence costs (the £50m being assumed to reflect provisions against effect of current mining) and the £130m pensions to past employees.
Source: NCB Accounts 1983/4.

Economic case against closures

The conclusion must be that the government cannot be said to be subsidising the production of coal. Sales of coal, even in the present depressed conditions, are practically enough to pay the miners and for the other inputs actually used to produce the coal, including a proper level of depreciation. The general state of the industry's finances cannot be used to justify in any way the NCB's pit-closure programme.

2. The basic case against pit closure

The basic economic case against pit closure is simple. The effect of closure is to reduce coal output by the contribution of the pit concerned. This is a cost to society which no longer has the coal at its disposal. In the present context of mass unemployment, numbers out of work will increase by the number of people who lose their jobs after the closure. There is accordingly no rise in production elsewhere to compensate for the fall in coal production. Society as a whole loses by the amount of coal production foregone.

Operating losses certainly do not, in themselves, justify closure. They do imply that the value of the coal produced is less than the various costs attributed to the pit. But to conclude that the pits should be closed pre-supposes that the resources which these costs represent would have been used elsewhere to produce something of greater value. If, on the contrary, those resources (both workers and equipment) would otherwise be idle, there is no real cost to society from their use in producing coal. Society as a whole gains the value of the coal. The miners gain the difference between their take-home pay at work and what they would receive if unemployed. If the value of the coal they produce exceeds what they gain the rest of society benefits as well. This is reflected in the fact that costs of closure which the government incurs (redundancy pay, dole and lost tax) exceed the operating subsidies which the government pays to keep the pits open.

Before justifying the argument in more detail it is worth illustrating it with the example of the so-called highest-cost pits. In 1983 the NCB claimed that the highest-cost 12 per cent of colliery output incurred £275m losses. These collieries employed about 40,000 miners. In addition, a further 35,000 or so other jobs were dependent on these pits.[3] Around a quarter of these were other NCB jobs (at pit, Area or HQ levels). The rest were in industries such as electricity, steel and engineering, which supply inputs needed by the pits. If the pits were to be closed and their losses eliminated, all these 75,000 workers would lose their jobs. But the country would lose the coal. The coal produced in these pits was worth around £475m (in 1982/3 prices).

Moreover, it was not only the miners and workers in supplying industries who gained from the pits being kept open. If it is assumed that they were all on average £70 per week better off in work than on the dole (a rather high estimate), they gained some £270m. But the pits produced £475m in extra output. So, after taking account of the amount required to pay the workers concerned, the rest of society actually benefited from the pits staying open to the tune of the £205m extra production at its disposal. This is reflected at the financial level by the effect on government receipts and payments. Whilst the government would have 'saved' £275m subsidy if the pits had been closed, it would have lost some £480m in lost tax revenue and through having to pay dole to the unemployed. So closing the so-called 'unprofitable' pits, whilst perfectly in tune with the NCB's task of increasing profitability, would have imposed substantial losses on the rest of society as well as on the miners concerned. In no sense, then, can these 'unprofitable' pits be labelled 'uneconomic' from the point of view of society.

3. The costs of closure

The benefit to the workers concerned of having jobs rather than being on the dole is obvious enough (though the exact financial advantage will depend on the workers' personal circumstances). But what, more precisely, is the impact of closing a colliery on government finances (and thus indirectly on the rest of society, via its impact on taxation)? The situation can be illustrated by taking a typical case where pit closure leads to a miner of 57 taking redundancy (either at the pit concerned or at a pit to which miners from the closed colliery are transferred). It is assumed that without the closure the older miner would have worked for a further five years. The person displaced from a job is initially the older miner, but after he would have retired anyway the loss of a job is borne by another person (the 'new' miner in table 4.2), who would otherwise have been taken on. A point frequently neglected is that for each 100 job losses for miners there will be about 87 lost elsewhere (around 25 in the NCB and the rest in supplying industries). Taking all these effects on employment into account, the pattern of costs of closure and subsidy savings to the government over the early years of the closure of an average 'uneconomic' pit, is shown in table 4.2.

It is assumed implicitly in the Henley (1984) study and explicitly by Davies and Metcalf (chapter 2) that pit closure leads to no job loss apart from the NUM members immediately concerned, implying that all other NCB employees both at the pit and at higher levels find other jobs immediately (they cannot be kept on by the NCB or else their costs,

Economic case against closures

Table 4.2 *Effect of closure on government finances*[4]
(£ per mining job lost)

	Redundancy pay etc. for older miner and lost tax revenue	Dole for 'new' miner and lost tax	Dole and tax lost for NCB staff and other workers	Total costs	Subsidy saved
Year	1	2	3	4 = 1+2+3	5
1	15,764	would	4,812	20,576	6,875
2	7,644	be	4,812	12,456	6,875
3	7,644	on	4,812	12,456	6,875
4	7,644	dole	4,812	12,456	6,875
5	7,644	anyway	4,812	12,456	6,875
6	would have retired	5,500	4,812	10,312	6,875
7	anyway	5,500	4,812	10,312	6,875

attributed to the pits, would not be saved), and that the same goes for all employees in affected supplying industries. No justification is given for these wholly implausible assumptions, which substantially cuts the adverse effect on government revenue of the pit closures. From table 4.2 it can be seen that even in later years the costs to the Exchequer (column 4) are far greater than the benefits from the subsidy (column 5), confirming the analysis in section 2. In the first year of course the costs of closure are enormous. On average over a seven-year period the costs of around £13,000 a year are nearly double the subsidy.

4. The effects of closure on individual pits

Using the information supplied to the NUM by the NCB in the *Operating Colliery Results*, these calculations for the economic effect of pit closure can be repeated for individual pits. The fact that closure is contrary to society's interests can then be demonstrated, in a vivid and immediate way, for individual collieries actually under threat of closure.

It should be emphasised that the information supplied by the NCB for individual pits is by no means complete. This makes the calculations more approximate than they would be if the full statement of each pit's costs was available. Moreover it is well known that individual colliery results fluctuate a great deal due to geological conditions; the NCB reported to the Monopolies Commission that colliery costs could fluctuate from year to year by as much as 30 per cent (MMC, 1983). In

Economics and accounting of the NCB

Table 4.3 *Costs of closure for threatened pits*
(£ per miner per week)

	If colliery is closed, cost to government revenue	Present level of subsidy to keep pit open	So to close pit means no loss to government of
Herrington	281	82	199
Cortonwood	295	74	221
Bullcliffe Wood	467	251	216
Snowdown	260	232	28

Note: the reason that the estimates of costs of closure in column 1 vary between pits is that the higher the costs other than miners' pay, the greater is the impact on other industries and thus the greater the costs of closure per *miner* affected.

extreme cases development work on the pit could mean that no coal was produced at all (Treforgan and Polmaise were examples in 1983), or that the pits' results were especially distorted (Selby and Snowdown). In addition there are ways in which colliery results can be made to look especially bad by loading extra overheads on to the pit or by holding back its output which leads to higher average costs. So no pit should be judged on a few months' results. But their analysis does at least give a valuable snapshot of the industry.

The calculations are based on (1) estimates, described in the previous section, of the costs to the government of unemployment of miners and other workers and (2) calculations of the number of workers affected in the NCB and in industries depending both on the NCB and on miners' spending. The precise assumptions and methods of calculation are explained in appendix 1. While the results are inevitably approximate they do allow a reasonable estimate to be made of the costs of closure of individual pits.

The calculations were carried out on the data for the 166 pits (the total number of pits in the British coalfield is 176 but in a few cases complexes of pits report jointly) operating prior to the strike, covering 29 weeks of 1983/4 before the overtime ban.

Whilst 103 pits are shown as reporting operating losses over this period, in not one case would closure have benefited government revenue. That is, on our calculations of the impact on and costs of unemployment, in every single case the 'subsidy' from the government required to cover the pit's reported operating deficit is less than what the government would lose in the form of dole payments, tax foregone and costs attributed to the pit which would not be saved. This can be illustrated with the examples of the pits which were immediately under threat at the beginning of the strike (excluding Polmaise where work being carried out was for 'development' and no results were reported).

Even Snowdown, burdened at the time with development work, which gave it much the lowest sales revenue per miner of all the NCB's pits (£103 per week), would have cost more to close than to keep open. On these estimates only three pits would have showed a gain to government revenue of being kept open of less than £100 per week per miner. The other three pits actually threatened with immediate closure would have cost the government around £200 per week more per miner to close than to keep open. The full list of pits, ranked in order of the net gain to the government from their being kept open, is given in table 4.4 in appendix 1.

The results can be looked at in another way. The 'worst' 20 pits (in terms of operating losses per tonne of coal) employed 17,600 miners, were producing at an annual rate of 4.7m tonnes and showed:

(1) operating losses running at a rate of £153m per year;
(2) costs of closure which would have totalled £267m per year; so
(3) the government was gaining some £114m per year from keeping the pits open and covering their operating deficits, rather than closing them and incurring the costs of closure.

Table 4.5 in appendix 1 allows this calculation to be done for any number of 'worst' pits by showing the pits (excluding in this case Snowdown and Selby Complex, whose results were especially affected by development work) ranked by the extent of government subsidy per tonne and with subsidy, costs of closure, and so on, cumulated for all pits up to and including the one in question. These more detailed pit-by-pit calculations, taking into account the pattern of redundancy payments and an estimate of the impact on industries dependent on the spending of workers affected, actually show substantially larger costs of closure than the simpler calculations outlined in section 2.

Whilst the results are, of course, dependent on the assumptions fed in (for costs of redundancy, etc.), the results are in fact very 'robust' in the face of changes in these assumptions.

(1) If it was assumed, most unfavourably to the case for keeping pits open, that we had exaggerated the true costs of closure by one-third, then only in the exceptional case of Snowdown would closure have benefited government revenue. Even then the gain would have been only a few pounds per miner per week, trifling in relation to the benefits of maintaining the jobs and incomes of the workers concerned.

(2) If, again very unfavourably, we ignore the 'multiplier effect' of closure on industries supplying the miners and others directly affected with goods and services, then again the only pit which shows a net benefit to the government from closure would be the exceptional case, Snowdown, whose reported results are not a reliable indicator of the longer-term position.

These results are devastating. On assumptions which, as appendix 1 shows, are by no means highly favourable to the case, there are no pits whatsoever whose closure would benefit government revenue. It implies that not only do the miners, and other workers directly and indirectly affected, benefit from keeping their jobs, but the rest of society also gains from the pits being kept open, as the 'subsidy' required is less than the costs of maintaining the workers concerned on the dole. It would require a whole battery of very unfavourable assumptions to make it possible to show revenue gains to the government from closure of even a handful of the highest-cost pits. The value of the coal produced makes every pit 'economic' once the interests of the miners and other workers affected, together with those of the rest of society, are taken into account.

5. The unemployment assumption

The most detailed attempt to examine the economic implications of pit closure, by Davies and Metcalf (chapter 2) for 'Weekend World', came to less unambiguous conclusions. The fundamental reason for this is that they assumed that workers displaced by pit closure do, over a period of time, find jobs. This means that, whilst the costs in terms of lost coal production are heavy immediately after pit closure, they are increasingly offset, and then more than offset, by increased production in other industries as displaced workers take up jobs which are more productive than those they were doing in mining.

This assumption is entirely responsible for their conclusion (p. 41) that 50–60 pits should perhaps be closed on average after 5 years. As they themselves admit, 'where there is a binding long-term constraint on employment because of permanent demand deficiency (that is, that displaced workers *cannot* find jobs – AG) ... *the pit should probably be left open to exhaustion*' (our emphasis).

Yet, under the present situation of mass unemployment what possible basis is there for asssuming that displaced workers *are* re-employed? It must be emphasised that the question is not simply whether or not the miners at the pits which are closed find re-employment, though NCB figures show that, of 43,141 mineworkers who have taken redundancy, only 0.2 per cent have obtained alternative employment.

Economic case against closures

Whether or not the NCB could maintain its guarantee of no compulsory redundancies is in fact irrelevant to the economics of the case. Even if all the coal miners (and others directly affected) found jobs at once, the loss of jobs at the pit concerned would still mean a corresponding fall in total employment if the re-employment of these miners simply meant that somebody else did not get a job. This would be the case, for example, if a miner moved to a nearby pit, but thereby deprived somebody else of the chance of a job there. This is a typical situation.

The only argument that Davies and Metcalf can muster in support of their assumption of the gradual re-absorption of those put out of work is the following: 'it could be argued that redundant mineworkers would *eventually* (their emphasis) create net extra jobs in the economy, either through entrepreneurial skills and/or through depressing the general level of the real wage' (pp. 32–3). Whilst no doubt a few mineworkers might set up on their own, it is quite implausible that this would create more than a handful of extra jobs. The rise in self-employment since 1979 has only offset a fraction of the decline in jobs for employees, and many of the people self-employed will be making a most marginal contribution to production as they huddle into the over-crowded occupations where costs of starting a business are small. Further, whatever orthodox economics might say, it is both highly unlikely that the addition to the dole queue would depress real wages and highly implausible that, if it did, there would be any new jobs created as a result (the fall in purchasing power if real wages fell would tend to reduce demand and therefore employment). The persistence of mass unemployment wholly discredits this theory.

It even sounds as though the authors are dubious about their own assumption when they say later, 'in the longer run, say five or ten years, some of the redundant miners are presumably going to find alternative jobs without displacing other workers by one of the above routes, especially if the economy ever returns to full employment' (p. 33). But there is no likelihood whatsoever of a return to full employment on present policies and thus no basis for assuming it as a way of justifying an unemployment effect of pit closures which declines over time. Indeed, it would be much more plausible to argue that pit closures will lead to *more* workers being unemployed in the longer run than are directly affected at the start, as the loss in purchasing power has secondary effects on other industries. The inclusion of this effect increased the costs of closure of the individual pits estimated in section 4 and strengthens the economic case against closure.

The study by Minford and Kung of Liverpool University (chapter 3) attacks the case against closure on two grounds. First they claim (p. 54) that it implies the 'ludicrous conclusion' that 'little or no change in the structure of the economy would ever be worthwhile'. It is self-evident that in a situation of full employment, rapid growth in new industries would require a contraction in the number of jobs in old industries. But with well over 3 million unemployed it is quite absurd to argue that the development of new industries is in any way inhibited by keeping open the pits. That is, unless you believe (as the authors may well do) that those out of work at present are 'voluntarily unemployed' and thus not available to take up work in sectors which are expanding.

Their second argument is that estimates, such as those in section 2, of the employment effects of pit closure ignore the fact that cutting subsidies to the pits would mean either that other public expenditure increases, or that taxes are cut and private consumption rises. Either way 'aggregate expenditure is not reduced nor consequently is aggregate demand for labour [reduced]' (p. 54). This argument is false. First, there is no reason to suppose that if the government spent less on supporting the coal industry then it *would* either increase public spending or reduce taxation. A major thrust of this government's policy has been to reduce public sector borrowing and, to achieve this target, cuts in one type of public spending cannot finance either increases in other public spending or tax cuts. But, even if taxes were cut, or other spending increased, this would not offset the impact on mining jobs.

Taking the (more plausible) case of tax cuts, a reduction in taxation of £275m saved by closure of 'uneconomic' pits would certainly increase demand for consumer goods. But the impact of this on employment would be much less than the 75,000 jobs lost through closing the pits. Taking into account some effect on savings, the number of new jobs which would result from the expenditure would be around 25,000 (see note 3). So the net fall in employment would be 50,000, with net unemployment costs of £310m. But this is not the end of the story. If the PSBR is not to *increase* as a result of this package of pit closures and tax cuts, then taxes would then have to be *raised* by £310m. This would more than wipe out the impact of the original tax cut. Far from offsetting part of the employment effect of closure, the requirement that pit closure leaves the balance between expenditure and taxation undisturbed actually increases the impact on jobs, as the cost of unemployment has to be financed by higher taxation, squeezing the economy even further. It would, ironically, only be if the £275m was diverted to 'subsidising' the same number of jobs in other industries as it presently supports in mining that there would be no employment effect, and this is the one use of the funds which is entirely ruled out by current government policy.

Minford and Kung claim that closing 4m tonnes of high-cost capacity would actually lead to a net *increase* in employment in the economy as a whole of some 18,000 (i.e. that new jobs created as a result of pit closure would run at about twice those lost). These figures are derived from the 'Liverpool Model', which must be a remarkable construction, probably the first ever economic model able to predict miracles.

6. Investment

The case for investment to redevelop and extend the life of existing pits is also enormously strengthened by analysing the effects on the economy, rather than simply looking at the NCB's profit and loss account. Just as NCB losses are no guide to whether to keep pits open when the alternative is unemployment, so the NCB's expected profits from additional investment are no guide to its economic contribution. If new investment allows workers who would otherwise be out of work to produce coal, then the whole of the value of the coal constitutes a return on the investment. To take an entirely hypothetical case, suppose an investment of £1m generates £2m of extra coal a year in a pit – if the costs of production and depreciation were also £2m per year, the NCB would see it is making no profit and thus would not incur additional interest costs to undertake it. But from society's point of view the return is £2m a year for an outlay of £1m, for without the investment the labour involved would produce nothing. The rate of return would be 200 per cent a year! Indeed, if the construction of the new development involved resources (construction workers, engineering workers, etc.) who would otherwise be unemployed, *its* real cost would also be far below its financial cost (thus further increasing the percentage return to society). On this basis the only pits where investment could not be justified would be those where the mineable coal was genuinely exhausted.

7. Imports and the price of coal

In the calculations for the costs of closure discussed so far it has been assumed that the NCB's figures for the average proceeds from sales of coal are correct measures of the value of the coal produced. But if the coal could be bought from abroad at a cheaper price than the NCB receives (from the CEGB or its other customers), should not the NCB's coal be valued at the costs of competitive imports? This after all shows what would have to be paid for the fuel if it was not supplied by the NCB.

Proponents of this argument usually take it as self-evident that imported coal is cheaper, frequently quoting figures which take little or no account of relevant transport costs. The most complete information

Economics and accounting of the NCB

was supplied by the CEGB to the Monopolies Commission and showed the position as of October 1982. This showed (MMC, 1983, p. 75) that imported coal under existing contracts was 8 per cent cheaper than NCB supplies to the Thames power stations (where transport costs favour imports), and that if the NCB had been able to take advantage of the depressed prices on the 'spot' market in Rotterdam they could have secured a price advantage of 26 per cent. But these benefits were entirely due to the exchange rate (£1 = $1.70). At present exchange rates (£1 = $1.20) imported coal under those contracts would be 30 per cent *more* expensive than NCB supplies and even spot coal slightly dearer.

Moreover, the import lobby never accept the logic of their own argument. If the NCB's coal sold to Thames stations should be valued at the cost of competitive imports, so should the coal sold to the Midlands stations where, being close to the pits, transport costs favour domestic coal. In 1982 imported coal under existing contracts would have cost 13 per cent more (at the exchange rate then prevailing) at the Ratcliffe (Notts) station than the NCB's coal, and spot coal would have only had a 6 per cent price advantage. At current exchange rates, imported coal at 1982 contract prices would cost 60 per cent more than NCB coal and even spot coal would be 33 per cent more expensive. If we guessed that on average competitive imports would cost 20 per cent more than NCB's coal, then revaluing the NCB's output at the competitive price would yield the NCB an extra £1,000 revenue; turning its alleged losses into huge profits.

Of course it would be stupid to base all the NCB's financial calculations on an import price which fluctuates wildly with the dollar price of coal and with the £/$ exchange rate. But nor is examination of the likely longer-run trend in the price of imported coal of much comfort to the coal imports lobby. The longer-run costs of production in the USA are currently estimated to give a break-even price of some $60–75 at Thames power stations (£50–60 at current exchange rates). A recent study came up with $75 per tonne as the most likely estimate of coal prices towards the end of the century; even at a rate of £1 = $1.50 this gives a landed price of around £50 per tonne, close to the present NCB price at the power stations.[5]

The suggestion of the import lobby is that at the likely price, large amounts of the highest cost NCB capacity would still be more expensive than imports and that the UK industry could only remain competitive by cutting out its high-cost pits. But in the context of mass unemployment this argument is wholly false. For if the resources in the high-cost pits would otherwise be unemployed the real costs of imports is not the price paid by the importer but that price plus the cost to the government of all

Economic case against closures

the unemployment caused by closure. It has already been shown that, given the present prices charged for NCB coal (and thus the present accounting losses on high-cost pits), there is not one pit whose closure would benefit government revenue. This means that the real cost of imports (price of imports, assumed to equal the NCB price, plus costs of closure) are greater than the costs of production of even the highest-cost pit. So the closure of a single pit could not be justified by reference to cheaper costs of imports.

Even twisting the assumptions further in favour of imports makes virtually no difference. If we assumed that the price the NCB charges was actually one-third above the competitive import price, which is really scraping around on the bottom of the plausible range of possibilities, only one pit judging by the 1983 results would be vulnerable to imports once the costs of closure are taken into account. And for that pit, Snowdown again, the 1983 results are not a real guide to the longer-term prospects.

8. Demand

But is the coal from the 'marginal' pits really worth anything, given the piling up of coal stocks in recent years? This stockbuilding, however, just like rising unemployment, reflects the government-induced contraction in the economy. If growth after 1979 had continued even at the slow rate achieved after the first 'oil shock', then production in 1984 would have been some 7 per cent higher and coal use correspondingly increased. Coal stocks, in October last year before the overtime ban, would have been under 30m tonnes, less than just before the disputes of 1971 and 1973. So there is no shortage of valuable uses to which the coal from the higher-cost pits could be put: to give one obvious example, if all pensioners had £1 per week extra to spend on fuel it would increase coal use by at least 1m tonnes per year.[6] The reason that coal sales are so low is that production and incomes are so depressed. Even the pre-1979 pattern of growth would have meant coal sales some 8m tonnes higher by 1984, which would have made the 4m tonnes per year reduction in capacity carried through in 1983/4 and planned for 1984/5 wholly unnecessary. Anything like full use of the economy's capacity would have implied a still higher coal demand.

9. New capacity

In the longer term, however, it is not only government-induced depression of sales which is threatening the markets for the coal produced by the higher-cost pits. New capacity, planned in the days

71

when a much more buoyant economy and hence coal market was anticipated, is expected to come on stream at a rapid rate over the next few years. Speaking early in 1984, NCB member H. M. Spanton said that 25m tonnes of new capacity was under construction (Spanton, 1984). This is precisely in line with the NCB's 1981 *Development Plan to 1990*, which shows new capacity of 25m tonnes being introduced in the years 1984/5 to 1990/1 (MMC, 1983, p. 92). Will this new capacity find a market?

Consumption of UK deep-mined coal was about 97m tonnes in 1983/4. (This was the level of capacity which the NCB was aiming for in 1984/5 with its March announcement of pit closures.) Mr Spanton said of the market for coal that 'little change is expected for several years with modest growth thereafter'. This was confirmed in the NCB's 1983/4 Report (p. 7) which 'looked forward to securing and developing a market for at least 100m tonnes a year of efficient deep-mined capacity'.

The combination of 25m tonnes of new capacity with sales stuck at 100m tonnes has devastating implications for the older pits. Given capacity of 101m tonnes at the beginning of 1984/5, 26m tonnes of higher-cost capacity would have to be closed over the succeeding seven years to 'make room' for the new mines and projects. This represents a rate of closure of older pits of practically 4m tonnes per year. The pit closure programme for 1983/4, and that planned for 1984/5, would therefore have to be repeated *each year* until 1990.

What would this rate of closure imply for jobs? Based on the figures for 1983/4 for each pit shown in table 4.5, the closure of the highest-cost 26m tonnes of capacity by 1990 would involve the closure of 70 pits and the loss of 69,000 mining jobs (leaving aside the impact on other NCB jobs and on workers in supplying industries). This would include 20 pits in South Wales, 7 in the North-East, 9 in the Barnsley area, 5 in Scotland and all 3 Kent pits. The Board have also stated to the NUM that within the same time-scale 50 per cent of the pits in South Notts and North Derbyshire will also close. It would not necessarily be precisely these pits which were closed, since economising on overheads might mean that the NCB saved more by even greater geographical concentration of the closures. Over 80 per cent of colliery losses would probably be eliminated.

The net loss of mining jobs would be less than the 69,000 or so which would go with the closures. The 25m tonnes of new capacity would involve some new jobs, though not very many. The 10m tonnes of capacity at Selby is expected to require only 4,000 miners (this is around five times the average productivity of existing pits). If the rest of the new capacity operated at half the Selby productivity level, then in total 16,000 new jobs would be created. So the effect of the introduction of the new capacity would be a reduction in mining employment of some 53,000 jobs by 1990 (leaving entirely out of account reductions in manpower, perhaps very substantial, at existing pits due to the introduction of new technology).

The NCB's real perspective for the next few years, therefore, is for the replacement of old capacity with new lower-cost capacity, rather than the closure of pits *and* loss of production. Does the economic case against pit closure still apply to closures under these conditions as well? Fundamentally the argument is unaltered. The case for replacing high-cost capacity with cheaper new pits is that resources (mainly workers) are released for more productive use outside the industry. As already argued, there is no chance in present economic conditions that this would occur. Installing the most up-to-date systems of production so that one worker can do the work of five is of no benefit to society as a whole if the four whose jobs are lost are unemployed.

The total value of output will be unchanged, which is another way of saying that society as a whole will neither gain nor lose. Those put out of work will suffer, since what they receive in redundancy pay and dole will be less than their net pay when at work. Their loss will be the rest of society's gain. But this gain will be far less than the difference in the NCB's costs on the new and the old pits. For closing the old pits leads to the government paying all the unemployment costs of closure. So the gain to the government (and thus the gain to the rest of society) is only a fraction of the cost and profit advantage to the NCB of replacing the old capacity with new. Moreover, to the extent that the rest of society gains, it is entirely at the expense of the jobs and incomes of the unemployed.

This can be illustrated very clearly for the projected replacement of 26m tonnes of old capacity with new. In 1983/4 the highest-cost 26m tonnes of capacity had operating costs of some £55 per tonne. Operating costs at Selby are expected to be £20 per tonne (MMC, 1983, p. 288). Assuming the other new capacity is substantially more costly then Selby might suggest an average cost of the new capacity of say £25 per tonne. A cost saving of £30 per tonne on 26m tonnes implies that the NCB's profits would benefit to the tune of £780m a year. But this gain to the NCB is no measure of the gain to the rest of society. Closure of the 70 pits would involve (annual) costs of closure of some £1,055m. To be set against this is the fact that some of those workers affected will be redeployed to the new pits (both directly and in the supplying industries). Taking into account the likely structure of costs on the new pits, the total net costs of closure (costs of closure of the old pits less those saved by redeployment on the new) come to some £680m. So the net benefit to the rest of society is only £100m (£780m less £680m), far less than the cost saving to the NCB. And it would all be at the expense of miners and other workers made redundant.

There can be no possible justification for such a policy. Even if the NCB passed on the benefits of its lower costs to other industries in the form of lower prices, most of this benefit would be taken back with the other hand as the government raised taxes to pay the costs of closure. Whatever slight net advantage remained would be paid for entirely by those who lose their jobs. In a situation of mass unemployment and stagnant demand the new capacity should only be introduced when existing pits are actually exhausted, or when a reduction in the working week for miners requires it be brought into use to meet demand. There is no basis whatever under present conditions for using the development of new lower-cost capacity as a justification for premature closing of older pits.

10. Future generations

There is a further argument against such a policy of closing older pits which would apply even in. conditions of full employment, where alternative work was available for those affected. The closure of such pits would mean that their reserves of coal could only be mined at a later date at far greater expense (since there are high engineering costs in reopening an old mine).

To make the ripping-out of the maximum amount of low-cost coal coincide with high rates of exploitation of the limited North Sea oil reserves seems to show the most flagrant disregard for the interests of the next generation. Much of the revenue from North Sea oil has been used to finance the mounting dole queues. The squandering of the best coal reserves would be even worse if the benefits of Selby and the other new pits are eaten up in paying dole to those directly put out of work by the introduction of this new capacity. E. F. Schumacher (at the time economic advisor to the Coal Board) put the case against premature closing of pits with mineable reserves nearly 25 years ago:

> It is a policy of doubtful wisdom and questionable morality for this generation to take all the best resources and leave for its children only the worst. But it is surely a criminal policy if, in addition, we wilfully sterilise, abandon and thereby ruin such relatively inferior resources as we ourselves have opened up but do not care to utilise. This is like the spiteful burglar who does not merely pinch the valuables but in addition destroys everything he cannot take (Schumacher, 1960).

In the present situation of mass unemployment it is doubly criminal, since it is not only mineral but human resources which are wasted, and since most of the apparent benefit from grabbing the best resources is swallowed up by ensuring that those wasted human resources can be kept alive.

Postscript

The arguments in this chapter were criticised on a number of grounds, both during the strike and thereafter. The most frequent objection was that the arguments contained in it could apply to any other industry as well as to coal; that there was no case for singling out miners for special treatment and that to support loss-making industries more generally would be a recipe for a backward economy, frozen into an inappropriate pattern of production.

It is perfectly correct that the general argument that it is better to have workers produce something of value rather than contribute nothing to the economy can be applied more widely than the coal industry. In my opinion this is a strength rather than a weakness. The coal miners' case was indeed part of a general case against unemployment, and one reason that their struggle deserved support was that they were attempting to fight against the logic of the market for which 'unprofitable' means 'uneconomic'.

Nor can it plausibly be argued that keeping open loss-making pits (or factories) would inhibit new industries. If new industries were short of labour then the case might be different. In a situation of full employment, the expansion of some industries necessarily requires the contraction of others; it might well be that the process of structural change required the running-down of older industries such as coal and this of course was what happened in the fifties and sixties. But this was not the case in the early eighties: the miners really were faced with the dole rather than well-paid jobs in high-tech industries. It is true that continuing government support would have been required to keep the pits open. But since it would have cost more to close them, as the chapter argues, it cannot be maintained that keeping them open would have deprived the government of finance with which it could have supported other activities.

It is perfectly valid criticism of the chapter that it did not deal with the broader issues of energy policy, which are taken up in other contributions in this volume (though the chapter does make an economic case against imported coal). It is certainly true that the longer-run case for a large coal industry depends on consideration of alternative energy sources. The case being argued here was a more limited one, which took it for granted that there were worthwhile uses of coal. The government's and NCB's case was based on the idea that financial profitability was *the* indicator of society's benefit; it was the foremost task of this chapter to criticise that position. Its central contention, that it was beneficial to keep pits open and miners working even at a financial loss, subsequently figured in a number of inquiries into, and studies of, individual pit closures (for example, St John's (Fisher *et al.*, 1985); Easington (Hudson *et al.*, 1984); Horden (Hudson *et al.*, 1985); Blyth Valley (Wade, 1985); Polkemmet (Cooper *et al.*, 1985); Bates (Blyth Valley, 1986)). Indeed the NUM had used the argument about the cost of pit closures in terms of unemployment pay, lost taxation, etc. for some time before the strike.

It was notable that in the report of the Independent Review, which recommended that Bates be kept open, these arguments were *not* deemed relevant; in effect the review body felt obliged to consider only the economic effects on the NCB. Indeed there is still an unfortunate tendency to equate *economic* with the narrow financial criterion of profit and loss to the enterprise concerned. Perhaps the most important point in the chapter is that this way of looking at the matter is fundamentally wrong. The impact on government financing, through dole payments, lost taxation and so forth is just as *economic* as the effect on the NCB's profits. These broader effects are (in economists' jargon) 'social', but the contrast implied is not with 'economic' but with 'private' (i.e. narrow). Of course there were important non-economic ('social' in the first sense) arguments against pit closures (destruction of communities, etc.), which should be taken into consideration. But there were also valid economic arguments for keeping pits open, once 'economic' was understood in the broad sense of improving the economic welfare of society. Many people, with sympathy for the social plight of the miners, felt that 'economics' was against them. This chapter attempted to show that this was not correct.

Appendix 1
Individual pits: methods of calculation

The NCB's *Colliery Operating Results* provide data on:
1. colliery manpower.
2. tonnes of coal produced.
3. costs per tonne.
4. profits.

The first stage is to calculate total revenue from sales (5) which equals total costs ((6 = (3)×(2)) plus profits (4). Total costs are then divided into total wage costs (7) and other costs ((8) = (6)−(7)). In the absence of information on wage costs for each pit, total wage costs for miners are estimated from average gross wage costs per NCB employee (£192 per week from NCB 1983/4 *Accounts*, p. 46) and the number of miners ((7) = (1)×£192).

The next stage is to estimate the effect of closure on employment of NCB employees other than miners and on workers in industries supplying the pits. It is assumed that one-quarter of non-wage costs are *not* saved by pit closure. Each pit's operating costs include allocations for depreciation and many overhead expenses (at Area and HQ level) which will not, or may not, be saved by closure. There is no information available on a pit-by-pit basis as to how important these costs are. Figures in the NCB *Accounts* for collieries as a whole suggest that these overhead-type expenses are well above one-quarter of non-wage costs. So, depending on how many of them may be saved by closure, the assumption used here that one-quarter of non-wage costs will not be saved by closure may be on the low side. Note, however, that the impact of this assumption on the calculation of the costs of closure is relatively slight, because if these costs were indeed saved then the impact on employment (in the NCB and elsewhere) would be greater.

To reach the figure for the impact of closure on non-mining NCB jobs and on jobs in supplying industries, the remaining 75 per cent of non-wage costs are presumed to be spent on production, 90 per cent of the value added to which takes place in the UK. Inspection of the 1979 *Input-Output Tables* (Central Statistical Office, 1983), table B, shows that the direct import content of NCB purchases is very low and that the pattern of its supplying industries suggests that an average import content of 10 per cent for its supplies is on the high side. Finally, the estimated savings of expenditure on domestic value added is assumed to have a proportionate effect on jobs. This loss of jobs (9) is estimated by dividing the figure for the weekly savings of $((8) \times 0.75 \times 0.90)$ by weekly value added per head in domestic commodity production (£225 per week in 1983 as calculated from *National Income and Expenditure*, 1984, tables 1.10 and 1.12) (Central Statistical Office, 1984).

The final estimated impact of closure on employment is the 'multiplier' effect on jobs as a result of the reduction in purchasing power of miners and others affected. One estimate for a comparable multiplier for the impact of a reduction in government expenditure is that these effects on employment are one-half of the initial first round effect (Britton, 1981, table 10.1). In order to allow for the fact that the impact on the spending of redundant miners may be less than the average because of the impact of redundancy payments, and also to err on the cautious side, an employment multiplier of only one-quarter was used. This means that the total effect on employment is:

(1) number of miners who lose jobs,

+(9) number of other workers affected in NCB and other supplying industries,

+(10) = $0.25 \times ((1)+(9))$ number of workers who lose their jobs as a result of the effect of reduced spending.

The total costs of closure are then estimated by assuming that the average cost to the Exchequer of an unemployed miner is £141 per week (calculated from table 4.2, averaged over a 10-year period), and that the average cost of other unemployed workers is £106 per week (a government estimate updated by Davies and Metcalf in chapter 2). So the total (weekly) costs of the unemployment resulting from pit closure is (11) = $(1) \times £141 + ((9)+(10)) \times £106$. To this has to be added the costs presumed not to be saved when the pit closes $(0.25 \times (8))$. If these total costs exceed the 'subsidy' represented by the pit's operating loss then closure does not benefit government revenue.

To derive the alternative, more unfavourable estimates in the first case (p. 65), costs of unemployment are reduced by one-quarter in the second case (p. 66), the multiplier effects are ignored, and in the third case (p. 71) operating losses are increased by one-quarter of total revenue. In order to emphasise that these calculations of the effects of closure are presumed to continue indefinitely as a result of the continuing impact on

78

unemployment, no attempt is made to estimate once-off costs of closure, such as making good the site of the colliery, etc., which the NCB reported to the Monopolies Commission averaged 20 per cent on pre-closure costs in the first year after closure, falling to 3 per cent in the third.

These calculations can be illustrated by taking the case of Cortonwood. Weekly tonnage (for the first 29 weeks of 1984) was 5,608.9. Costs per tonne were £58.21, so that total weekly production costs were £326,494. Given average manpower of 839, and the assumed weekly gross wage costs of £192 per week, the total weekly wage costs were 839×£192 = £161,088: this leaves non-wage costs as the difference between total costs and wage costs (£326,494−£161,088 = £165,406).

Assuming that one-quarter of these non-wage costs would not be saved by closure, and that 90 per cent of the non-wage costs which are saved would have been spent on domestic value added, yields a figure for the reduction of expenditure in other industries (and on other NCB employees) of £111,649 (= £165,406×0.75×0.90). When this is divided by the figure for average value added per head of £225 per week it gives the estimate of the number of workers affected in the NCB and elsewhere as 496. The multiplier effect on employment as a result of reduced spending by miners and others is assumed to be one-quarter of the total employment effect in the NCB and supplying industries, i.e. 0.25×(839+496) = 334. The total costs of closure are then calculated from the number of miners affected (839) and the assumed cost of redundancy, dole and tax loss spread over a ten-year period (£141 per week), plus the number of other workers affected (496+334), and the assumed cost to the government of their being unemployed (£106 per week), plus the quarter of non-wage costs assumed not to have been saved by closure. This gives a weekly total of £118,017 (in respect of miners unemployed), plus £87,980 (in respect of other workers unemployed), plus £41,351 (costs not saved). Expressing this as a weekly sum per miner (£247,318 ÷ 839) gives a weekly figure of total costs of closure of £295 per miner per week. Given an average operating loss (or 'subsidy') of £74 per miner per week, the net gain to the government from keeping Cortonwood open, on the basis of the results in 1983, was £221 per miner per week.

A recent study (see chapter 5) of the NCB's accounting practices estimated that 23 per cent of Cortonwood's total costs would not be saved by closure. This is nearly double the amount assumed in our calculations, which confirms that in this respect our estimates of the total costs of closure are on the low side.

Economics and accounting of the NCB

Table 4.4

BA	Barnsley	NN	North Nottinghamshire	SN	South Nottinghamshire
DC	Doncaster	NY	North Yorkshire	SW	South Wales
ND	North Derbyshire	SC	Scotland	SY	South Yorkshire
NE	North-East	SM	South Midlands	WN	Western

				£ per miner per week			
Name of pit		Manpower	Tonnes per week	Revenue	Profits	Cost of closure	Net gain from pit being open
Thoresby	NN	1,426	37,337	1,000	451	399	850
Betws New	SW	683	11,141	994	223	542	765
Bagworth	SM	868	21,513	817	265	401	666
Caphouse Dby	BA	458	9,461	834	179	467	647
Kellingley	NY	2,203	46,177	782	225	404	629
Silverwood	SY	1,488	20,978	645	180	344	524
Ellington	NE	2,203	37,229	625	147	353	500
Ledston Luck	NY	449	7,794	616	148	346	494
Welbeck	NN	1,319	22,036	606	164	329	493
Clipstone	NN	1,434	17,980	580	153	320	473
Ollerton	NN	1,163	17,707	583	140	330	470
Harworth	NN	1,205	17,748	568	108	341	449
Silverdale	WN	881	11,987	524	157	281	438
Hem Heath	WN	1,886	26,581	553	103	334	438
Ireland	ND	751	11,374	569	63	371	434
Bilsthorpe	NN	1,229	18,780	552	83	347	430
Pye Hill	SN	1,031	15,107	526	128	301	429
Bersham	WN	481	6,557	558	58	367	425
Sharlston	NY	1,179	17,028	541	88	336	425
Golborne	WN	811	10,917	542	71	349	419
Marine	SW	640	7,743	530	71	340	411
Ferrymoor	BA	565	8,278	537	31	371	402
Royston Drift	BA	567	8,799	551	−27	417	391
Whitwell	ND	831	11,158	516	27	360	387
Thurcroft	SY	870	8,827	488	71	313	384
Highmoor	ND	583	9,871	525	0	383	383
Bick Par	WN	1,196	14,674	496	53	330	383
Annesley	SN	1,003	13,825	507	28	354	381
Whittle	NE	777	9,860	481	74	307	381
Daw Mill	SM	1,336	17,013	526	−11	390	380
Dearne Valley	BA	389	5,284	512	13	366	379
Mansfield	NN	1,415	16,349	515	−1	378	376
Sherwood	NN	929	14,059	562	−88	464	376
Bevercotes	NN	1,401	18,214	493	30	343	373
Bolsover	ND	1,004	11,708	479	45	324	369
Renishaw	ND	560	7,408	487	27	341	368
Cotgrave	SN	1,754	23,488	462	68	298	367
Holditch	WN	699	6,800	494	8	358	366
Baddesley	SM	994	12,501	460	62	301	363
Manton	SY	1,283	14,846	451	68	291	359
Wath	SY	706	8,810	464	39	318	357
Arkwright	ND	778	9,582	484	1	356	357
Frances	SC	699	7,987	460	36	318	354

Economic case against closures

Table 4.4 (*cont.*)

			£ per miner per week			
Name of pit		Manpower	Tonnes per week	Revenue	Profits	Cost of closure	Net gain from pit being open
Markham	ND	2,211	27,432	476	5	348	353
Point of Ayr	WN	693	8,275	459	33	319	352
Treeton	SY	723	7,101	451	43	307	350
Lea Hall	WN	2,256	26,794	455	32	317	349
Creswell	NN	1,046	12,901	456	30	319	349
Allerton	NY	1,266	16,759	447	33	311	345
Deep Navigtn	SW	772	7,582	425	58	281	339
Wearmouth	NE	2,387	23,187	438	28	309	337
Gedling	SN	1,536	15,027	419	61	275	336
Maltby	SY	1,414	15,802	428	32	299	331
Taff Merthyr	SW	681	7,570	446	−1	333	331
Fryston	NY	1,077	12,239	440	−3	330	327
Sutton	NN	729	9,033	455	−33	359	326
Wolstanton	WN	987	8,607	453	−35	359	324
Sutton Manor	WN	778	7,576	448	−25	350	324
Prince of Wales	NY	1,360	18,751	490	−107	430	323
Florence	WN	1,365	15,396	447	−30	352	322
Bold	WN	1,116	11,970	444	−25	347	322
Westoe	NE	2,378	25,562	442	6	313	319
Dawdon	NE	2,032	20,517	413	17	299	316
Barnburgh	SY	984	10,499	415	12	304	316
Shirebrook	ND	1,884	23,256	446	−44	360	316
North Gawber	BA	774	8,095	401	34	281	315
Linby	SN	1,043	10,040	410	5	306	310
Yorkshire Mn	DC	1,461	12,965	393	35	275	310
Markham	DC	1,512	15,088	402	17	292	309
Shireoaks	SY	913	10,908	409	0	308	308
Houghton	BA	1,535	16,133	425	−31	338	308
Vane Seaham	NE	1,587	15,838	415	−12	319	308
Grimethorpe	BA	1,743	17,212	404	−1	306	304
Calverton	SN	1,502	15,095	407	−15	316	301
Goldthorpe	DC	1,074	13,093	394	8	293	301
Warsop	ND	1,297	13,655	413	−32	331	299
Kiveton Park	SY	810	8,955	380	28	271	299
Brenkley	NE	525	6,545	415	−41	338	297
Merthyr Vale	SW	664	5,343	410	−34	331	297
Whitwick	SM	747	8,653	395	−12	306	294
Littleton	WN	1,871	18,940	396	−16	309	294
Bilston Glen	SC	1,990	17,946	376	11	279	290
Rawdon	SM	1,176	12,433	375	6	282	288
Emley Moor	BA	247	2,728	420	−103	381	279
Markham	SW	595	4,692	377	−31	307	277
Easington	NE	2,552	23,147	384	−54	327	273
Wheldale	NY	873	8,897	381	−48	321	273
Penallta	SW	647	5,413	343	8	260	268
South Kirby	BA	1,471	16,108	403	−108	374	266
Trelewis	SW	296	3,819	442	−185	449	264

Table 4.4 (*cont.*)

			£ per miner per week			
Name of pit		Manpower	Tonnes per week	Revenue	Profits	Cost of closure	Net gain from pit being open
Frickley Sth	DC	1,813	16,685	350	−17	280	264
Oakdale	SW	867	6,753	373	−59	322	264
Silverhill	NN	1,209	11,638	365	−54	314	261
Kingsley Drift	BA	444	6,056	480	−274	531	257
Cwm Coedely	SW	1,274	9,453	358	−58	312	255
Rossington	DC	1,564	13,480	340	−36	287	251
Bentley	DC	1,038	9,427	334	−26	276	250
Donisthorpe	SM	1,046	10,117	342	−49	296	248
Comrie	SC	703	6,127	325	−28	272	244
Hatfield	DC	1,465	11,622	319	−29	268	239
Hawthorn	NE	3,117	26,702	345	−78	317	239
Park Mill	BA	365	3,372	375	−137	375	238
Bentinck	SN	1,749	16,042	339	−72	309	237
Barrow	BA	1,263	9,263	346	−95	328	234
Askern	DC	1,259	10,182	323	−64	294	229
Parkside	WN	1,703	11,868	330	−81	309	228
Hucknall	SN	1,132	10,700	330	−85	312	227
Six Bells	SW	487	3,587	320	−74	298	225
Agecroft	WN	874	7,784	347	−127	350	223
Moorgreen	SN	1,001	9,072	316	−75	297	222
Dodworth	BA	1,261	9,853	303	−52	273	221
Cadley Hill	SM	921	7,875	312	−69	290	221
Cortonwood	SY	839	5,609	315	−74	295	221
Bullcliffe	BA	309	3,162	403	−251	467	216
Horden	NE	1,807	12,377	329	−116	332	215
Nostell	NY	613	5,518	320	−105	319	214
Darfield	BA	709	5,531	313	−94	306	212
Brookhouse	SY	706	5,629	295	−65	277	211
Dinnington	SY	933	5,746	287	−56	266	209
Woolley	BA	1,747	12,686	300	−84	292	208
Abercynon	SW	1,116	8,575	304	−91	299	207
Savile	NY	521	4,241	307	−102	308	206
Polkemmet	SC	1,370	7,434	270	−39	243	204
Brodsworth	DC	2,069	13,799	282	−63	266	204
Ackton Hall	NY	1,326	10,319	306	−111	313	202
Herrington	NE	709	4,274	286	−82	281	199
Tower	SW	655	3,286	267	−50	249	198
Abernant	SW	835	3,830	273	−74	268	194
Monktonhall	SC	1,662	13,820	272	−75	268	193
Ashington	NE	659	5,733	292	−111	304	193
Glasshoughtn	NY	602	5,099	298	−130	320	190
Bates	NE	1,651	15,126	289	−133	317	184
Kilnhurst	SY	505	3,110	275	−125	302	177
Bedwas	SW	599	3,556	259	−126	293	167
Nantgarw	SW	638	3,754	282	−171	337	165
Celynen Nth	SW	570	3,042	257	−129	293	164
Penrikyber	SW	649	3,146	236	−99	260	161

Economic case against closures

Table 4.4 (*cont.*)

Name of pit		Manpower	Tonnes per week	£ per miner per week			Net gain from pit being open
				Revenue	Profits	Cost of closure	
Cynheidre	SW	1,033	3,832	243	−121	279	158
Manvers	SY	1,169	7,060	243	−122	280	157
Babbington	SN	1,031	9,555	312	−256	411	155
Killoch	SC	1,894	9,474	235	−119	272	154
Blaenant	SW	698	6,871	255	−156	309	153
Measham	SM	368	2,685	257	−174	322	148
Abertillery	SW	448	2,190	226	−126	271	145
Sacriston	NE	263	1,269	220	−121	264	143
Coventry	SM	1,383	9,115	245	−186	322	137
Seafield	SC	1,791	10,026	225	−150	286	136
Mardy	SW	773	2,808	208	−133	264	131
Aberpergwm	SW	317	1,169	223	−165	294	129
Desford	SM	410	2,871	225	−173	301	128
Selby Complex	NY	866	5,483	204	−148	271	123
Barony	SC	791	3,341	191	−132	252	121
Betteshanger	SM	1,143	5,050	211	−169	289	120
Tilmanstone	SM	894	3,803	204	−163	281	118
Garw	SW	689	3,073	208	−172	289	117
Blidworth	NN	1,053	5,178	216	−206	316	111
Hickleton	DC	896	3,424	170	−126	235	108
Cadeby	SY	954	4,179	178	−153	257	104
Newstead	SN	1,210	7,165	187	−180	281	101
Birch Coppice	SM	974	6,343	197	−200	300	101
St Johns	SW	881	3,354	169	−153	252	99
Celynen Sth	SW	470	1,685	167	−213	289	99
Snowdown	SM	539	1,117	103	−232	260	28

Economics and accounting of the NCB

Table 4.5 *Cumulative costs of closures*

BA	Barnsley	NN	North Nottinghamshire	SN	South Nottinghamshire
DC	Doncaster	NY	North Yorkshire	SW	South Wales
ND	North Derbyshire	SC	Scotland	SY	South Yorkshire
NE	North-East	SM	South Midlands	WN	Western

		Profits per tonne	Manpower	Tonnes (millions)	Profits (£m)	Cost of closure (£m)	Net gain from pit being open (£m)
Name of pit				on annual basis – cumulative up to pit shown			
1 Celynen Sth	SW	−59.5	470	0.1	−5.2	7.1	1.9
2 Aberpergwm	SW	−44.7	787	0.2	−7.9	11.9	4.0
3 Blidworth	NN	−41.8	1,840	0.5	−19.1	29.2	10.1
4 St Johns	SW	−40.2	2,721	0.7	−26.1	40.7	14.6
5 Garw	SW	−38.5	3,410	0.9	−32.2	51.1	18.8
6 Tilmanstone	SM	−38.4	4,304	1.1	−39.8	64.2	24.3
7 Betteshanger	SM	−38.3	5,447	1.4	−49.8	81.4	31.5
8 Mardy	SW	−36.7	6,220	1.5	−55.1	92.0	36.8
9 Hickleton	DC	−33.0	7,116	1.7	−61.0	102.9	41.9
10 Cynheidre	SW	−32.6	8,149	1.9	−67.5	117.9	50.4
11 Barony	SC	−31.2	8,940	2.1	−72.9	128.3	55.4
12 Cadeby	SY	−30.9	9,894	2.3	−80.5	141.1	60.6
13 Birch Coppice	SM	−30.7	10,868	2.6	−90.6	156.3	65.7
14 Newstead	SN	−30.5	12,078	3.0	−101.9	174.0	72.1
15 Nantgarw	SW	−29.1	12,716	3.2	−107.6	185.2	77.6
16 Coventry	SM	−28.2	14,099	3.7	−120.9	208.4	87.4
17 Babbington	SN	−27.6	15,130	4.2	−134.6	230.4	95.7
18 Seafield	SC	−26.8	16,921	4.7	−148.6	257.1	95.7
19 Abertillery	SW	−25.8	17,369	4.8	−151.5	263.4	111.8
20 Sacriston	NE	−25.0	17,632	4.9	−153.1	267.0	113.8
21 Desford	SM	−24.7	18,042	5.0	−156.8	273.4	116.5
22 Bullcliffe	BA	−24.6	18,351	5.2	−160.8	280.9	120.0
23 Celynen Nth	SW	−24.2	18,921	5.4	−164.6	289.6	124.9
24 Measham	SM	−23.8	19,289	5.5	−167.9	295.8	127.7
25 Killoch	SC	−23.8	21,183	6.0	−179.6	322.6	142.8
26 Bedwas	SW	−21.2	21,782	6.2	−183.5	331.7	148.0
27 Penrikyber	SW	−20.5	22,431	6.4	−186.8	340.5	153.4
28 Kilnhurst	SY	−20.3	22,936	6.6	−190.1	348.4	158.1
29 Manvers	SY	−20.2	24,105	7.0	−197.5	365.4	167.7
30 Kinsley Drift	BA	−20.1	24,549	7.3	−203.8	377.7	173.7
31 Horden	NE	−17.0	26,356	7.9	−214.7	408.9	194.0
32 Abernant	SW	−16.2	27,191	8.1	−217.9	420.5	202.4
33 Blaenant	SW	−15.8	27,889	8.5	−223.6	431.7	208.0
34 Glasshoughtn	NY	−15.3	28,491	8.8	−227.7	441.7	214.0
35 Park Mill	BA	−14.8	28,856	9.0	−230.3	448.8	218.5
36 Bates	NE	−14.5	30,507	9.8	−241.7	476.0	234.3
37 Trelewis	SW	−14.3	30,803	10.0	−244.5	482.9	238.4
38 Ackton Hall	NY	−14.3	32,129	10.5	−252.1	504.5	252.4
39 Agecroft	WN	−14.2	33,003	10.9	−257.8	520.4	262.6
40 Blaenserchan	SW	−13.6	33,424	11.0	−259.8	527.0	267.2
41 Herrington	NE	−13.6	34,133	11.2	−262.8	537.4	274.6
42 Barrow	BA	−12.9	35,396	11.7	−269.0	559.0	290.0

Economic case against closures

Table 4.5 (*cont.*)

Name of pit		Profits per tonne	Manpower	Tonnes (millions)	Profits (£m)	Cost of closure (£m)	Net gain from pit being open (£m)
		on annual basis – cumulative up to pit shown					
43 Ashington	NE	−12.7	36,055	12.0	−272.8	569.4	296.6
44 Savile	NY	−12.6	36,576	12.2	−275.6	577.7	302.2
45 Darfield	BA	−12.1	37,285	12.5	−279.1	589.0	310.0
46 Abercynon	SW	−11.9	38,401	12.9	−284.4	606.3	322.0
47 Nostell	NY	−11.7	39,014	13.2	−287.7	616.5	328.8
48 Parkside	WN	−11.6	40,717	13.8	−294.9	643.9	349.0
49 Woolley	BA	−11.6	42,464	14.5	−302.5	670.4	367.9
50 Cortonwood	SY	−11.1	43,303	14.8	−305.7	683.3	377.5
51 Tower	SW	−10.0	43,958	15.0	−307.4	691.8	384.3
52 Six Bells	SW	−10.0	44,445	15.2	−309.3	699.4	390.0
53 South Kirby	BA	−9.9	45,916	16.0	−317.6	728.0	410.4
54 Brodsworth	DC	−9.4	47,985	16.7	−324.3	756.7	432.3
55 Emley Moor	BA	−9.3	48,232	16.8	−325.6	761.6	435.9
56 Dinnington	SY	−9.2	49,165	17.1	−328.3	774.5	446.1
57 Hawthorn	NE	−9.1	52,282	18.5	−341.0	825.9	484.8
58 Monktonhall	SO	−9.0	53,944	19.2	−347.5	849.1	501.5
59 Hucknall	SN	−9.0	55,076	19.8	−352.5	867.5	514.9
60 Moorgreen	SN	−8.3	56,077	20.3	−357.4	882.9	526.4
61 Brookhouse	SY	−8.2	56,783	20.6	−358.8	893.1	543.2
62 Cadley Hill	SM	−8.0	57,704	21.0	−362.1	907.0	544.8
63 Askern	DC	−8.0	58,963	21.5	−366.3	926.2	559.8
64 Bentinck	SN	−7.8	60,712	22.3	−372.8	954.3	581.4
65 Prince of Wales	NY	−7.8	62,072	23.3	−380.4	984.7	604.2
66 Cwm Coedely	SW	−7.8	63,346	23.8	−384.2	1,005.4	621.1
67 Oakdale	SW	−7.5	64,213	24.2	−386.8	1,019.9	633.0
68 Polkemmet	SC	−7.1	65,583	24.6	−389.5	1,037.2	647.5
69 Dodworth	BA	−6.6	66,844	25.1	−392.9	1,005.1	662.0
70 Easington	NE	−6.0	69,396	26.3	−400.1	1,098.5	698.2
71 Sherwood	NN	−5.8	70,325	27.0	−404.4	1,120.9	716.4
72 Silverhill	NN	−5.6	71,534	27.6	−407.8	1,140.7	732.8
73 Donisthorpe	SM	−5.0	72,580	28.1	−410.5	1,156.8	746.3
74 Wheldale	NY	−4.7	73,453	28.6	−412.7	1,171.4	758.7
75 Merthyr Vale	SW	−4.2	74,117	28.9	−413.9	1,182.8	768.9
76 Rossington	DC	−4.2	75,681	29.6	−416.8	1,206.1	789.3
77 Wolstanton	WN	−4.0	76,668	30.0	−418.6	1,224.5	805.9
78 Markham	SW	−3.9	77,263	30.2	−419.5	1,234.0	814.5
79 Hatfield	DC	−3.6	78,728	30.8	−421.7	1,254.4	832.7
80 Shirebrook	ND	−3.5	80,612	32.0	−426.0	1,289.7	863.7
81 Longannet	SC	−3.5	83,548	33.6	−431.7	1,336.1	904.4
82 Brenkley	NE	−3.3	84,073	33.9	−432.8	1,345.3	912.5
83 Comrie	SC	−3.3	84,776	34.2	−433.8	1,355.2	921.4
84 Warsop	ND	−3.1	86,073	34.9	−436.0	1,377.5	941.6
85 Houghton	BA	−2.9	87,608	35.7	−438.4	1,404.5	966.2
86 Bentley	DC	−2.9	88,646	36.2	−439.8	1,419.4	979.7
87 Florence	WN	−2.6	90,011	37.0	−441.9	1,444.4	1,002.6
88 Sutton	NN	−2.6	90,740	37.5	−443.1	1,458.0	1,015.0

Economics and accounting of the NCB

Table 4.5 (*cont.*)

Name of pit		Profits per tonne	Manpower	Tonnes (millions)	Profits (£m)	Cost of closure (£m)	Net gain from pit being open (£m)
				on annual basis – cumulative up to pit shown			
89 Sutton Manor	WN	−2.6	91,518	37.9	−444.1	1,472.1	1,028.1
90 Bold	WE	−2.6	92,634	38.5	−445.6	1,492.2	1,046.8
91 Frickley Sth	DC	−1.8	94,447	39.4	−447.2	1,518.6	1,071.7
92 Royston Drift	BA	−1.7	95,014	39.9	−448.0	1,530.9	1,083.2
93 Littleton	WN	−1.5	96,885	40.9	−449.5	1,561.0	1,111.8
94 Calverton	SN	−1.5	98,387	41.7	−450.7	1,585.7	1,135.3
95 Vane Seaham	NE	−1.2	99,974	42.5	−451.7	1,612.1	1,160.7
96 Whitwick	SM	−1.0	100,721	42.9	−452.2	1,624.0	1,172.1
97 Daw Mill	SM	−0.8	102,057	43.8	−452.9	1,651.1	1,198.5
98 Fryston	NY	−0.3	103,134	44.4	−453.1	1,669.6	1,216.8
99 Grimethorpe	BA	−0.1	104,877	45.3	−453.2	1,697.3	1,244.4
100 Taff Merthyr	SW	−0.1	105,558	45.7	−453.3	1,709.1	1,256.1
101 Mansfield	NN	−0.1	106,973	46.5	−453.4	1,736.9	1,283.8
102 Shireoaks	SY	0.0	107,886	47.1	−453.4	1,751.5	1,298.4
103 Highmoor	ND	0.0	108,469	47.6	−453.4	1,763.1	1,310.0
104 Arkwright	ND	0.1	109,247	48.1	−453.3	1,777.5	1,324.4
105 Markham	ND	0.4	111,458	49.5	−452.7	1,817.5	1,365.0
106 Linby	SN	0.5	112,501	50.0	−452.4	1,834.1	1,381.8
107 Westoe	NE	0.5	114,879	51.3	−451.7	1,872.8	1,421.2
108 Rawdon	SM	0.5	116,055	51.9	−451.4	1,890.1	1,438.8
109 Rufford	NN	0.6	117,510	52.6	−451.0	1,914.1	1,463.2
110 Goldthorpe	DC	0.7	118,584	53.3	−450.5	1,930.4	1,480.0
111 Holditch	WN	0.8	119,283	53.7	−450.2	1,943.4	1,493.3
112 Penallta	SW	0.9	119,928	54.0	−449.9	1,952.1	1,502.3
113 Dearne Valley	BA	1.0	120,317	54.3	−449.6	1,959.5	1,510.0
114 Barnburgh	SY	1.1	121,301	54.8	−449.0	1,975.1	1,526.2
115 Bilston Glen	SC	1.2	123,291	55.7	−447.9	2,004.0	1,556.3
116 Dawdon	NE	1.7	125,323	56.8	−446.1	2,035.6	1,585.7
117 Markham	DC	1.7	126,835	57.6	−444.7	2,058.6	1,614.0
118 Whitwell	ND	2.0	127,666	58.2	−443.5	2,074.2	1,630.7
119 Annesley	SN	2.0	128,669	58.9	−442.1	2,092.6	1,650.6
120 Renishaw	ND	2.1	129,229	59.3	−441.3	2,102.5	1,661.3
121 Ferrymoor	BA	2.1	129,794	59.7	−440.4	2,113.4	1,673.1
122 Bevercotes	NN	2.3	131,195	60.6	−438.2	2,138.4	1,700.3
123 Creswell	NN	2.4	132,241	61.3	−436.6	2,155.7	1,719.3
124 Allerton	NY	2.5	133,507	62.2	−434.4	2,176.2	1,742.0
125 Kiveton Park	SY	2.5	134,317	62.7	−433.2	2,187.6	1,754.6
126 Lea Hall	WN	2.7	136,573	64.1	−429.5	2,224.8	1,795.6
127 Point of Ayr	WN	2.8	137,266	64.5	−428.3	2,236.3	1,808.3
128 Wearmouth	NE	2.9	139,653	65.7	−424.9	2,274.6	1,850.1
129 Maltby	SY	2.9	141,067	66.5	−422.5	2,296.6	1,874.5
130 Wath	SY	3.1	141,773	67.0	−421.1	2,308.3	1,887.6
131 Frances	SC	3.2	142,472	67.4	−419.8	2,319.8	1,900.5
132 North Gawber	BA	3.3	143,246	67.8	−418.4	2,331.1	1,913.2
133 Bolsover	ND	3.9	144,250	68.4	−416.0	2,331.1	1,932.5
134 Yorkshire Mn	DC	3.9	145,711	69.1	−413.4	2,368.9	1,956.0

Economic case against closures

Table 4.5 (*cont.*)

Name of pit		Profits per tonne	Manpower	Tonnes (millions)	Profits (£m)	Cost of closure (£m)	Net gain from pit being open (£m)
				on annual basis – cumulative up to pit shown			
135 Ireland	ND	4.2	146,462	69.7	−410.9	2,383.4	1,972.9
136 Bersham	WN	4.3	146,943	70.0	−409.4	2,392.6	1,983.5
137 Bick Par	WN	4.3	148,139	70.8	−406.1	2,413.1	2,007.3
138 Treeton	SY	4.4	148,862	71.2	−404.5	2,424.6	2,020.5
139 Baddesley	SM	4.9	149,856	71.8	−401.3	2,440.1	2,039.3
140 Cotgrave	SN	5.1	151,610	73.0	−395.1	2,467.3	2,072.7
141 Golborne	WN	5.3	151,421	73.6	−392.1	2,482.0	2,090.4
142 Bilsthorpe	NN	5.5	153,650	74.6	−386.8	2,504.2	2,117.9
143 Whittle	NE	5.8	154,427	75.1	−383.8	2,516.6	2,133.3
144 Marine	SW	5.9	155,067	75.5	−381.4	2,527.9	2,147.0
145 Manton	SY	5.9	156,350	76.3	−376.9	2,547.3	2,170.9
146 Deep Navigtn	SW	5.9	157,122	76.7	−374.6	2,558.6	2,184.5
147 Sharlston	NY	6.1	158,301	77.6	−369.2	2,579.2	2,210.5
148 Gedling	SN	6.2	159,837	78.4	−364.3	2,601.2	2,237.4
149 Thurcroft	SY	7.0	160,707	78.9	−361.1	2,615.4	2,254.8
150 Hem Heath	WN	7.3	162,593	80.3	−351.0	2,648.2	2,297.7
151 Harworth	NN	7.4	163,798	81.2	−344.2	2,669.6	2,325.8
152 Ledston Luck	NY	8.5	164,249	81.6	−340.8	2,677.7	2,337.3
153 Caphouse Dby	BA	8.7	164,709	82.1	−336.5	2,688.8	2,352.7
154 Ellington	NE	8.7	166,908	84.0	−319.7	2,729.3	2,409.9
155 Pye Hill	SN	8.7	167,939	84.8	−312.9	2,745.4	2,432.9
156 Ollerton	NN	9.2	169,102	85.7	−304.4	2,765.3	2,461.3
157 Welbeck	NN	9.8	170,421	86.8	−293.2	2,787.9	2,495.1
158 Bagworth	SM	10.7	171,289	87.9	−281.2	2,806.0	2,525.1
159 Kellingley	NY	10.7	173,492	90.3	−255.6	2,852.3	2,597.1
160 Silverdale	WN	11.5	174,373	90.9	−248.4	2,865.2	2,617.1
161 Clipstone	NN	12.2	175,807	91.8	−237.0	2,889.2	2,652.3
162 Silverwood	SY	12.8	177,295	92.9	−233.1	2,915.7	2,692.8
163 Betws New	SW	13.7	177,978	93.5	−215.2	2,934.9	2,720.0
164 Thoresby	NN	17.2	179,404	95.4	−181.8	2,964.5	2,783.0

Appendix 2
The economic impact of the strike

There have been a large number of estimates of the economic impact of the dispute. The purpose of this section is to put together the best available figures for the various costs, in terms of lost production, of the strike up to the end of September 1984 and to show how they have been borne by miners, by the NCB, by the government and by other industries. Finally estimates for the effect on the balance of payments are reported.

(a) The loss of production

The economic cost of the strike to society is the loss of production involved, in the coal-mining industry, in supplier and customer industries and more widely.

(1) *The fall in coal output.* This is obviously much the biggest effect on total production (or GDP). According to the NCB in negotiation with the NUM (September 1984), the total loss of production over the period of the dispute (that is, including both the overtime ban and the subsequent strike action), was 52m tonnes. Adding on an extra 3m tonnes to take the calculation up to the end of September, and reckoning the saleable price in 1984/5 at £42 per tonne[7] yields a figure for the total value of lost coal production of *£2,310m.*[8]

(2) *Supplier and customer industries.* The effect of reduced production in the industries supplying coal with *current* inputs (electricity, engineering products, etc.) is already included under (a). But in addition, work on capital projects was virtually halted at most of the pits. This capital programme was worth £689m in 1983/4. Taking into account that to some extent mining machinery may have been stockpiled (rather than not produced), a central estimate would be that production of *capital goods and construction* for the NCB was cut in half, which represents a loss, for the first 29 weeks of the strike, of some *£200m.*

Economic case against closures

Table 4.6 *Impact of the dispute on production*

	£m
Lost coal production	2,310
Reduced production of mining investment goods	200
Reduced rail services	130
Extra electricity costs	500
Reduced consumption of UK goods by miners' families	210
Total quantifiable loss	3,350

The other industry closely linked to coal which suffered reduced production is railways, where revenue was cut by the reduction in coal transport. These losses are put at £4½m per week – a total of *£130m*.[9]

The main customer to suffer in the dispute was the electricity industry whose costs increased as a result of burning oil rather than coal.[10] These are said by the CEGB to have been around £20m per week.[11] Allowing for a slow build-up to maximum oil burn on the one side (and some extra expense to the CEGB through running coal stations out of merit order), a central estimate of these costs would be *£500m*.

(3) *Indirect effects*. The most important indirect or 'second round' effect is that the cut in miners' pay reduced their spending and therefore demand for consumer goods. This in turn led to a fall in production in the consumer goods and services sector. Given the cut in production of coal, the cut in miners' take-home pay is estimated at some £370m. If miners and their families were able to make up for one-quarter of this cut by running down savings (including the postponement of hire purchase and mortgage payments), and if one-quarter of the spending was on imported goods and services, then the total effect on consumption and thus production of domestic commodities would amount to *£210m*.[12]

(4) *Total impact*. The reduction in miners' consumption is only the most easily quantifiable of an almost endless list of second-round effects. For example, a rise in taxation to cover the losses in government revenue (see below) leads to further major reductions in consumer spending. The impact of reduced miners' spending has further ramifications as workers in the consumer goods industries earn less and in turn can spend less. The effect of the strike probably raised interest rates in the UK and reduced business confidence leading to lower investment. None of these are readily quantifiable. But together they ensure that despite the inevitable uncertainty surrounding the estimates of the items which have been quantified, their total (see above) certainly constitutes a *substantial underestimate* of the total effects.

89

Economics and accounting of the NCB

The quantifiable loss in production was running at around £105m per week, in 1984, the equivalent of nearly £5 per week for every person at work in the country.

(b) Who bears the cost of a coal strike?

Lost production means lost income in the industries concerned. Workers' take-home pay is cut, nationalised industries' and private firms' profits are reduced and the government's tax receipts fall. These losses are not additional to the lost production, but show rather which sectors of the economy bear the brunt.

(1). The economic cost to the *miners* is their loss in take-home pay *and* pension contributions (less some £16m of social security)[13]: *£405m.*

2. The loss to the *government* is comprised of:

(i) Extra nationalised industry losses. The NCB was reported to be losing some £27½m per week during the strike (reckoned on colliery profit and loss accounts).[14] Assuming that in the absence of the strike it would have lost some £7½m per week as in 1983/4, this means that the effect of the strike added some £20m per week. Adding this to the NCB's estimate of £200m losses in 1983/4 due to the dispute gives a total loss to the NCB of £700m.[15] Losses in steel,[16] rail and electricity make the total for nationalised industry losses up to £1,445m.

(ii) Tax and national insurance contributions lost. The biggest effect here is from tax and national insurance paid by miners (some £135m – see note 12). Reduced VAT paid by miners, and lower taxes paid by those affected in other industries brings the total of lost tax revenue to around £300m.

(iii) Additional policing costs are estimated (conservatively) at £125m. This gives a total for the costs to the government as:

Losses in nationalised industries	£1,445m
Losses of tax revenue	£300m
Additional policing costs	£130m
Extra social security	£16m
Total	£1,891m

It has been suggested (Henley Forecasting Centre, 1984, p. 24) that such an effect on government revenue is less important because it can be accommodated within the government's 'contingency allowance'. This is quite false because either the contingency allowance would otherwise not have been spent (in which case government borrowing would have been lower), or it could have been spent on something useful.

Economic case against closures

3. The rest of the identifiable costs of lost production are reflected in lower wages and profits in other industries and total some £1,000m.[17]

(c) The balance of payments

The economic impact of the dispute has not in the main been reflected in reduced consumption. Despite the huge cut in production, consumption was maintained by stocks of coal being run down and by importing more goods and exporting less (mainly oil). This cushioning of the immediate effect of the strike did not make the loss of production any less relevant as the real measure of the cost of the dispute. Stocks have to be rebuilt and extra exports have to be produced to pay for the additional imports brought in during the strike. The deficit on the balance of payments is a reflection of how the real cost of the dispute, the loss of production, has been felt in the economy. This is not an extra cost in the sense of being added to the loss in production, but it does have some significance as the indicator to one aspect of the strike's impact. Phillips and Drew estimate 'the balance of payments cost is at least £234 million per month', which implies a total effect of some £1,500m so far (*The Economic Analyst*, 1984, p. 12).

NOTES

1 Unless otherwise specified all figures in this part come from the NCB's *Report and Accounts* for 1983/4 (NCB, 1984).
2 *National Income and Expenditure*, 1984, tables 5.4, 6.2, 11.7, 12.4 (Central Statistical Office, 1984).
3 The figures in this section are calculated as follows: according to the Department of Energy, 1983 the worst 12% of NCB capacity incurred losses of £275m and employed 40,000 workers. From the 1982/3 NCB accounts (NCB, 1983, p. 81), 12% of colliery production was worth £475m. Losses of £275m implies that operating costs were £750m, estimated from *NCB Accounts, National Income and Expenditure* 1983, and 1979 *Input-Output Tables* as:

Miners' wages	£370m
Other NCB salaries	£80m (represents 8,000 jobs)
Bought-in goods and services of which:	£300m (represents 27,000 jobs),
Indirect taxes	£30m
Wages	£200m
Gross profits	£70m

Economics and accounting of the NCB

Total costs to the government from closure are estimated as:
£180m: income tax and national insurance lost
£60m: value added tax on inputs and worker consumption lost
£195m: dole payments
£30m: profits tax lost
£15m: nationalised industries profit lost

The net gain to workers involved is £245m (£650m gross wages, less £180m direct taxes, less £195m dole payment, less £30m VAT on workers' consumption). Gain to other employers is £25m and to government is £205m (£480m costs of closure less £275m subsidy). In order to avoid complication the text includes the £25m profits in with gains to the workers concerned.

4 For simplicity we have used the Davies–Metcalf (chapter 2) estimates for columns 2 and 5, and to calculate column 3 (which is simply 87% of the full figure shown in column 2) to reflect the incidence of unemployment elsewhere. These are based on government estimates and the NCB estimate of the average subsidy to the 12% highest cost of capacity. Column 1 was calculated by the NUM Social Insurance Department. It is applicable to a 57-year-old man who has been in the industry for 34 years and who it is assumed would otherwise have retired at 62. As well as tax lost it comprises Weekly Benefit and Unemployment Benefit Equivalent. In the first year the lump-sum payments under EPCA and RMPS are included. The payments total some £35,000 over a 5-year period. This is consistent with the Department of Energy (1983) estimates.

5 Louis Turner, 1984. The long-run costs of production are from the *Financial Times*, 4 July 1984.

6 Calculated from *Family Expenditure Survey*, 1982, table 11.

7 This is the figure in the NCB *Accounts* (p. 58) for 1983/4 of £39.7 per tonne for colliery output, adjusted up by 6% assuming coal prices rise in line with general inflation.

8 This estimate accords closely with official and independent estimates. The government (*Economic Trends*, August 1984, p. 3) says that 'It is estimated that the dispute reduced the output measure of GDP by about ½% in the first quarter of 1984 and about 1¼% in the second quarter. Most of the reduction is the direct effect of lower coal output.' The National Institute (1984, p. 3), suggests the same figures for the loss of coal production itself. Assuming a similar loss of 1¼% of GDP in the third quarter yields a total loss of around £2,300m for the period January–September 1984.

9 Report made by Iron and Steel Trades Confederation to NUM at a meeting in September.

10 Note that these extra fuel costs do represent reduced domestic production in the UK because the more expensive oil comes from abroad (or would have been sold abroad), thus reducing value added within the UK as compared with the use of cheaper coal. Conversely, the losses incurred by BSC (put around £5m per week) as a result of higher transport costs cannot be regarded as a loss of production. Rather they represent a reduction of value added by the steel industry, compensated for by greater value added by road haulage.

Economic case against closures

11 As reported to the Electricity Council on 5 September 1984.

12 The NCB reports figures for lost miners' wages of £530m. Given average rates of income tax and national insurance and miners' pension contributions, and our assumptions about consumption, this total would be split as follows:

	£m
Reduction in wages	530
− Reduction in taxation and National Insurance	135
− Reduction in pension contributions	25
= Reduction in take-home pay	370
= Reduction in savings	90
+ Reduction in consumption of UK goods	210
+ Reduction in consumption of imported goods	70

13 NUM Social Insurance Department.

14 The NCB *Operating Colliery Results*, August 1984.

15 This estimate of £500m for losses during the 1983/4 financial year is identical to that of the *National Institute Economic Review*, 1984, p. 8.

16 Report made by Iron and Steel Trade Confederation to NUM at a meeting in September.

17 In national accounting terms the loss in production should be reduced by the costs of policing which are regarded as an addition to GDP. Such an adjustment has not been made here. The net loss in income in other industries would be correspondingly reduced.

REFERENCES

Blyth Valley Borough Council (1986), 'A Case for Bates Colliery'.

Britton, A. (ed.) (1981), *Employment, Output and Inflation: The National Institute Model of the British Economy*, London: Heinemann.

Central Statistical Office (1983), *Input-Output Tables for the United Kingdom 1979*, London: HMSO.

    (1983, 1984), *National Income and Expenditure*, 1983 and 1984 editions, London.

Cooper, D., J. Bird and W. Sharp (1985), *Report of the Public Inquiry into the Proposed Closure of Polkemmet Colliery, Whitburn*, Linlithgow: West Lothian District Council.

Department of Employment (1983), *Family Expenditure Survey 1982*, London: HMSO.

Department of Energy (1983), *Appendices to the Minutes of Evidence before the House of Lords European Communities Committee (Sub Committee F)*, pp. 302–3, London: HMSO.

The Economic Analyst (1984), Aug/Sept, London: Simon and Coates.

Economics and accounting of the NCB

Economic Trends (1984), August, London: Central Statistical Office.

Financial Times Energy Economist, no. 33 (July 1984) London.

Fisher, A., Fothergill, S., Morgan Rev. J. I. and Rees G., 'St John's Colliery, Maesteg: the Proposed Closure of: Report of a Public Inquiry' (1985), Cardiff: Mid-Glamorgan County Council.

Glyn, Andrew (1984a), 'Propped up with Prejudice, *Guardian*, August 7.

(1984b), 'When Coal not Dole is the Best Choice', *Guardian*, May 28.

Henley Centre for Forecasting (Sept. 1984), 'The Cost of the 1984 Coal Industry Dispute', London.

Hudson, Peck and Sadler (1984), 'Undermining Easington', Work and Employment Unit, Department of Geography, University of Durham.

(1985), 'Mismanaging Horden', Work and Employment Unit, Dept. of Geography, University of Durham.

Monopolies and Mergers Commission (1983), *National Coal Board: A Report on Efficiency and Costs in the Development, Production and Supply of Coal by the NCB*, 2 vols, Cmnd. 8920, London: HMSO.

National Coal Board (1983, 1984), *Accounts 1982/3 and 1983/4*, London: NCB.

National Institute, Economic Review (1984), August.

Schumacher, E. F. (1960), 'Coal: The Next Fifty Years' in *Britain's Coal*, Report of a NUM Study Conference.

Spanton, H. M. (1984), 'Exploiting the Plan for Coal Investment', *Mining Engineer*, May, pp. 533–8.

Turner, L. (1984), *Coal's Contribution to UK Self-Sufficiency*, Aldershot: Gower.

Wade, E. (1985), 'Coal Mining and Employment: A Study of the Blyth Valley', Eldon House Regent Centre, Newcastle upon Tyne: Open University.

5

NCB accounts: a mine of mis-information?

A. J. BERRY, T. CAPPS, D. J. COOPER,
T. M. HOPPER and E. A. LOWE

Introduction

The current problems in the National Coal Board are likely to cost everyone in Britain a great deal, not least in terms of higher electricity prices and taxes. Accounting measurement of profit is central to the debate about pits and pit closures. Yet little public attention seems to have been paid to the underlying accounting reports that identify pit profit and loss.

This chapter is intended to demonstrate the limitations of the use of accounting statements, drawn up in a manner consistent with conventional accountancy practice, for use in public debate in the justification of cost savings attributable to plant closures. We use the colliery profit and loss account – the F23 – of the NCB to illustrate fundamental arguments. Pit closures in the NCB are highly topical and we would hope that our analysis would prove useful to any independent colliery review body which may be set up, such as that under the recent NCB/NACODS (National Association of Colliery Overmen, Deputies and Shotfirers) agreement.

Careful scrutiny of NCB accounts produces the conclusions that they fail to form an adequate basis for informed management decisions, since they are almost bound to be misleading in any attempts to identify the changes in expected future cash flows consequent upon particular pit closures. While we are not in a position to state whether these documents are used for pit closure decisions, the information contained in them *is* used in public justification for such decisions.

The standard accounting statement for pits – the F23 – is, as far as can be ascertained, used as a blueprint for making budgets, projections of pit

Originally published in *Accountancy*, January 1985. A reply by B. Harrison, the then NCB board member for finance, 'Pitfalls of academic accounting', is in the same edition, p. 13. Comments were made on an earlier draft of this article by the NCB, but the authors stress that the opinions expressed remain entirely their own.

95

profit and loss in the future and, more importantly, to justify decision-making, at least in public debate. Its decision-making rationale cannot therefore be ignored. Yet for this purpose, as will be shown, the F23 is fundamentally flawed.

First, though, a word of caution. We wish to distance ourselves from the political arguments about the management's 'balance sheet' attitudes or the social costs/benefits of employing miners. Decisions in any intelligently run business (and we regard the NCB as such) may be made on the basis of general business strategy and assessments of future market opportunities, as well as the industrial relations implications of change. It is important to appreciate that many different documents and kinds of information may be used to make pit closure decisions. Our concern is to focus on the financial economic rationale for decision-making and the extent to which the routinely produced accounting statements would form an adequate basis for the justification of such decisions. The source material for our analysis is all publicly available, either in the NCB's annual reports and accounts or in the Monopolies and Mergers Commission (MMC) report on the NCB (1983).

Given that the MMC criticised the NCB for not producing pit or Area balance sheets, it is ironic that the NCB has been accused of having a 'balance sheet mentality'. For the F23, a major budgeting, control and accountability document, is a profit and loss account. (A pro-forma F23 is shown as appendix 3.9 in the MMC Report, vol. 2, pp. 56–7.)

The F23 may be designed to be used predominantly for control and accountability purposes. The 'bottom-line' of the document (in terms of pit profit or loss and cost per tonne) has, however, been widely used to justify pit closure decisions and to identify the alleged cost savings arising from the closure of a pit. Such use is misleading and does not provide a sensible basis for debate on pit closure for the following reasons:

1. Given the interdependence within the NCB, and within the energy sector (e.g. oil, gas, the Central Electricity Generating Board (CEGB)), and with other nationalised industries (e.g. British Rail and British Steel Corporation), there are major problems in determining a fair and reasonable revenue figure for sales proceeds in economic and financial terms for the NCB as a whole and individual collieries in particular.

2. The accounts are prepared on an absorption basis. It is exceedingly difficult to appraise the relative contribution of a pit (let alone a production face within a pit), as such information is not collated on an ongoing basis. Emphasis is instead concentrated on profit/tonne and unit costs. Given that many costs appear to be fixed, volume is therefore encouraged at a time of over-production.

A mine of mis-information?

Table 5.1 *Coal-mining operating statement*

Collieries	**1984**			**1983**		
	m tonnes			m tonnes		
Saleable output	89.9			104.3		
	Amount £m	Per tonne saleable £	Total cost %	Amount £m	Per tonne saleable £	Total cost %
Turnover	3,642			3,954		
(Decrease) in stocks of finished goods	(76)			(10)		
Other operating income	5			12		
Value of production	3,571	39.70		3,956	37.95	
Operating grants	–	–		4	0.03	
Total income	3,571	39.70	–	3,960	37.98	–
Costs						
Wages, including allowances in kind	1,290	14.35	31.0	1,436	13.77	33.6
Wages charges	483	5.37	11.6	489	4.68	11.4
Materials and repairs	858	9.54	20.6	909	8.72	21.2
Mining contract work	11	0.12	0.3	11	0.11	0.3
Power, heat and light	188	2.09	4.5	199	1.91	4.7
Salaries and related expenses	122	1.35	2.9	125	1.20	2.9
Other operating exes	571	6.35	13.7	503	4.83	11.8
Overheads and services	313	3.48	7.5	319	3.06	7.4
Depreciation	330	3.66	7.9	286	2.75	6.7
Total costs	4,166	46.31	100.0	4,277	41.03	100.0
Operating (loss)	(595)	(6.61)	–	(317)	(3.05)	–

Note: The saleable outputs shown above exclude tonnage extracted in the course of capital roadway development.

The above forms part of the coal-mining operating statement from the NCB's 1983/4 *Annual Report and Accounts*. While individual collieries vary in their proceeds and costs per tonne, the table provides an average for these across all collieries and uses almost the same account classification as the F23.

3. Not all costs included are related to current pit operations, e.g. early retirement costs and Area and HQ overheads.
4. Depreciation is included, but more as a bookkeeping convention than because it is a relevant cost for decision purposes. A capital charge would be more relevant, if extremely subjective.
5. Most importantly, the F23 is an historic account. Such accounts are unreliable for predicting expected future profits, especially given the uncertain geology and lengthy developmental work in deep mining.

What follows details the above criticisms: table 5.1 indicates the total *income* from coal mining, whereas the F23 statement refers to *proceeds*. While the calculation of both figures has the appearance of being both easy and objective, this is not so, largely due to major interdependencies in the energy market, as discussed below.

Profitability

Approximately 70 per cent of coal output is sold to the CEGB. The price is determined by complex negotiations the results of which have considerable impact on the *apparent* profitability of both organisations. For example, in the 1950s the NCB was forced to sell imported coal in the home market at a price lower than the cost of importing it. Current price agreements with the CEGB are set above the price for coal on the international spot market but considerably below the cost of oil with equivalent heat output. Further, there are considerable difficulties in using market prices as a basis for planning. For example, the volume of available imported coal is relatively small and subject to a number of vagaries. The volume and price of Polish coal owes as much to that country's foreign exchange problems as to the cost of production, and Poland cannot be regarded as a reliable supplier of cheap coal. The net cost in the UK of coal from Australia, South Africa and North America depends heavily on transportation costs, exchange rates, and so on. Changes in international freight rates dramatically affect the price of imported coal, as does the movement in the respective currencies. And without large investment in coal-handling facilities in British ports it would not be possible to import coal in large volumes. Thus calculation of proceeds represents a classic example of the problems of transfer pricing between interdependent units (in this case, the NCB and CEGB). The suggestion that imputed market prices represent an objective solution to these problems ignores the contrived and volatile nature of the market for coal.

Currently, collieries are credited with a selling price based on a formula relating quality to contracted selling prices. This present generous arrangement for marginal production, together with the low marginal costs of increasing production in the short run, leads colliery managers to believe that, in order to increase pit profitability and/or to reduce unit costs, it is desirable to maximise the volume of output. This is because proceeds are credited to saleable output rather than the coal actually sold and, as we will show below, many of the costs included in the F23 statement are fixed in nature, at least within the relatively short time horizons of most colliery managers.

Overproduction

It is hardly surprising that one outcome of these accounting treatments, and the emphasis placed on unit costs per tonne, is that in conditions of depressed demand, overproduction and increasing stockpiles have resulted. The way in which proceeds are realised means that stocking issues have not been perceived as the concern of pit managers.

In some organisations investment decision-making is mainly based upon incremental capital budgeting criteria, project by project. In others, such as the NCB it would seem, the 'bottom-line' profit figure for current operations is an important guide in justifying investment decisions before incremental economic criteria are applied. Assessments of colliery performance thus run the considerable risk of becoming self-fulfilling prophecies: reported high performance yielding high investment and output allocations, both of which contribute to low unit costs. The opposite consequences occur for reported low-performing collieries.

Pits are not independent units either in relation to their costs or their proceeds. For example, transfer prices issues arise again with regard to proceeds because coal is of variable quality and is frequently mixed or blended. This mixing involves transferring coal between pits; the selling price recorded is based on the notional selling price and thereby affects the recorded profitability of the pits involved in the transfer. In addition, given that a number of geographically adjacent collieries may be mining the same coal seam, the decision as to which colliery is allocated which coal faces will affect reported profitability.

The figure for proceeds in the F23 pit profit and loss account could, therefore, include coal which has been sold, transferred to other collieries and that which is produced for stock. Each category may be credited with different prices.

We have not analysed all components of colliery costs – for example, we have avoided the discussion as to whether wages and wage charges (which together in 1983/4 represent some 42 per cent of total colliery costs) are fixed or variable, and what the costs to the nation are of employing men in coal mining, as this depends on the assumed alternatives to employment in coal mining. Instead we have focussed on cost interdependencies and the allocation of costs to pits. These issues are crucial in assessing the meaning of the suggestion in the NCB annual report that in 1983/4 the average cost per tonne was £46.31 and in the MMC report (1983) that in 1981/2 'there were collieries where costs were over £100 per tonne' (*ibid.*, p. 167) and that 'the financial impact (on both profit and loss account and cash flow) of the worst 5 per cent is understated in table 8.4 (which showed a loss of £166m)' (*ibid.*, p. 169).

The second largest component of average costs is the charge for materials and repairs. Such a cost category might be assumed to represent variable costs of consumables used in coal getting. Elements such as timber, adjustable supports and belting may indeed vary with the rate of extraction and be avoidable if coal production is stopped at a particular pit. However, materials and repairs include charges for the hire of Area plant pool equipment. Charges are intended to apportion costs of this equipment in relation to usage at the specific pit. The MMC criticised the basis of the charge, suggesting that it did not reflect an economic charge as no allowance was made for interest or profit.

Cost interdependencies

Plant pool charges illustrate cost interdependencies between pits. The charge is, in effect, an allocated share of central costs. Rental charges are likely to depend on the usage of the equipment and it is therefore probable that the charge to a pit will be dramatically affected by the actual or budgeted usage of the equipment at other pits. Further, the closure of a pit will not, in the short run, reduce the total costs to be allocated but could result in a greater share of costs being allocated to each of the remaining pits. In the event of a pit closure, similar consequences of higher charges for surviving pits could occur with allocations involved in 'other operating expenses' and Area and national overheads.

Many textbooks discuss the advantages and disadvantages of marginal and full costing in decision-making. While there are undoubted benefits to full costing, it is generally agreed that marginal costing is more appropriate for decisions such as the closing of pits, an approach which the NCB claims to follow. Items in the mining operating statement such as mining contract work, power, heat and light, salaries and related expenses at the colliery level are all likely to disappear, even in the short run, if a colliery closes. These items comprised under 8 per cent of the total costs in 1983/4. On the other hand, the remaining items in table 5.1

are unlikely to alter directly with changes to the level of production at a specific pit.

No doubt a proportion of the 'other operating expenses' would be avoided if a pit closed. This item also includes surface damage costs, central coal preparation plants, Area survey costs, pumping, closure expenses, the voluntary early retirement scheme (VERS) and redundancy costs, most of which will not be reduced even in the longer term by a pit closure. Indeed some of these items, most particularly voluntary early retirement and redundancy costs have, according to the MMC, been rising most rapidly in recent years.

The issue of surface damage costs is complex. It is intended that the charge included in the F23 should relate to expected claims for damage due to current operations. However, claims have risen dramatically in recent years from £132m to £245m between 1983 and 1984. One consequence of these unanticipated increases has been that part of the cost is an allocation arising out of underprovision in respect of past production. Thus the allocation of £2.73 per tonne for deep-mined coal in 1984 is a mixture of costs related to current and past production. The closure of any particular pit may leave some past subsidence costs to be borne.

The exact allocation of costs for early retirement and pit closures cannot be identified from table 5.1. However, the MMC indicates that for 1981/2 it amounted to 83p per tonne. Yet these costs are not related to current production and are likely to be increased if capacity is reduced. From such information as we can glean from published sources, a cost somewhere between 83p and £3.56 of the £6.35 'other operating expenses' are fixed, and this does not include any allowance for the possibly fixed nature of central coal preparation facilities, survey costs and pumping of water from pits (both current and abandoned).

Overheads and services were 7.5 per cent of unit costs in 1984 and comprised Area and Headquarter-related costs. These costs, which are allocated on the basis of net operational expenditure, output and manpower, have also risen in real terms in recent years. These too are largely fixed costs for the colliery and will not be immediately reduced by a pit closure decision. However, in the medium term we suggest a substantial proportion will remain 'sticky' (although the NCB maintains that these will disappear in the medium term).

Depreciation represents 7.9 per cent of average annual costs. This charge includes fixed assets at the pit (but only since the reconstruction of fixed assets in 1973), equipment in the plant pool and write-downs of equipment due to colliery closure. Depreciation of assets at the pit is not affected by closure; the original cost would merely be written off at a quicker rate. It is, of course, unlikely that these assets would have significant resale value (although a proportion may well be salvaged for use elsewhere).

The depreciation charge is indeed a sunk cost and does not relate to actual rates of extraction. All depreciation rates depend upon subjective judgements, such as size of reserves left, or bookkeeping rules, e.g. maximum periods of write-off, or judgements of what constitutes capital or revenue. For example, we understand major drivages are capitalised whereas lesser ones are not. Whatever, depreciation is a spreading of historical cost which may have little relevance to future decisions. It would be of considerable relevance, however, to include an interest charge for the use of fixed assets. This was not done at the time of the MMC report but reported comments by Mr Butler, the NCB director-general of finance, suggested that the NCB was introducing a capital charge. Of course, given the limited sources of NCB finance (it borrows predominantly from the Treasury, not commercial sources), the rate charged would be contentious, as would be the value placed on the assets used by a specific colliery.

Cortonwood

Clearly, what is relevant is the future rather than the past – that is, estimates of capacity, associated costs and net cash flows. However, these are not the accounts produced for public scrutiny. Inevitably such estimates rely on judgement and are capable of being challenged. Yet might not such assessments, given their crucial national importance and their inherent uncertainty, be much improved by wider public debate? Recourse to historical cost statements carries the danger of misleading rather than enlightening the current debate over the future of the coal industry. To take just one example of historical data – the suggested closure of Cortonwood Colliery, which precipitated the recent strike. In 1981/2, the MMC (1983) indicated that its receipts were £44.3 per tonne and its operating costs were £50.5 per tonne, resulting in a tonne loss of £6.2 (approximately £1.7m in total). Yet if we assume that the fixed-cost element (represented only by other operating expenses, overheads and depreciation) in that year was approximately the same proportion of total costs as in 1984, then between 17.2 and 23.1 per cent of the unit cost of £50.5 would not be avoided by the decision to close Cortonwood. That mine would, at least in 1981/2, have contributed between £2.49 and £5.45 per tonne to NCB operating performance (on 1984 assumptions). These figures would still include some partly allocated costs such as plant pool and previous years' subsidence costs. However, they do not include any charge for capital used in the pit. Apart from these considerations of

A mine of mis-information?

Table 5.2 *Short-run contribution analysis of Cortonwood Colliery*

	1981/2 F23	Assumptions		
Per tonne		1 1983/4 basis	2 1981/2 basis	3 1981/2 basis
	£	£	£	£
Net proceeds	44.30	44.30	44.30	44.30
(Operating costs)	(50.50)	(50.50)	(50.50)	(50.50)
Profit/(Loss)	(6.20)	(6.20)	(6.20)	(6.20)
Less Unavoidable costs:				
Surface damage		2.73	2.44	nil
VERS		1.14	0.83	0.36
Depreciation		3.99	2.78	2.78
Overheads and services		3.79	3.94	3.94
Total		11.65	9.99	7.08
Contribution		+ 5.45	+ 3.79	+ 0.88

Assumptions. All three assumptions are based on published statistics in which some of the average costs are unclear. Assumptions 2 and 3 are based on a consideration of 1981/2 costs, as against 1981/2 revenue, to meet the argument that Assumption 1 draws upon 1983/4 costs.

1. Based on assumption of average costs for 1983/4. The range of contribution would be between + £2.49 and + £5.45 (see text). Assumes depreciation of 7.9% of annual average, and overhead and services costs of 7.5% of unit costs.

2. Based on assumption of average costs for 1981/2 (see appendix 3.3 of MMC Report, vol. 2). Assumes depreciation of 5.5% which reflects a lower level of depreciation in 1981/2 than in 1983/4 due to major projects (e.g. Selby), which are included in 1983/4 figures. Overheads and services are based on 7.8% of unit costs, which reflects a higher level than in 1983/4 due to certain reorganisations in 1981/2.

3. Assumptions as in 2 above, except for surface damage which reflects 'perfect knowledge' regarding this cost, which would render it totally avoidable. Additionally the cost of the VERS has been calculated on the cost remaining to the NCB after government subsidies.

103

avoidable cost, the receipts of £44.30 per tonne credited to Cortonwood are also unreliable for general reasons discussed above. If all output is saleable then the proceeds credited may be reasonable. If, however, the output is not readily saleable, then the proceeds credited may be too high. But this depends upon other policy considerations.

A short-run contribution analysis for Cortonwood, according to varying assumptions regarding the applicable costs and the nature of their avoidability, is shown in table 5.2. Circumstances can dramatically change in mining regarding markets for specific coal grades, geology, etc. Therefore, this analysis may not be a definitive representation of expected future costs and revenues. Indeed, it is subject to numerous assumptions about whether costs at Cortonwood behave similarly to the average costs in NCB collieries. But it does indicate the difficulty of informed public debate about pit closures on 'uneconomic grounds'. The question remains about how 'uneconomic' is defined, from whose perspective and over what period.

Colliery production programmes are, of course, established within a longer-term national production planning programme. While the F23 is a financial representation of these production programmes which indicates problem areas, constructed as it is on accounting conventions it is not an adequate basis for an analysis of the consequences of economic decisions taken about any particular pits.

This demonstrates how difficult it is for an informed public debate to take place upon contentious issues of pit closures. But we trust that it will be part of a constructive debate within which the information for any colliery review body may be established.

Postscript

The original article was written to draw attention to the considerable difficulties and uncertainties attached to identifying and measuring what constituted an economically viable pit or otherwise. As the strike lengthened and increased in bitterness this fact increasingly seemed to be disregarded, not least by government spokesmen. Publication of the article was delayed a month, following NCB allegations that the original contained errors and misunderstandings. Further, the NCB were concerned about the use of privileged and confidential information, because the authors had been conducting research on management control and accountability within the NCB for several years, the results of which had been fed back to and discussed with NCB managers at various levels (Capps *et al.*, 1984; Berry *et al.*, 1985). However, eventually the NCB acknowledged that this article drew only from publicly available sources.

A mine of mis-information?

After meeting representatives of NCB management the authors decided to publish an amended version, incorporating additional information given, but maintaining the essential arguments intact. We were not amenable to suggestions that publication should be delayed until after the strike, for we believed that public interest and debate over-rode obligations to management within the industry.

Both prior to and after publication the article attracted considerable media and parliamentary attention, fueled in part by media allegations that the NCB had tried to suppress it. Much of the comment misunderstood the article by seeking to purport that we had *'proved'* the NCB calculations, especially those for Cortonwood, were wrong, rather than noting the inherent difficulties of making *any* single point estimate of pit profitability. In a sense the Prime Minister's dismissal of the article in parliamentary questions in December 1985, by stating that accounting is done by mirrors and can therefore be made to prove anything, came close to the spirit of the article. Unfortunately her logic was not carried through when she went on to state that such calculations did nothing to address the fact that the industry was losing money. As both this and other chapters in this volume illustrate, whether or not the NCB was being subsidised is dependant upon the mode and level of analysis adopted. In polarised conflicts inherent ambiguities in data tend to be disregarded.

The response of the NCB was to attach a reply to the article, restating their allegations that the article contained errors and misunderstandings. In addition they hired four 'eminent' accountants to help them with a more detailed response. After nearly a year of private investigation within the NCB the consultants produced a report (Custis *et al.*, 1985), published by the NCB. Opinions on the report varied dramatically. The NCB press release quoted the NCB Director-General of Finance as stating, 'This confirms our considered view made at the time the article was prepared, that it contained major misunderstandings and inaccuracies and also serious misconceptions. Those allegations could not be left unchallenged and now the record has been put right.' However *The Times* Finance and Industry Editorial (*The Times*, 1985) had a different perception, referring to the NCB report as 'An eminent study in time-wasting'. They went on to say, 'Unfortunately the eminent accountants seem to have devoted their attention to picking holes in the article under review rather than address the wider issues which it raised when it was published at the height of the pits dispute ... The question about how best the NCB should account for its financial performance still remains unanswered.' This view was shared by much of the professional accounting press. In fact the NCB report, whilst exceedingly narrow, does implicitly and explicitly support many of the points made in the *Accountancy* article, though disagreeing on balance with its opinion that these render the F23s to be 'fundamentally flawed', and it omitted to refer to the authors' indication that this assessment was for decision-making purposes. The NCB response is more interesting as an illustration of attempted news management, rather than as a contribution to considered analysis.

From the conduct of the industry since publication, we suspect the accounting issues raised in the article remain largely unaddressed, though we have reason to believe that management are seeking means of rectifying some of the technical deficiencies in their procedures. For example, though costs of capital are now to be calculated for individual pits, the latest planning documents suggest that 'costs' are still being treated in an unproblematical way. Perhaps not surprisingly, the arguments about the contestable nature of accounting information are being used by the NUM, but seem not to be used by the NCB in their negotiations with government and customers. The implicit call in the article for an energy policy (from which reasoned accounting allocations may be made) has not yet been adopted.

REFERENCES

Berry A. J., T. Capps, D. J. Cooper, P. Ferguson, T. M. Hopper and E. A. Lowe (1985), 'Management Control in an Area of the N.C.B.: Rationales of Accounting Practice in a Public Enterprise', *Accounting, Organizations and Society*, vol. 10, n. 1, pp. 1–27.

Capps T., D. J. Cooper, T. M. Hopper, E. A. Lowe and J. Mouritsen (1984), 'Accountability and Control within the North Derbyshire Area of the NCB', Report to the NCB and the ESRC, Selected for Deposit in the British Lending Library, December 1985.

Custis P. J., D. Morpeth, E. Stamp and D. P. Tweedie (1985), *Report of an Independent Committee of Enquiry on Certain Matters Relating to the Affairs of the National Coal Board*, London: NCB.

Harrison, B. (1985), 'Pitfalls of Academic Accounting', *Accountancy*, vol. 96, no. 1097, p. 13.

Monopolies and Mergers Commission (1983), *National Coal Board: A Report on Efficiency and Costs in the Development, Production and Supply of Coal by the NCB*, 2 vols., Cmnd. 8920, London: HMSO.

National Coal Board (1984), *Annual Report and Accounts 1983/4*, London: NCB.

The Times (1985), Finance and Industry Editorial, 25 October, p. 21.

6

How large a coal industry?

P. W. ROBINSON

Introduction

In the first nine months of the recent dispute, neither side attempted to advance its cause by reasoned argument. 'Negotiations' made little headway against a starting position of non-negotiable demands, so that the dispute settled into a trial of strength. In chapter 9 we describe the background to the dispute; here we attempt to go a stage further by presenting estimates of the number of people who can profitably be employed in the industry. We show that the number is crucially dependent on the price of coal and the costs of producing it. It also depends on which definition of 'uneconomic pits' is used, and what definition of marginal (avoidable) costs. We recommend using a strict definition of 'uneconomic' but a generous interpretation of avoidable cost, and suggest that on this basis the current level of profitable employment in the industry is some 160,000. However, future employment prospects depend on how coal prices move in relation to costs of extraction.

Coal costs, demand and employment

The miners' strike raised a number of fundamental economic issues about UK energy policy. How large a coal industry do we need? What exactly is meant by an uneconomic pit? Is there a case for keeping uneconomic pits in existence against the day when the oil runs out? There has been no informed debate on these questions. During the strike public attention was focussed instead on very short-term issues, notably how long coal stocks would last and what proportion of miners would be working by Christmas.

The NUM stipulated no pit closures except on geological grounds. The Coal Board insisted on its right to close uneconomic pits. But what this

The original version first appeared in *Economic Outlook*, December 1984.

Economics and accounting of the NCB

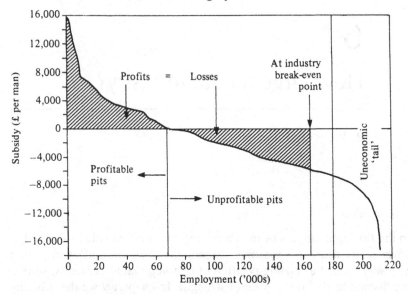

Fig. 6.1 Mining employment and subsidy per man in 1981–2.

meant in practical terms – how many jobs would be lost if 'uneconomic' pits were closed – was barely discussed. If every pit is closed where the avoidable costs of production exceed revenue then the industry faces further drastic contraction. The analysis of the year 1981/2 carried out in the October *Economic Outlook* (reproduced in chapter 9) showed that only 66,000 of the then 218,000 work force would have jobs if every pit were required to break even. If on the other hand the Coal Board had insisted on closing only the most uneconomic of the high-cost pits, for example to the point where *the industry as a whole* broke even, then there would have been jobs for 165,000 miners.

These employment estimates are shown on fig. 6.1, which illustrates the NUM position on the two possible interpretations of the Coal Board's position. The figure has been derived from data in the Monopoly and Mergers Commission Report (1983) on the coal industry, which gives detailed information on the industry for the year 1981/2. The figure, which is based on a detailed analysis of individual pits, shows the level of profit or subsidy in each colliery, expressed in pounds per man employed. Pits below the zero line are loss-makers. When total employment is greater than 165,000 the cumulative losses from the unprofitable pits exceed the profits made on the efficient pits, and the industry as a whole runs into deficit.

Figure 6.1 helps us to understand why the miners chose to make a stand in 1984. The industry had shrunk from nearly 220,000 to under

How large a coal industry?

180,000 men since 1981/2 when the so-called 'tail' of uneconomic pits was so clearly identified in the Monopoly and Mergers Commission Report. The 'tail' had thus been considerably thinned, if not entirely eliminated. From then on cuts arguably threatened the body, not the tail. There is a point of inflexion on the cost curve somewhere around the 180,000 mark beyond which the slope starts to change rapidly, and the case for closures becomes overwhelming. Those closures have in the main already occurred. The industry is now on a long and virtually straight cost curve with no obvious stopping point. The NUM must therefore feel that if they are going to resist further closures they must do so now. For, if they accept the logic of a reduction below 180,000 to 160,000, what is to stop the Coal Board pushing them to 140,000, 120,000 or lower?

Suppose the miners' fierce resistance to further closures, following a period of three years in which some 35,000 mining redundancies were peaceably agreed, does reflect their fears that a further 100,000 jobs could disappear. Is a compromise possible whereby the NUM is persuaded to accept the principle of closure on economic grounds in return for a guarantee that the principle will not be pursued to the point where the industry is completely decimated?

If such a compromise is sought, then further discussion of the economics of the industry will be needed. Figure 6.1 provides a useful framework of analysis but it is out of date. We have therefore used the information about particular pits contained therein to construct a picture of the industry as it might have looked in 1984 had there been no strike. The crucial assumption is that costs and prices in *each pit* moved since 1981/2 in line with the average for the industry. The change between 1981/2 and 1983/4 is given in a recent NCB Report (NCB, 1984). We assume no underlying change in the relationship between costs and prices in 1984/5 and have put in a notional 5 per cent increase to bring the figures close to 1984 prices. We discuss below how the situation would change if there were changes in these cost–price relationships (which we call the coal terms of trade).

Although the position of individual pits may change markedly at any moment for geological reasons, the overall shape of the industry's cost curve shown in figs. 6.1 and 6.2 has proved fairly stable. However, its slope and level shifts in response to cost and price movements. Since 1981/2 there has been a deterioration in the coal terms of trade (costs have risen more than prices), and the break-even points for particular pits and for the industry as a whole changed. As fig. 6.2 shows, the number of jobs available in profitable pits had by 1984 shrunk to just under 60,000. Since there is a smaller surplus with which to subsidise the operations of the less efficient pits, the number of people who can be

Economics and accounting of the NCB

Table 6.1 *Cost and price movements since 1981/2 (deep-mined coal)*

	1981/2	1982/3	1983/4	1984/5 (estimate)
Average selling price				
£/tonne	35.6	37.9	39.7	41.5
% change	8.5	6.5	4.7	5.0
Avoidable costs				
£/tonne	39.5	41.0	46.3	48.6
% change	13.2	3.9	12.9	5.0

Source: NCB *Annual Report*, 1984, plus London Business School estimates.

employed before deep-mining operations as a whole start to make a loss has also shrunk to under 140,000. This is substantially less than the break-even point in 1981/2, and well below the actual 1984 level of employment. The change between 1981/2 and our estimates for 1984/5 illustrates vividly the impact of variations in the coal terms of trade on employment prospects in the industry.

The coal dispute was about shutting down high-cost pits. Figure 6.2 enables us to relate pit closures to costs per man of keeping pits open. Figure 6.3 presents the same information in the form of the total subsidy required at each level of employment. If the industry were cut back to 60,000 men its surplus would be maximised. Any expansion beyond this point reduces the cash available to the Coal Board for investment in efficient pits and eventually plunges the industry as a whole into deficit.

The size of the surplus or deficit does not just depend on how many pits are left open. It also depends on the price at which coal can be sold on world markets, and the cost of producing such coal in the UK. The amount of coal that can be profitably produced is highly sensitive to the relationship between costs and prices. The point is illustrated by fig. 6.4, reproduced from the Monopolies and Mergers Commission's (1983) examination of the industry in 1981/2. In that year the volume of profitable production was just under 50m tonnes, the point at which the cost curve crosses the price line. Clearly if the price is raised to £40 per tonne the volume of profitable output rises to over 70m tonnes. And if costs were cut by 10 per cent volume would rise further to nearly 90m tonnes. In other words, the volume of profitable output is highly sensitive to the coal terms of trade. The sensitivity has been explored in a series of simulations in which coal prices and miners' wages have been changed

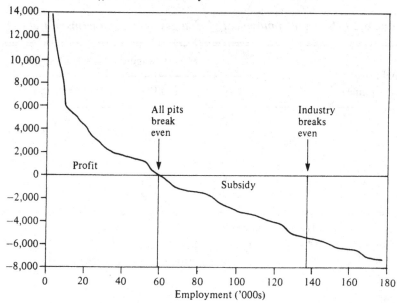

How large a coal industry?

Fig. 6.2 Mining employment and subsidies estimated cost, £ per man in 1984/5.

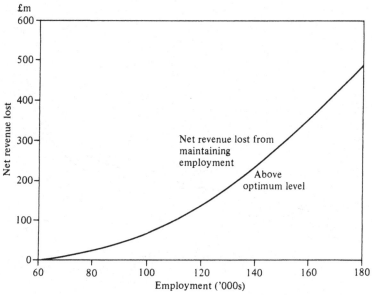

Fig. 6.3 Mining employment and net revenue.

111

Table 6.2 *Effects on employment of changes in the coal terms of trade*

Coal price (£ per tonne)		Miners' wages (£ per week)		
		£156	£173	£190
38	A	52	29	18
	B	107	76	53
42	A	73	59	52
	B	172	138*	108
46	A	89	70	60
	B	>180	168	135

A Employment '000s, in profitable pits.
B Employment '000s, if industry as a whole breaks even.
* Central case – estimate of underlying position of the industry in 1984/5.

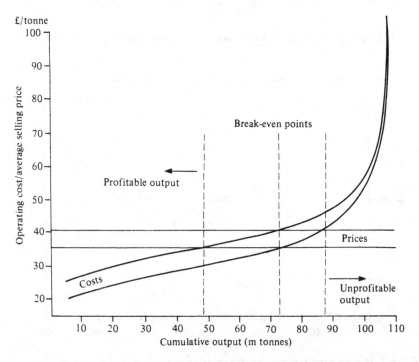

Fig. 6.4 Costs, prices and profitable output.

Table 6.3 *Effect of employment of productivity changes*

			Base line productivity	High productivity (+10%)
low coal price ⎫	−10%	A	52	80
low wages ⎬		B	107	175
base case		A	59	92
		B	138	>180
high coal price ⎫	+10%	A	60	90
high wages ⎬		B	135	>180

A, B: see footnote to table 6.2.

from their (estimated 'normal') 1984 level. The results of these simulations are shown in table 6.2.

Table 6.2 shows the effect of varying coal prices and wages by 10 per cent. It illustrates the difficulties faced by those who have to plan the future of the industry. Variations in the price of coal can change total employment at industry break-even points by huge amounts in either direction. Under these circumstances any 'Plan for Coal' is likely, sooner or later, to become outdated. It is simply not possible to lay down rigid long-term plans for the volume of production or employment where there is so much uncertainty about relative prices. The table also illustrates the extent to which the level of profitable employment in the industry has been eroded by wage increases. At a weekly wage of £156 – which is what the miners might be earning if they had not climbed to the top of the earnings league – the industry break-even point would not be far below present levels of employment.

One way of stabilising employment would be to relate wages in the industry to the price of coal. If we look at the outcomes on the diagonal of table 6.2, total profitable employment fluctuates relatively little if prices and wages move in the same direction – though a 10 per cent wage cut will not fully offset a 10 per cent fall in prices because wages constitute only half of total costs. Thus, as coal prices and wages fall, the coal terms of trade worsen and profitable employment falls.

In all the simulations shown in table 6.2 productivity is the same. However, there have been substantial variations in productivity in the past. All things being equal a 1 per cent rise in productivity reduces unit costs by 1 per cent (whereas a 1 per cent cut in wages reduces unit costs by only ½ per cent). So in table 6.3 we show the effect of re-running the simulations shown on the diagonal of table 6.2, feeding in a 10 per cent productivity improvement.

Economics and accounting of the NCB

The results are fairly dramatic in terms of employment, and emphasise the point that in an industry which is not governed by volume targets but is allowed to produce as much as it profitably can, productivity improvements *increase* employment. Such productivity increases may come about either through better working practices or through new investment. However, the case for new investment (which may also increase the level of profitable employment in the industry) is subject to the usual criterion that there is an adequate return on the capital employed.

What practical relevance do the simulations shown in tables 6.2 and 6.3 have to the present dispute? Clearly a wages cut or productivity increase of 10 per cent is not immediately in prospect. But if the figures are regarded as alternative views of the year 1990 (expressed in today's prices), then the tables show that employment levels over the medium term are highly dependent on wage and productivity performance at any level of demand.

What is avoidable cost?

All the above calculations are based on the definition of operating cost used in the Monopolies and Mergers Commission Report (1983). It has been argued, for example by Andrew Glyn (see chapter 4) and more recently by Berry *et al.* (see chapter 5), that that definition is not an appropriate criterion for determining pit closures. It is common ground that the relevant concept is *avoidable* cost. The Coal Board definition of operating cost includes provisions for depreciation, for repair of surface damage and past employee costs. If these costs are not *avoided* by closures, they should not be included in the comparison of marginal costs and revenues which is the basis of closure decisions.

Surface damage is the easiest case to deal with. Although it is true that the Coal Board cannot avoid paying out compensation for pit damage, it *will* avoid creating future damage liability if it ceases mining. It must therefore be right to include a provision for prospective subsidence claims in the cost of mining new coal. The cost of compensating for past subsidence is a reasonable estimate of the likely subsidence costs from future operations.

Depreciation is more difficult. The Coal Board has constantly to choose between buying new equipment or accepting higher repairs and maintenance costs on old equipment. In the very short term a repair may seem like a cost which is avoidable if a pit is closed, while depreciation is unavoidable. But over a longer time horizon, when the machine comes up for replacement, that too is avoidable. (Individuals face the same choice with domestic equipment: in the longer term the money set aside

114

each month to replace the car when it finally wears out is just as much an avoidable cost as the money spent on running repairs. Both can be avoided by giving up motor transport.)

By contrast with these two cases, the money spent on past employee costs does not seem to be avoidable. Closing a pit cannot reduce the pension costs of past employees. The latest NCB report (NCB, 1984) shows that these costs contribute 8 per cent of total operating costs. It therefore seems appropriate to reduce operating costs by this amount in any calculation of the marginal effect of closures.

Another important argument that we have not so far discussed relates to the variability of costs from year to year. A pit which is unprofitable this year may easily be profitable again next year. Fluctuations of 15 per cent in costs from year to year are not unusual in the industry. If we wish to avoid closing any pit which, though unprofitable today may well make a profit in future, a 15 per cent margin must be built in. This implies a permanent subsidy to the industry as a whole – though not to any particular pit – which could perhaps be justified as an insurance against possible energy shortages as oil and gas resources are depleted.

To take account of both these points we have re-run the calculations underpinning fig. 6.2, reducing costs by 25 per cent. These results suggest that some 160,000 people are currently employed in pits which are potentially profitable on this definition. This figure has been derived by applying the most stringent criterion of profitability (that is, that every pit must break even, not just the industry as a whole). This is the correct criterion for the optimum allocation of resources within the economy and recognises in full the principle of closure of 'uneconomic' pits. But by combining this strict definition of *profitability* with a minimalist definition of *cost* – to give the maximum benefit of the doubt to marginal pits – we arrive at a figure which should be easily achievable via voluntary redundancies on the presently available terms.

However, it must be recognised that there can be no permanent guarantee of employment in the coal mines. In this respect coal is just like any other industry. A fall in the coal price is a signal that less coal is needed. Unless the NCB can capture an increasing share of the world market by holding down costs, employment in the industry must fall if the price falls. Any other solution would in the long run lead to a serious misallocation of the nation's resources.

Postscript

My background paper, reproduced in chapter 9, originally appeared in the October 1984 issue of *Economic Outlook*, but its publication coincided with *The Sunday Times'* discovery of Mr Scargill's so-called Libyan connection, which somewhat reduced the attention paid to it in the press. However, when I used the material in talks and seminars the response was very positive. So I decided to carry the work a stage further, and explore the sensitivity of my calculations of the numbers who could be profitably employed in the industry to variations in the price of coal and the wages and productivity of coal miners. It was that article which is reproduced in this chapter and which appeared in the December 1984 issue of *Economic Outlook* in a slow news week. It received the greatest interest and publicity.

Subsequent to the dispute ending, and the later collapse of oil prices, I have re-analysed the situation within my existing methodology. The results of this analysis are contained in the postscript to chapter 9.

REFERENCES

Monopolies and Mergers Commission (1983), *National Coal Board: A Report on Efficiency and Costs in the Development, Production and Supply of Coal by the NCB*, 2 vols., Cmnd. 8920, London: HMSO.
National Coal Board (1984), *Annual Report and Accounts 1983/4*, London: NCB.

PART II

Economic strategies of NCB management

7

The economic case for deep-mined coal in Scotland

G. KEREVAN and R. SAVILLE

A critique of NCB corporate planning

Since the *Plan for Coal* (1974) was initiated, the NCB has invested £6.3bn (1983 prices). Any reasonable corporate planning exercise should be willing to examine a range of scenarios, and be insistent on re-examining assumptions and data before making decisions about terminating productive capacity. We will argue that the NCB, particularly in the Scottish Area, has been weak in its corporate planning, too narrow in its time-scale for reorganisation relative to uncertainties in world prices and markets, and has planned on inadequate or misleading data. We follow:

1. The Monopolies and Mergers Commission (MMC) Report in criticising the inadequacy of Area planning and statistics, which casts *prima facie* doubt on the NCB's ability to make acceptable projections (MMC, 1983, para. 19.6).
2. The 1983 MMC Report, and other MMC Reports on nationalised industries, which cast doubt on the adequacy of corporate planning and investment appraisal techniques in the public sector.
3. Both Andrew Glyn (see chapter 4) and Berry *et al.* (see chapter 5) in criticising the Area and colliery accounting procedures as adequate financial planning tools, thus raising a question mark over suggestions to close particular pits in the short run.

The relationship of NCB Area planning to national corporate planning and its inadequacy

The MMC Report (1983) on the NCB noted:

> balance sheets are not prepared in any normal form at deep mine Areas or other formations ... There is a lack of the necessary information that would enable management to base

119

its decisions on an understanding of the cost of the capital
likely to be involved, or the real profitability or otherwise of
individual operations ... The NCB has explained to us that
there are difficulties in providing, even at Area level, adequate
information to enable the balance sheets and other financial
statements to be set up and maintained (MMC, 1983, paras
19.25 and 19.26).

We can confirm, from our analysis of NCB documentation, that pit
and Area financial statistics are seriously inadequate for forward planning. In essence the MMC was criticising the NCB and its Area
management for 'flying blind'. This casts serious doubts over the reliance
that can be placed on NCB Scottish Area forecasts, and it suggests that
an ill-informed management might be prone to rapid somersaults in
decision-making – because its basic approach will be an empirical
reaction to short-term events unguided by a proper understanding of
underlying trends. This has happened in the case of Cardowan and
Polmaise.

The MMC made a number of recommendations as a result of these
findings:

We recommend that the NCB should make the necessary
changes to its accounting system and organisation to enable
the deep mine Areas and other formations to have adequate
financial information and to be operated, as far as possible, as
separate business units both for planning and for day-to-day
management purposes (MMC, 1983, para 19.28).

However, the NCB reaction to the Report was to reject out of hand the
MMC recommendation:

The Board considered that the Commission's recommendation
that deep-mined Areas should operate as far as possible as
'separate business units' was not clearly defined and that the
Commission had failed to consider wider questions of
fundamental importance which would be associated with such
a change (NCB, 1984, p. 9).

What lies behind this rejection? The MMC's recommendations are
broadly in line with recent reorganisations in nationalised industries,
devolving management into 'profit centres' or functional business units,
e.g. British Rail organising around activities such as freight. The NCB's
rejection can only be speculated on, but it would seem consistent with a
desire by the national Board to retain central control. But why?

The case for deep-mined coal

The NCB is a large multi-plant, multi-product business facing heavy competition in a crowded market. Its preferred strategy is to axe productive capacity to match short-term supply and demand. In common with other large or multi-national companies, individual area operations may be scheduled for closure as part of the overall corporate plan, irrespective of their local or individual profitability. A case in point was the closure of the Massey Ferguson plant at Kilmarnock, which was viable in its own right but was not consistent with the Massey Ferguson corporate plan to concentrate production of new lines in France. Thus the rather curt rejection of the MMC recommendations by the NCB may indicate simply the desire of the Board to be in a position to axe large sections, or all, of the Scottish (and Welsh) capacity, not in terms of local Area viability but as a by-product of a general strategy conceived in London. To turn the Scottish Area into a 'business unit' and to seek more rational planning information would be a barrier to a design conceived irrespective of Scottish deep-mining viability in the longer term.

By way of, admittedly, anecdotal confirmation of such an assessment, one of the authors had a long conversation with Professor A. D. Bain, a member of the MMC till December 1982, when he resigned over the government's refusal to uphold MMC objections to the take-over of the Scottish mining-equipment firm Anderson Strathclyde. He suggested that the greatest factor accelerating the decline of Scottish business autonomy was not the influx of foreign multi-nationals but rather the post-war growth of London-managed nationalised industries which had subordinated Scottish economic needs to so-called national strategies.

By way of a judgement on the weight to be placed on Scottish Area statistics and forecasts, we could cite Polmaise, where £15.8m was invested over a number of years only to see plans to open the colliery abandoned. This example could be repeated from other Areas: for example, Cortonwood's closure precipitated the recent strike, but capital developments had been taking place prior to the closure order.

The limitations of NCB corporate planning

The 1983 MMC Report made significant criticisms of NCB planning:

> The NCB's longer-term planning has been deficient in a
> number of important respects . . . plans have been designed to
> support the NCB's submission for investment finance, they
> have not permitted assessment of whether funds provided in
> the past have been well spent . . . The plans have not

demonstrated the robustness of the NCB's chosen course . . .
(MMC, 1983, para 5.71).

A series of MMC investigations of nationalised industry operations
since 1980 have indicated the same criticism, namely 'investment
appraisal optimism'. Most nationalised industries raise the bulk of their
capital investment finance from the government, mostly through loans.
There is little prospect that a government will let a nationalised industry
close down, or place the burden of redundancies on management
(though British Airways is something of an exception on the latter
point). Thus in nationalised industry after nationalised industry a corporate planning method and management culture has emerged hinged on
this 'dependent' relationship with the state.

Managers plan in volume terms (more power stations, more airliners)
and rig their forecasts ('appraisal optimism') in order to secure state
loans. A huge deficit is often the best grounds for going to government
for money for a major new capital investment optimistically designed to
raise efficiency and competitiveness to cure the deficit. A curious
symmetry emerges when we consider nationalised industries primed for
privatisation: they become 'profitable' according to their formal balance
sheets in order to attract buyers: witness British Airways' £180m surplus
(1983/4). None of this is to suggest that investment in national industries
is not vital, but there is evidence, especially from MMC reports, that this
'appraisal optimism' syndrome is reducing the marginal efficiency of
investment. This has led the MMC, and the Serpell Report on British
Rail (1983), to condemn various nationalised industry Boards for acting
against the public interest. Interestingly, the remit of the MMC Report
(1983) into the NCB specifically excluded consideration of the public
interest. The import of this discussion is to suggest, on MMC evidence,
that nationalised industry and NCB planning may have an ulterior
motive. Namely, presenting evidence to the government in such a way as
to maximise potential loans and grants rather than to give a true picture
of the business or its long-term prospects.

When the present government came to power in 1979 it called on the
NCB to break even by 1984. By December 1983 a new Coal Industry Act
increased the NCB's cumulative net borrowing limit to £5.5 bn and
extended grants to eliminate Board deficits to March 1986, with the
Secretary of State for Energy having the power to provide up to £2bn in
such grants for the three financial years of 1983/4 till 1985/6. What
produced this change?

In 1981 the NCB 'bounced' the government into increased funding by
theatening an accelerated closure programme and risking a major

industrial dispute with the NUM which the government was not then willing to contemplate. A substantial increase in deficit grant soon followed. In order to 'solve' the over-capacity and to reduce deficit grants to the NCB – and presumably to reduce the labour force and thereby the strength of the NUM – government has supported the investment programme (another £691m in 1984 despite the suggested glut of coal in world markets). This produces two dubious side-effects. First, the NCB is largely free from any real pressures to consider the opportunity cost or cost-effectiveness of its investment programme, for, though it pays interest to the government on investment loans, that self-same government covers the interest by deficit grants. The net effect – for the NCB – is free use of large amounts of capital. This has led the NCB to go for 'luxury' investment projects with extensive inputs of high technology. But a serious case can be made for a different modernisation programme, economising on investment funds but seeking still to increase capacity in line with the 'Plan for Coal', which would have used less sophisticated but heavier mining equipment to win bigger amounts of coal from existing reserves in existing pits. This would have had particular relevance in the Scottish Area.

The second side-effect is that by meeting appraisal optimism with large-scale investment through loans, the government is itself creating the increase in interest debt payments which, in the formal accounting, represent a huge 'loss' which then has to be covered by a deficiency grant payment. If the government acted like a private venture capitalist and took shares in the NCB rather than using its power to dictate a loans structure, then NCB finances would look significantly different. For instance, if the NCB were given the same deal that British Airways is demanding – the conversion of 65 per cent of their government debt into equity – then £303.5m of the NCB's supposed loss in 1984 would disappear. When it is noted that the bulk of NCB investment is located in the central English pits, but that the burden of the interest payments is borne nationally, then a case can be made for saying this represents discrimination against the operating economics of the low-investment areas like Scotland (who suffer doubly by seeming to have lower productivity because of the low investment).

The convolutions of the appraisal optimism syndrome are further complicated in the Scottish Area by the interaction of the NCB with another nationalised industry, the South of Scotland Electricity Board (SSEB), which is prone to the same corporate planning and investment pressures. A criticism of the SSEB is that it has placed even more emphasis on physical volume planning. Leaving aside the point about the failure to synchronise the investment plans of the energy industries, we see the SSEB trying to reduce its short-term costs by reducing coal purchases, while adding to the surplus capacity that is causing these problems by completing Torness nuclear power station. The symbiosis of two nationalised industries, the NCB Scottish Area and the SSEB, neither of which is constrained by normal market pressures, and both of which have largely administered pricing and investment structures, means that neither taken separately, and certainly not the weaker NCB Scottish Area, can be understood in crude terms of short-run excess capacity or high cost. For the data on which such a judgement could be made is heavily biassed.

Accounting systems: NCB income from coal sales to the electricity supply industry

In the original version of *The Economic Case* considerable attention was paid to the work of Andrew Glyn and Berry *et al.* As this covers similar ground to these articles (reprinted as chapters 4 and 5), it has been omitted here. The text which follows is limited to discussion of NCB income from sales of coal to the CEGB and the SSEB, which amplifies comments in chapters 4 and 5.

One problem of the 'flawed' accounting procedures of the NCB relates to the income which the NCB receives from coal sales to the CEGB and the SSEB. The problem dates back to nationalisation in 1947 and the decision to base the main investment programmes of the NCB on money loaned from the Exchequer, with only a part of capital costs subsumed under the costs of each colliery. The Standing Commission on Energy and the Environment (appointed in 1978 and abolished in 1981) noted (1981) that the 'NCB's financial performance was considerably inhibited by an informal pricing policy with the government. The NCB was encouraged to meet its capital requirements by Exchequer borrowing rather than by price increases and self-financing.' Since 1947 the preference of the NCB and the Treasury has been to maintain a low price for coal with major expenditures completed with Exchequer loans. The result is an unnecessarily poor financial performance on the part of the NCB.

Yet the government has every intention of maintaining the 'profits' of the electricity supply sector. This was made clear in the Report from the House of Commons Energy Committee (1984). The Committee noted that the sharp rises in electricity prices after 1979, coupled with the artificially low prices of coal compared with oil, meant that the electricity supply industry 'is currently self-financing and expects its capital requirements will be financed from internal sources over the period 1983/4 to

1989/90'. Moreover, the increase in revenue has enabled huge payments to be made to the Treasury. The projected payment for 1984/5 is £740m. The chairman of the Electricity Council confirmed that this minus external financing limit (EFL), 'was *not* an agreed figure and that it had been "imposed" on the industry without the normally expected degree of consultation'. While taking this sum from the electricity industry the Treasury will 'lend' the NCB its capital requirements and charge it 10–12 per cent interest on a fixed loan.

The Treasury spokesmen admitted that their current agreement on pricing coal sold to the CEGB 'had the direct effect of reducing the NCB's revenue and thus of increasing the level of deficit support'. The Treasury could do something about the NCB's 'fictitious' losses as they have an overall responsibility for policy for the nationalised industries, 'especially on pricing and investment'. The Committee tried to probe the reasons behind the imposition on the Electricity Boards, but the Secretary of State for Energy refused to answer many of the questions about the relationship of the EFL to the public sector borrowing requirement, or on government pricing policy. 'We were thus denied information about the differing perspectives of the Departments which in our view is essential to a proper understanding of the Government's position and the considerations which gave rise to it.' Further, the Committee stated that,

> The Treasury witnesses did not strengthen their case by the manner in which they chose to present it to the Committee. An honest statement of the constraints placed upon their freedom to speak would have been more acceptable than the disingenuous claim that they knew no more about the Electricity's Council's views than they had read in the newspapers. The inability of the Treasury to present their own case in a cogent and serious manner can only encourage the assumption that they do not themselves believe that it would survive close scrutiny.

Statement of NCB's case for reducing Scottish deep-mining capacity, and summary of inadequacies in NCB's position

This section attempts to present the commercial arguments of the NCB for reducing capacity in the Scottish Area, and suggests that these arguments are problematic and open to criticism. The NCB's case may be summarised as follows:

1. While oil price rises in 1973 and 1979 made coal a cheap energy source on a world scale (25–65 per cent cheaper than oil in most parts of

the globe), nevertheless coal demand has not grown fast enough to match the increase in world output. Though world consumption of coal rose 30 per cent in the decade 1973–83, coal-mining capacity was still 20 per cent above demand in the three biggest Western producer-countries (Canada, USA and Australia).

2. This excess capacity has kept world coal prices low on international markets.

3. 25m tonnes of extra capacity will come on stream from new investment through the rest of this decade. This extra capacity will have trouble finding a market. Therefore the NCB must accelerate the decommissioning of older, high-cost capacity as the new pits come on stream.

4. Much of this high-cost capacity is, according to NCB figures, situated in Scotland. The 1984 NCB *Accounts* show that the Scottish Area made a financial loss of £74m on a turnover of £202m. This was the worst performance relative to turnover of any region, including South Wales. Cost per tonne of deep-mined coal in Scotland was £53.80 against the NCB average of £45.31. Average loss per tonne was £13.96.

5. On a pit-by-pit basis, only two of the nine operating mines or mine complexes in Scotland are credited with being in (marginal) profit in the 29 weeks till the start of the overtime ban preceding the recent dispute (as indicated in the NCB's own Operating Accounts). If the NCB were to follow the logic of its own statements on reducing high-cost capacity up to circa 25m tonnes of output to offset new capacity this decade, then at least five pits in Scotland would be decommissioned (computed by counting the number of high-cost Scottish pits in the total numbers of UK pits accounting for the highest-cost 25m tonnes of current NCB output, according to the NCB's own Operating Accounts).

6. A Scottish Area draft budget projection for 1985/6 (Smith and Harrison, 1984) has recently been made public by the STUC, and it gives an indication of the sort of further capacity cuts the Scottish Area NCB is willing to contemplate: namely a reduction to eight collieries by 1985/6, and the cessation of capital replacement at three more pits, indicating a likely short-term closure of these operations.

7. In response to the publication of the draft budget projection for 1985/6, an NCB spokesman stated: 'Producing units in the twenty-first century will include the Frances Seafield complex, the Longannet mines, Bilston Glen and Monktonhall' (*Scotsman*, November 1984). However, while noting that few business enterprises would feel confident about predicting the functioning of individual productive units 16 years in advance, this total is a clear reduction to five pits (using the NCB's method of counting pit units as presented in the Operating Results). The

same spokesman proceeded to cast doubt on the future of the Ayrshire pits of Barony and Killoch on geological grounds, and was noticeably silent on the future of Polkemmet, which is directly linked to the problematic existence of Ravenscraig Steel Works.

8. Finally, the NCB statement in the *Scotsman* should perhaps be taken as a 'best case' scenario. All other things being equal, the overwhelming logic of the NCB strategy is to sharply reduce excess capacity outside of the new mining complexes of central England. That excess capacity burden, in the NCB's terms, can override previously held medium-term Area plans. Witness the decision to close the Polmaise development pit before it came on stream and despite £15m of investment.

The NCB's case rests primarily on the view that the Scottish Area pits are in the high-cost/low-productivity tail-end of British production, and that this tail-end must be cut off to match supply with demand and thereby release inefficiently used resources to other ends within the UK and Scottish economies. We take issue with this scenario on the following five points.

(i) Following the MMC (1983) and Berry *et al.* (chapter 5), we note a lack of adequate financial data at Scottish Area and pit level on which one could make with any reasonable degree of business confidence the sweeping closure decisions that the Scottish Area NCB is contemplating.

(ii) We note grave inadequacies in the productivity measures used by the NCB and conclude that, since productivity is a function of past investment programmes in an industry as capital-intensive as deep-coal mining, short-run productivity scores are not a good guide to closure decisions.

(iii) We raise doubts about the short-term wisdom of reducing output of Scottish coal, with its low sulphur content, only to replace it with coal of a much higher sulphur content from either central English pits or imports. The social and economic costs of the subsequent increase in acid rainfall damage will have to be met elsewhere in the economy or in Europe.

(iv) We calculate that the hidden long-run costs of colliery closures borne by the Exchequer and the taxpayer far outweigh the short-run savings to the NCB. It would be cheaper to the Exchequer to retain present Scottish capacity until market conditions improve in the 1990s, irrespective of the new capacity which will also come on stream this decade.

(v) Finally, we discount the view that, in the present economic climate in Scotland, any substantial amount of labour or other resources released from coal mining will be reabsorbed by the economy. Thus the closure programme will have a marked detrimental effect on the overall Scottish economy, and in particular could lead to a cumulative and interactive collapse of coal, BR freight and Ravenscraig steel production.

The weaknesses in the NCB's Scottish Area scenario and in planning systems and information in Scotland

How good is the managerial decision-making behind the Scottish Area NCB's closure plan? Consider, by way of evidence, the following statement from the MMC Report: 'Area Directors do formulate what the NCB calls "strategies" for their Areas. These are not quantified in terms of the resulting effects on Areas' costs or profits, or in terms of the time by which they should be accomplished' (MMC, 1983, vol. 1, para 7.124). Not surprisingly, most of the paragraph is censored from the published record. Here we have Area directors formulating 'strategies' which take no account of costs, financial returns or timing. It is against this background that we examine the Scottish NCB's case for reducing capacity.

The MMC records that accountability meetings between the NCB and Area managers restrict budgetary discussions to the year in question. Scottish Area planning is thus restricted to the short run, prey to over-hasty responses to sudden developments, and at the mercy of highly centralised national NCB budgetary planning. Are single-year budgetary figures for colliery profit and loss good enough for planning? For instance, 1984 NCB Operating Results for Scotland show only two pits in profit. Even, for the sake of argument, accepting these figures at their face value, they are not sufficient grounds on which to draw immediate conclusions regarding closure. Who says so? The NCB in its evidence to the MMC.

> The NCB pointed out that the results of a particular colliery for a single year may not be representative and said that over the seven-year period 1974–75 to 1980–81 the cost per tonne for a colliery varied from its average cost per tonne by 16 per cent, so that there could be variation from one year to another by over 30 per cent up or down (at constant prices) (MMC, 1983, vol. 1, para 3.31).

Because of the nature of mining work with its unexpected geological problems and safety questions, year-to-year results can alter dramatically. Therefore only a medium-term view of colliery operations and performance is likely to be accurate. We must be certain when reacting to short-term demand fluctuations (such as the rising value of sterling in the

The case for deep-mined coal

Table 7.1 *Colliery operating results for Scottish Area 1981/2*
(£/tonne)

Colliery	Net proceeds	Unadjusted operating costs	Operating cost − 25%	Unadjusted surplus/loss	True operating surplus/loss
Polkemmet	45.5	54.5	40.9	(9.0)	4.6
Frances	35.3	53.1	39.8	(17.8)	(4.5)
Barony	36.4	50.2	37.7	(13.8)	(1.3)
Killoch	32.3	49.0	36.8	(16.7)	(4.5)
Comrie	31.7	48.3	36.2	(16.6)	(4.5)
Seafield	35.4	44.1	33.1	(8.7)	2.3
Bilston Glen	38.1	42.7	32.0	(4.6)	6.1
Monktonhall	30.1	38.3	28.7	(8.2)	1.4
Longannet	29.7	31.2	23.8	(1.5)	5.9

Source: MMC, 1983, Vol. 2, p. 30.

early 1980s raising export prices) that individual pits are not penalised because of equally short-term production problems yielding an unflattering financial picture in a given year.

Following our own work on local Scottish Area accounts, and the work of Berry *et al.* (chapter 5), we note that the 1983/4 NCB *Accounts* (p. 58) indicate that something between 20 and 25 per cent of so-called operating costs are non-avoidable overheads payable whether or not production takes place. If we were to apply, say, a 25 per cent reduction in operating costs per tonne at Scottish pits, we see a transformation in their profitability. Take the colliery operating results in the very bad year of 1981/2, when every Scottish pit was registered as loss-making (table 7.1). Five pits were making genuine operating profits: Polkemmet, Comrie, Seafield, Bilston Glen, Monktonhall and the Longannet Complex. Only the smaller pits still appear to make operating losses. Taking the Scottish Area as a whole for 1981/2, the operating loss claimed by the NCB was £33.8 per tonne on a cost of £39.6 per tonne. But if we deduct the overheads 'loaded' onto operating costs at the rate of 25 per cent, we get a more genuine operating cost for Scotland of £29.7 per tonne and an Area profit of £3.35 per tonne.

These calculations refer only to operating costs and take no account of capital payments. No economy can operate without sufficient returns to reconstitute capital invested. Without some measure of the productivity of capital in various uses we would have no idea how to deploy capital resources between competing ends. But it remains a first rule of business that if an enterprise is covering its out-of-pocket operating expenses plus contributing towards capital costs, then you don't shut down the business.

Besides, in the Scottish case there is a distortion of the accounts on the capital side. Investment in Scottish mining has been excluded from eligibility for regional development grants (RDG). Until this year's changes in RDG, much of the private sector, including the oil industry, was an automatic recipient of large government subsidies towards capital investment. Investment in coal-mining was excluded from such grants under the present government. Instead the government lends the NCB its capital requirements at a market rate, and then 'subsidises' the industry when it cannot pay the interest. If the NCB were given regional aid like a private sector company, its interest charges would be reduced and its performance would look healthier. The method of subsidising the private sector via regional aid distorts private sector returns in a favourable way, while the method of subsidising the NCB distorts returns in an unfavourable way. The MMC was at pains to comment that these rules should be changed 'in particular to ensure that capital investment in new mines, or to extend the economic life of existing mines, attracts the same level of grants as would be available to other industries' (MMC, 1983, vol. 1, para 19.21).

Weaknesses in productivity assessment

No society can afford to be indifferent to the productivity of its industrial resources and low-productivity enterprises must eventually be closed in favour of higher-productivity enterprises. In the case of Scottish deep-coal mining, the NCB *Accounts* indicate a grave situation of lower than average productivity and thus underline the arguments for closure. Productivity is measured in output per manshift (OMS). OMS is the saleable output of coal produced on average per miner per shift. In 1983/4, Scottish OMS was 1.94 tonnes, which was lower than any Area except South Wales. However, two serious criticisms can be made of the OMS calculation. First, OMS is a crude productivity measure. It is a brute measure of physical output, regardless of the cost or difficulty of production, measured against only one sort of input, namely labour. Coal mining is a highly capital-intensive industry and will become more so as a result of new technology. A truer productivity measure (inputs : outputs) should take into account capital costs as well as labour. Secondly, if output is as much a reflection of machinery as labour in mining, then a current low OMS merely reflects historic low levels of

Table 7.2 *NCB deep-mines capital expenditure by Area 1974/5 to 1981/2 (average 1981/2 prices)*

Area	Total £m	Existing pits with major investment programmes costing over £1m
N. Yorkshire	730	5
Barnsley	408	9
Western	405	12
N. Notts	397	11
North-East	374	9
Doncaster	353	9
S. Wales	316	14
S. Midlands	310	8
S. Yorkshire	280	12
S. Notts	272	5
N. Derbyshire	244	6
Scotland	200	4

Source: NCB reproduced in MMC, 1983, vol. 2, p. 65.

investment rather than current inefficiency. A low Scottish OMS could be the result of investment starvation. The figures recorded in the MMC Report (1983) show that Scotland has had a low investment record. For the years 1974/5 to 1982/3, in an industry with a long lead time between investment and increased production, Scotland had the lowest absolute level of investment of any NCB Area. (Areas are obviously of different sizes; nevertheless reference to the 1984 *Accounts* shows the Scottish Area with a much lower than average capital endowment per miner) (table 7.2). A hard view might be that we have to deal with the here and now. Irrespective of past investment decisions, the situation is that there is low Scottish productivity relative to the prices that can be obtained for Scottish coal.

This argument can be countered on two grounds. First, assuming that a given Area or pit does have lower-than-average productivity, it is no serious strategy to 'cure' the problem by writing-off millions of pounds worth of capital in a short-term attempt to cut capacity. The fact that it takes roughly ten years to bring new coal on stream means that coal supply and demand are extremely difficult to synchronise. Low productivity, provided a pit is contributing above its genuine marginal operating costs, should be rejected as a reason for immediate closure. The normal business strategy in these circumstances would be to examine the pace of investment in new capacity, and look again at what short-term improvements in productivity might be gained in existing capacity.

This brings us to the second counter argument. Present-day Scottish Area productivity is subject to a number of constraints which can be removed in the short term. But these constraints are the result of the closure programme itself. For instance, there is evidence that at Cardowan, as in a number of other pits, a long-term decision by Scottish Area NCB to close the pit resulted in a slow reduction in capital investment in drivages. By the end of the financial year 1982/3 no further capital expenditure on drivages or anything else was earmarked for Cardowan. Such uncertainty, coupled with local industrial relations problems, produced a high rate of absenteeism. This affected short-term OMS. A management decision to run down the pit produced the low OMS which justified the action. This was easily reversible. Confidence in the pit's future and better Area management could have reduced absenteeism to normal levels. Since the method of working at Cardowan was manpower-intensive, some limited form of heavy mechanisation would have yielded positive productivity increases in a short time. Cardowan is further proof of the NCB's obsession with highly complex and expensive forms of capital investment at the expense of intermediate forms of technology which would boost productivity at the older pits. NCB planners think in volume terms and are seduced by big new mining projects rather than more cost-effective, if less exciting, attempts to improve productivity in existing operations by, say, crash use of heavy-duty equipment.

The MMC Report (1983) gives powerful evidence of this NCB rejection of a low-cost route to increased productivity: 'Our own estimates suggest that an extra minute's increase in running time per shift on all faces could, given no other restrictions on the flow of coal, increase output by over 800,000 tonnes per year' (MMC, 1983, vol. 1, para. 7.61). It could be achieved at very little cost, and certainly much less than through reliance on 'super' pits. For instance, underground railway systems could be improved to allow more time at the face. The MMC (1983) also recommended more cost-effective use of overlapping shifts on the German model.

Dr Robinson (in chapter 6), using figures from the MMC Report (1983), suggests that the current level of employment in the industry could be maintained even on the NCB's operating assumptions as to costs, provided there was a 10 per cent increase in productivity. This is not an impossible target to achieve over the rest of the decade using the sorts of methods mentioned above. Dr Robinson, echoed by the *Economist* (1984b), offers an alternative, namely a 10 per cent wage cut. Wage costs are in the order of 42.6 per cent of NCB operating costs. This is not

The case for deep-mined coal

any different a proportion from that of a so-called low-cost producer of deep coal. Labour costs in a typical Australian deep mine constitute approximately 41 per cent of total costs (Schultz, 1984). The issue with respect to raising productivity is not high wage costs in mining – average weekly earnings in mining in Scotland in 1983 were less than the average for all manufacturing industries. It lies rather in the NCB's obsession with 'super' pits at the expense of a more modest but cost-effective way of using men and machines. The new super pits will leave some 50 per cent of the coal reserves in the ground because of the nature of the high-tech machinery used. It is this 'uneconomic' and 'wasteful' approach to mining which now has to be justified by arbitrarily cutting capacity in other Areas such as Scotland.

The failure of the NCB's marketing plan to defend the production of low sulphur Scottish coal as an aid to reducing acid rain

Proper business planning should build on a marketing strategy for the product. Scottish Area management has singularly failed to note the advantages of continuing to produce coal with a lower sulphur content over that produced in the newer pits of central England. Undoubtedly this is linked to the Scottish Area's biggest customer being the SSEB. The electricity boards have been reluctant to admit responsibility for sulphur emissions, and the resulting acid-rain damage.

It is our contention that the importance of low-sulphur coal in the period while we develop the technology to cure the acid-rain problem gives a strong marketing rationale for continuing to maintain Scottish deep-mining capacity intact through the 1980s. Scottish coal seams are among the best in Europe with regard to quality for consumers, for industry and for electricity generation. They have a high calorific value, combined with low ash and sulphur contents (see table 7.3). The figures in table 7.3 come from systematic NCB sampling techniques at five collieries. The normal range of sulphur and ash contents in European coal are on the higher side of the range 0.5/0.6 per cent sulphur to above 2 per cent, and 3 to 30 per cent plus for ash. Scottish coal comes out especially well, as suitable for all uses, in particular those which require a low sulphur content.

The cost to the Exchequer and the taxpayer of the Scottish pit closure programme

The NCB's case for closing a significant part, if not all, of Scottish capacity is that the Scottish Area contributes to the high-cost 'tail' of excess output. But what should be meant by uneconomic? In the case of

Economic strategies of NCB management

Table 7.3 *Quality of coal from five Scottish collieries*

Colliery	No. of seams	% ash	Calorific value	% sulphur
Cardowan	5	3.3/6.2	34,700	0.60/0.68

Cardowan: This is a good-quality coking coal of rank 501/502 used as a blender for steel-production in Scotland. Is especially good for forge work. It commands a high price on the international market.

| Monktonhall | 5 | 4.9/8.3 | 30,180/34,440 | 0.72/1.01 |

Monktonhall: 98% of coal from Monktonhall goes to the SSEB. The pit has huge reserves, and as future work would be mainly under the Forth, subsidence costs would be negligible.

Barony	3	4/10	34,000/34,500	1.00
Polmaise	1	9/14	30,000/31,000	0.51/0.75
Polkemmet	2	6.0/9.0	32,000/33,000	0.75/0.80

Polkemmet: produces a good-quality coking coal. Coal rank code 501/502. This colliery has been the subject of an extensive investigation and public inquiry in June 1985, organised by the West Lothian District Council (Cooper *et al.*, 1985).

the Scottish pits we are presented with a *prima facie* case that the taxpayer is subsidising the mining of coal. Hence Scottish pits should be closed, and the resources returned to more productive use in other industries. But herein lies the central weakness of the 'uneconomic' pits argument: there is no evidence whatsoever that in the present economic climate the termination in part, or in whole, of the Scottish mining industry will lead to its workers, capital and purchasing power being transferred to any other economic sector. Such a termination will be a net loss to Scottish economic activity and add considerably to the already pronounced de-industrialisation of the Scottish economy.

Manufacturing employment in Scotland has fallen by almost a quarter of a million since 1971. Unemployment stands in excess of 300,000 or 14 per cent of the work force. If we add the 75,000 subsidised jobs provided through special employment measures, and the 11,400 individuals removed from the statistics by the April 1983 decision not to count men over 60 not claiming unemployment benefit, then the total is nearer 400,000. Employment in the public sector, excluding the nationalised industries, fell since 1979, and is predicted to fall even further (Scottish Office, 1984, p. 5). Manufacturing jobs that are created, in the semi-conductor fabrication sector, for instance, fall in large measure to

134

women: total female employment in Scotland has risen from 787,000 in 1971 to around 875,000. None of this would seem to indicate any optimistic prospect of labour shed from mining being absorbed in great numbers into the local economy, given the current economic climate. According to the Scottish Office, the only areas of employment demand or skills shortage in the local economy are part-time female service employment, and specialist manpower in electrical and electronic engineering (*ibid.*, p. 7).

In terms of capital and other material resources being redistributed to 'productive' sectors by the closure of the Scottish pits, it is well to remember that the bulk of fixed investment in the Scottish economy – over two-thirds of the total – comes from the public sector. If the state cuts spending on Scottish coal merely to reduce total public spending in order to make income-tax reductions, then there is no redirection of capital and material resources within Scottish industry at all. The result, inasmuch as individuals eventually receive an income-tax boost, is to boost demand for goods made in areas where the manufacturing base remains intact, for example the EEC and Japan, but there is a net fall in Scottish investment as the state cuts its involvement in coal.

There is little current economic evidence to indicate that the Scottish economy would respond to a minor boost in consumer demand brought about by tax cuts. Apart from low value-added food processing from alcohol, there are few consumer goods manufacturers. The strategic capital and intermediate goods manufacturers in Scotland are dependent on industrial and public sector demand. Scottish manufacturers suffered a sharp fall in output in 1982 and 1983, while total UK manufacturing output was rising, as a result of falling orders in mechanical engineering, steel tubes and forgings. The consequences of the loss of deep-coal mining as an industrial purchaser can be reasonably inferred.

However, the foregoing arguments assume that closure of coal-mining capacity in Scotland represents a reduction in state expenditure and no corresponding utilisation of the 'freed' resources by the private sector. In fact there is a further consequence. The NCB is but a part of UK Ltd. Its finances are part of the overall financing of the Exchequer. There is overwhelming evidence that, given the circumstances outlined above, there is a significant increase in the financial costs to the British Exchequer of such closures, which will in the medium term raise the tax burden imposed by the Exchequer.

Economic strategies of NCB management

Table 7.4 *Cardowan Colliery 1982/3 operating figures (000£)*

Net proceeds	8,309
Total costs made up of:	15,730
Wages	5,738
Wage costs	3,141
Power, heat, light	829
Materials	1,857
Plant hire	1,000
Area overheads	775
National overheads	507
Other expenses etc.	1,883
Loss	6,736

Evidence for a net rise in Exchequer costs as a result of Scottish pit closures: Cardowan as a case study

On the basis of NCB *Accounts*, closing Scottish pits will cost more to the Exchequer, and ultimately the taxpayer, than retaining them until the world demand for coal rises significantly in the 1990s. We examine the evidence for this claim using figures for Cardowan Colliery for 1982/3 (see table 7.4), which was scheduled for closure just prior to the recent dispute.

First, the direct financial savings to the NCB and the Exchequer of closing Cardowan: nearly £16m was paid out for net proceeds of only a little over £8m; savings, £6,736,000. In 1982/3 there was on average some 1,100 miners at Cardowan, so the saving per miner employed per week was £6,736,000 divided by 1,100 divided by 52. That is a saving of £118. But if those miners are not re-employed, or if some of the younger miners are transferred to take jobs at other pits but once there displace older miners taking voluntary redundancy, then a chain-reaction sets in which adds other costs to the Exchequer far outweighing this gain of £118 per miner per week. The 'new' post-closure costs which have to be offset against these savings are four-fold, as shown in table 7.5.

(a) *Direct costs of lost mining jobs*: redundancy payments, voluntary or otherwise; lost tax revenue from filling the job which will have to be made up elsewhere, either by higher taxes on the remaining working population or by increased government debt; and assuming that our redundant miner would have reached normal retiral age, avoidable continued expenditures on unemployment benefits for youngsters who would have succeeded to the job on the miner's retiral, plus their 'lost'

136

The case for deep-mined coal

Table 7.5 *Exchequer financial loss resulting from closure of Cardowan Colliery: summary of calculations contained in text based on 1982/3 operating figures*

	£ per miner per week
Financial 'saving' from closure	118
Financial costs involved in closure:	
Redundancy payments and tax loss	(142)
Lost tax and dole for estimated 395 supply workers who lose jobs as a result of reduced NCB demand	(38)
Lost tax and dole for estimated 374 workers put out of work by general decline in consumer spending	(36)
Overheads at Cardowan transferred elsewhere	(28)
Total costs	(244)
Net costs to Exchequer of closing Cardowan	(126)

tax payments if they had worked.

(b) *Indirect costs of jobs and business lost elsewhere in the economy as a knock-on effect of reduced mining expenditures*: the aforementioned redundancy, tax and dole losses will be repeated for jobs lost in mining suppliers, and jobs lost to the economy as a result of a reduction in consumer spending due to increased unemployment.

(c) *Non-wage overhead costs which cannot be terminated even with the closure of the pit*: due to the non-standard and dubious accounting practices of the NCB a significant proportion of the total operating costs charged to each pit are nothing to do with the day-to-day coal-mining operations of the colliery, and would remain after shut-down (see Berry *et al.*, chapter 5).

(d) *Lost rates to local authorities*: mining operations are major payers of rates to local authorities; e.g. Monktonhall Colliery in Lothians paid some £160,000 in rates in the financial year 1981/2: the loss of a colliery adds to the local rates burden or implies an increase in rate support grant from the Exchequer.

We shall now proceed to try and calculate the above 'new' post-closure costs and set them against the supposed Cardowan savings of £118 per miner per week. We will follow the method adopted by Andrew Glyn (see chapter 4) to calculate (a) – the direct costs of a lost mining job to the Exchequer. The figures in table 7.6 (calculated by the NUM Social Insurance Department) assume a 57-year-old man who has been in the industry for 34 years and who would otherwise have retired at 62. As well

Table 7.6 *Exchequer costs of closing Cardowan Colliery*

		Redundancy payments etc. for older miners plus lost tax revenue (£)
Year	1	15,764
	2	7,644
	3	7,644
	4	7,644
	5	7,644
	6	5,500
	7	5,500
	8	5,500
	9	5,500
	10	5,500
Total over ten years		73,840
Average over ten years		7,384 per annum
Weekly average over ten years		142

as tax lost, the figures include weekly benefit, and unemployment benefit equivalent. In the first year, the lump-sum payments under the Employment Protection (Consolidation) Act and the Redundant Mineworkers Payments Scheme (RMPS) are included. The payments total some £35,000 over the five-year period. This is consistent with the Department of Energy (1983) estimates (House of Lords, 1983). A further breakdown of RMPS allowances is in the MMC Report (1983, vol. 2, app. 8.1). To the extent that miners of different ages or different years of service take redundancy, then this average figure will be distorted. But on past experience, and for single pit closures, it will stand as a rough approximation.

So, for a saving of £118 per miner per week, the Exchequer will need to support the NCB by £142 per miner per week over the first ten years. Even allowing for a 16 per cent reduction in the extra costs we still see the Exchequer better off keeping Cardowan afloat than closing it down. The NCB Scottish Area has not published exact figures for the projected redundancies following on from the closure of Cardowan nor details of the ages and service records of the miners who would be redundant. But we hazard that even if our figure of £142 per miner per week cost of closure was too high, then taking into account the further costs of redundancies elsewhere and passed-on overhead costs, the closure of Cardowan on grounds of being 'uneconomic' is ludicrous.

To calculate the indirect cost of jobs and business lost elsewhere as a

The case for deep-mined coal

knock-on effect of a pit closure ((b) above), we first calculate the number of additional jobs lost. In the front line will be jobs dependant on NCB purchases. While simple logic dictates that pit closures must lead to a loss of jobs in supplying industries, calculating the precise losses is difficult. Much will depend on the degree of local purchasing and the extent to which the new pits in central England will create compensating increases in materials purchases. Following Glyn (chapter 4), we assume that 75 per cent of non-wage costs are 'saved' by pit closure as per the national average in the NCB *Accounts*. That gives, in the Cardowan case, a figure of £5,138,250. This figure would have been spent on such things as supplies, heat, power, light etc., i.e. on production contributing to value added in the UK economy. Inspection of the 1979 *Input-Output Tables for the UK 1979*, table B (Central Statistical Office, 1983), shows that the direct import content of NCB purchases is no more than 10 per cent. Therefore some 90 per cent of non-wage purchasing contributes to domestic value added. So, if at Cardowan closure took out of the economy £5,138,250 of purchases of other value added, and 90 per cent was in the UK, then £4,624,425 of UK value added to domestic output is eliminated by the loss of Cardowan. According to the *National Income and Expenditure* tables (Central Statistical Office, 1984, tables 1.10 and 1.12), the weekly value added per British worker in 1983 was £225. Therefore, and very crudely, if we divide £225 into any weekly loss of purchasing of industrial output, we attain some idea of the jobs further at risk. The Cardowan loss of supplies purchases in the UK was £4,624,425 per annum, or £88,931 per week. Divided by £225, representing a worker at risk, we find a figure of 395 jobs will be eliminated in addition to the Cardowan jobs.

Glyn (chapter 4) proceeded to use figures produced by Davies and Metcalf (chapter 2) which estimate an average cost for other unemployed workers to the Exchequer of £106 per week. So the approximate 395 jobs eliminated by the loss of NCB purchases at Cardowan cost the government an additional 395×£106 per week, that is, £41,870 per week or, dividing by 1,100, £38 per Cardowan miner eliminated. This is on top of the direct extra cost of £142 per individual miner, or £180 in total. Compare this to the 'saving' of £118 per miner per week.

It is legitimate to criticise this calculation on the grounds that some of the lost purchasing of supplies etc. will be substituted by the development of the 26m tonnes of new capacity in central England. Unless all such purchasing was substituted for, this criticism merely reduces the size of the extra costs involved in shut-down, and still leaves us well in excess of the supposed savings.

At this point, we introduce a Scottish element into the purchasing

139

Economic strategies of NCB management

calculation. It is highly unlikely that any significant reductions in local spending by the Scottish Area NCB will be compensated for *in Scotland* by additional materials purchasing through the new English pits. In other words, the loss of material purchasing by Scottish pit closures does produce a once-and-for-all and permanent reduction in Scottish output and does therefore lead to a permanent exterior job loss of Glyn's proportions. This point can be verified by reference to the *Scottish Input-Output Tables* (Henderson, 1984). These indicate that the Scottish coal and coke industry (basically the NCB) purchased £100.6m of supplies from Scottish industry, compared to only £30.1m from the rest of the UK and £7.9m from the rest of the world (*ibid.*, vol. 2, table 6). These tables are for 1979, but we assume that little has happened to change the ratio of purchases even if the absolute expenditure and price levels have altered. It remains true that the overwhelming bulk of Scottish Area purchases (such as hiring equipment, construction timber, mining equipment, SSEB electricity) are from the Scottish economy itself. These local purchases will die with the loss of Scottish collieries.

There is a complementary way of calculating the knock-on employment loss from a Cardowan-type closure, using wholly Scottish figures. This involves reference again to the *Input-Output Tables* for Scotland. The Industry Department for Scotland calculates employment multipliers for individual Scottish industries. That is, estimates of precisely the employment and output effects on the rest of the Scottish economy of a given change in a particular industry. It must be noted that such multipliers are extremely crude. They assume a marginal change to a permanent set of inter- and intra-industry relationships, and eliminate wholesale change in technology or economic growth. These multipliers are based on the Scottish economy as it was in 1979 before the major recession and before major economic change in coal, steel etc. Nevertheless, with all these caveats, we can test the impact of a Cardowan-type loss on the rest of the Scottish economy. Table 8, in Henderson (1984, vol. 3, p.56) indicates an employment multiplier in the Scottish coal and coke industry of 1.340 (includes intra-industry transactions). That is, for a given change in employment in the industry there will be a 1.340 change in overall Scottish employment. So for a loss of 1,100 Cardowan jobs there will be a total loss of 1,100×1.34, or 1,474; or a change over and above the colliery redundancies of 1,474−1,100 = 374. This is quite close to Glyn's original rough estimate for the UK additional job-loss of 395. It is again necessary to point out the provisional nature of such calculations; but they give a rough order of magnitude sufficient to cast a reasonable doubt over the claim to 'save' Exchequer and taxpayers' money through the Cardowan or similar colliery closures.

140

The case for deep-mined coal

But we have other calculations to make. The loss of jobs at each colliery plus the loss of jobs in supplying industries will lead to a further drop in the consumer spending of the newly redundant workers. This consumption multiplier can be variously calculated. Glyn (chapter 4) follows calculations in Britton (1983), noting that the impact of a reduction in public expenditure on employment is one-half of the initial first-round effect. In order to allow for the probability that the impact on spending of redundant miners may be less than the average because of the impact of redundancy pay, and to err on the cautious side, Glyn arbitrarily reduces the consumption multiplier to 25 per cent. That is, the first-round number of jobs lost is multiplied by 0.25 to get the additional jobs lost as redundant miners and supply workers fail to purchase their normal quota of consumer products. In terms of our Cardowan figures, that would be 1,100 miners plus 395 supply workers (1,100+395 = 1,495) plus a further quarter of that total (1,495×0.25 = 374). That gives a total unemployment increase of 1,869. Those 374 workers made redundant by the loss of purchasing power by the 1,100 miners and 395 supply workers will have to be paid unemployment benefit and will cease to pay tax. Using our previous figure of an average cost to the Exchequer of £106 per redundant worker per week, we reach the following conclusion: 374 workers redundant, costing £106 per week, amounts to a total of 106×374 = £39,644. That is, an extra cost of £36 per redundant Cardowan miner. Add this to the £142 direct cost per redundant Cardowan miner, plus the £38 per week cost per miner of the redundant supply workers, and we get the total cost of £216 cost per miner per week. And the savings were only £118 per miner per week.

The estimation of the consumption multiplier in the Scottish context might give a different figure from the 25 per cent used by Glyn. For instance, a recent study commissioned by the Scottish Trade Union Congress (Smith and Harrison, 1984) used a consumption multiplier of only 10–15 per cent. A more cautious consumption multiplier estimate could be justified on the basis that at this point in the recession, given a huge reduction in manufacturing capacity to date, further fluctuations in demand are unlikely to have the larger consequences they did at the start of the down-turn. Thus, on a 10 per cent consumption multiplier, we would see extra jobs lost on our Cardowan figures of (£1,100+395)×0.1, which gives approximately 150. An extra round of consumption-related redundancies of 150 costs the usual £106 per week to the Exchequer or an annual cost of £826,800; which is an extra £14 per week per redundant Cardowan worker, or £194 in total – still well ahead of the supposed savings of £118. The true figure for Scotland should probably lie between the Glyn and STUC estimates. On the higher side, it could be argued that much of the consumption loss will be concentrated in localised mining communities and that will have a particularly marked effect on the local economy.

We now come to the third 'cost' of the Cardowan closure, the non-wage overheads which cannot be saved and which will have to be passed on to other pits. They include Area and National overheads, subsidence costs, previous redundancy costs and depreciation on lost equipment still being paid for by government loans. The pit in operation provided proceeds of £8.3m towards these costs. The costs of not mining must be borne elsewhere.

The Cardowan figures tell us that Area, National and other expenses for 1982/3 were £3,165,000, or 46 per cent of non-wage costs. Some elements of these costs will no doubt disappear: for instance, the heading 'Other operating costs' also includes transport charges, rents, rates, insurance, dirt disposal and coal stocking. But Cardowan, for reasons we can only speculate about, appears to have had its costs 'loaded' in great measure with non-production items such as to make the pit appear 'unprofitable'. The relative proportion of Area, National and Other expenses to total non-wage costs at Cardowan is greatly in excess of the proportion at other Scottish pits for which we have operating figures, for instance Monktonhall or Polkemmet.

Of the £3,165,000 non-production overheads included as 'operating costs', we will assume that an arbitrary but generous 50 per cent are really saved. Therefore £1,582,500 is passed on to other NCB accounts. That works out at £28 per week per redundant miner. When this is added to £142 direct costs, the £38 costs of redundant supply workers, and the £36 costs of workers made redundant by a fall in general consumption, we get a total of £244 per miner per week. That is double the 'savings' of £118 per worker per week gained by closing Cardowan. Our estimate could be reduced dramatically and it would still be cheaper for the Exchequer and the taxpayer to keep the pit open. We could add further closure 'costs': lost rates, lost vehicle licences and lost VAT, but these adjustments would only make the case against closure more compelling.

The crux of the Scottish NCB case is that the Scottish pits are producing the high-cost 'tail' of national production which cannot find an economic market today. Therefore productive capacity must be dismantled, as it was in steel and shipbuilding before. But the high-cost argument falls to the ground if those costs are merely transferred elsewhere via the Exchequer, or even increased in the process. We only end up with reduced productive capacity (when the rest of the world is in fact increasing its coal production) while the Exchequer funds the continuing costs – now transferred to the Social Security budget –

The case for deep-mined coal

through general taxation or the public sector borrowing requirement. It is just as 'rational' an economic calculation to suggest maintaining Scottish productive capacity till the market expands and with it the demand and technology stimulus to the local economy. Such a course is 'profitable' when considered from the social and economic needs of Scotland as a whole.

Scottish Area NCB management in action: Polmaise as a case study

The picture is conjured up of Area managers wrestling with elderly high-cost collieries reaching the end of their useful producing lives and plagued by geological difficulties. The 'rational' economic decision is to close down and switch the emphasis to pits where big capital investment programmes hold out the prospect of low costs to compete with imported coal. This scenario is fixed in the public mind, but from any reasonable interpretation of the management practice it does not square with reality. Drawing on the MMC (1983) Report we have established a different picture:

(a) Area directors' 'strategies' are not quantified in terms of the resulting effect on costs, profits or in terms of time-scale, i.e. their 'strategies' are crude prognostications about what they would like to do, not serious plans (MMC, 1983, para 7.124);

(b) the co-ordination of Area management is weak and imprecise, giving rise to 'possibilities of confusion and divided responsibility' (MMC, 1983, para 7.131);

(c) such financial and other data provided in Colliery Operating Results are inadequate and misleading (MMC, 1983, para 19.25);

(d) Area operations have insufficient autonomy (MMC, 1983, para 19.27);

(e) the national NCB management, which consists of mining engineers rather than managerial or marketing strategists (MMC, 1983, para 19.29), has launched a massive investment programme with inadequate planning or capital investment appraisal (MMC, 1983, paras 5.71, 5.75, 5.76).

Putting these points together, we discover a management which launched a massive investment programme in new capacity under the *Plan for Coal* (1974) without proper planning and controls, and without proper co-ordination with the Areas. This growth in capacity was much later in coming on stream than similar post-oil crisis coal projects abroad, leaving the NCB to enter a market which had become highly competitive. The result has been a panic move to reverse the process, again ill-conceived, to cut capacity at any cost. Meanwhile Area directors, who

143

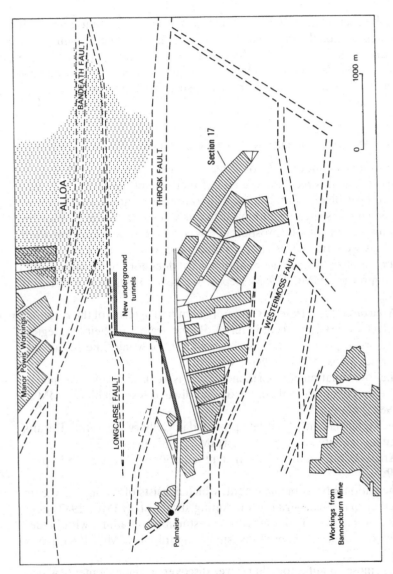

Fig. 7.1 The Hirst seam.

are operating on woefully inadequate cost data and whose 'strategic' planning is limited to physical production volumes, have been caught out by this change in policy. They have been told to get rid of capacity, to 'bring supply into line with demand'.

Here we come to the crux of the matter. What capacity do they eliminate? In the Scottish Area we have an example of the out-turn of this National and Area management practice. In January 1984, shortly before the recent dispute, the Scottish Area NCB announced the closure of Polmaise Colliery near Stirling. Polmaise had been closed for three years to undergo a major capital investment programme costing £15.8m. Despite this, the Scottish Area NCB reversed its longstanding investment programme in a trice and abandoned a modernised pit which was about to come on stream. Why? Because the central question for the NCB is not in fact the so-called high-cost tail of capacity (a designation which the poor cost data generated by the NCB makes difficult to quantify and whose extent even the ultra-cautious and strictly monetarist London Business School has queried) (see Robinson, chapters 6 and 9). Rather, the NCB is really concerned with cutting capacity wherever and whenever it can get away with it, even if it is newly modernised pits like Polmaise.

Historical background to the Polmaise closure decision

In 1979 the NCB decided, in consultation with the union and the local NUM, to cease existing production in the area between the Throsk fault and the Westermoss fault (see fig. 7.1) even though substantial workable reserves existed in the Hirst seam to the east of section 17 of around 1.5m tonnes. It was agreed to invest some £22m in developing parallel underground tunnels in this seam which would enable the coal between the Throsk fault and the Bandeath fault to be exploited. This involved driving two parallel tunnels from which other smaller tunnels would push out and the coal then be removed by connecting up the tunnels with longwall mining equipment. A good illustration of this procedure can be seen on the geological and mining map (fig. 7.1) on the Manor Powis workings and between the Throsk and Westermoss faults. It should be pointed out that the existence of the Longcarse fault was known before the investment programme started, and the estimates of capital expenditure took this into account. The Area manager of the NCB in Scotland assured the work force that this investment would provide work for 700–750 miners for at least thirty years, and follows similar assurances to men at the Bannockburn and the Manor Powis mines, whose work force was transferred to Polmaise in recent years, when those pits were shut.

Economic strategies of NCB management

Table 7.7 *Expenditure under investment programme at Polmaise*

Year	£ per year	£ cumulative
1980–1	3,287,000	3,287,000
1981–2	4,120,000	7,407,000
1982–3	4,646,000	12,053,000
1983–4 (to Dec. 1983)	3,748,000	15,801,000

From 1980 to October 1983 some £15,801,000 (see table 7.7) was expended in surface buildings and in underground tunnels, installing two Dosco coal-cutting machines, and in rebuilding the railway line from Polmaise to Stirling to carry the coal. The work went according to plan and within the allocated budget. The absenteeism rate was one of the lowest in the UK, there were no industrial stoppages and industrial relations at the pit were described as good. On 5 July 1983, however, the Area director of the NCB in Scotland ordered the work force to be locked out of the pit. The dispute was sent to arbitration and the 'umpire', the ex-Lord Provost of Edinburgh, found no justification in the NCB action and awarded the miners £40,000 in back pay. This lockout may be an indication of the about-turn in thinking about Polmaise within the NCB.

The NCB's case for shutting Polmaise

The Scottish Area NCB has shifted ground on the reasons for closing Polmaise despite the big investment programme. While we hesitate to resort to a conspiracy theory of management, we feel this at least indicates the strong possibility that, over and above any local factors, there were capacity reducing pressures being exerted from above. The NCB produced three reasons to justify the closure of Polmaise, two of which have dropped from view. First, they argued that the pit was affected by faulting which had not been anticipated in 1979 and that this was sufficiently serious to warrant abandoning it. The extent and thickness of each seam below Polmaise – including the Hirst seam – is known from boreholes and previous mining activity, as is most of the 'faulting' which the seams encounter. Figure 7.1 shows the fault lines with their names, their extent and the relationship to coal reserves and to previous workings. In the opinion of those we have spoken to, including the miners at Polmaise, the faulting referred to by the NCB was the existing Longcarse fault which a few weeks' work at a low marginal cost would have proved. Secondly, the NCB turned to problems of the ash content of the coal. The proper seam sample of the Polmaise coal gives readings of between 9 and 14 per cent, well below that required for power stations and most industrial uses. The NCB, however, quoted a sample from the last production face of 1979 contaminated with workings (etc.) from the underground tunnel. This was, of course, only one example and misleading to use when assessing the potential of Polmaise. We have to state that had the NCB found an unacceptable ash content *before* starting their investment programme, this would have provided the kind of case which the House of Commons Public Accounts Committee could have investigated. More recent pronouncements by the Board have been concerned with market problems for Polmaise output, and reflect the real cause of the proposed shutdown. So how much coal would be available from Polmaise?

Some 1,350,000 tons of coal is now available, without further development of roadways. The area of coal available for mining in the Hirst seam, between the Bandeath and the Throsk faulting, is approximately 6,100 metres by 1,100 metres with a seam thickness which varies from 5–6ft, and total reserves of 9m tonnes, of which the NUM experts suggest that around 5.4m tonnes would be available for extraction. As developed to date the pit would benefit from one of the best machine available time ratios of any Scottish colliery based on a modern underground railway system to transport miners and materials for 85 per cent of the distance from the bottom of the shaft to the face (the UK average is only 67 per cent). These facilities allow for over six hours to be available for face work and the continuous running of machinery. The latest NUM estimate (following the NCB figures) is for a minimum of 700 miners (face plus surface) to work 300,000 tonnes for 4½ years with around 2 years to complete the investment programme; this would lead to a minimum of 10–15 years' workable coal reserves, though the actual figure could be up to 30 years.

An annual output of upwards of 300,000 tonnes would place Polmaise among the smaller Scottish pits. Its real problem is that it is 'inconvenient' to National and Scottish Area management to have even modest increments to Scottish output, as it goes against the centrally dictated rationalisation plan which aims to concentrate production in the new southern super pits.

Economic strategies of NCB management

The economic and social costs of terminating Polmaise and the effect on the Central Region of Scotland

In its original form this section repeated the exercise conducted for Cardowan for the Polmaise colliery. It is omitted here.

The pit is situated in the depressed Central Region of Scotland where unemployment stands above the Scottish average. The loss of Polmaise colliery represents the loss of a major input to the local economy. The projected output from Polmaise is around 300,000 tonnes of coal per annum. At the 1984 Scottish average cost of production per tonne of coal (£53.80), that output would indicate an operating expenditure of approximately £16,140,000 per year, i.e. £53.80×300,000. On top of operational costs, further capital expenditure would take the annual colliery expenditure to, say, £18m or so.

What does an annual expenditure of £18m represent in terms of the Central Region economy? The latest available *Regional Trends and Accounts for Scotland* (1983) record the Gross Domestic Product for Central Region to be £3,588 per head in 1981, the latest year for which figures are available. In other words, the value of the economic activity in Central Region each year is roughly £3,588 for every individual in the area.

The population of Central Region according to the 1981 census was 273,000. Multiplying GDP per head by the total population gives a monetary estimate of the value of economic activity in Central Region circa 1981 of £979,524,000, i.e. just under a billion pounds. Therefore the relative weight of Polmaise in the Central Region economy is roughly £18m as a percentage of £1bn, or just under 2 per cent, though some of this £18m will be spent outside the region. Now 2 per cent might not immediately sound significant, but for a single enterprise to register on this scale for a whole economy is dramatic. On a UK equivalent basis, a factory would have a yearly expenditure of over £5½bn, or approximately the NCB's entire 1983/4 expenditure. To put it another way, the relative scale of the termination of Polmaise in terms of the Central Region economy is approaching that of shutting down the whole NCB for the UK economy.

An alternative scenario for Scottish coal: what is the problem?

In his chairman's statement prefacing the 1984 NCB *Accounts*, Mr MacGregor states a çlear intention to 'reduce output by a further 4 million tonnes in 1984/5, which would achieve the required supply/

148

demand balance and give the industry a stable base capacity of 100 million tonnes'. That represents a reduction in capacity since 1974 of over 25 per cent. Scottish deep-mined output has fallen from 8.7m tonnes in 1974 to 5.3m tonnes in 1983/4, a reduction of almost 40 per cent. If Mr MacGregor is serious about a 'stable base capacity of 100 million tonnes' while putting in 22m extra, then another 22m tonnes of existing capacity must come out. This spells a bleak future for 'marginal' coalfields like those in Scotland. One would be forgiven for believing that coal was a declining industry. Despite the much-vaunted *Plan for Coal* (1974), the past decade has seen a massive cut in capacity, the closure of 76 collieries and general rationalisation of the industry. In other words, the British disease.

Now consider the following statement by one of Britain's leading experts on company management:

> In 1950, world ship launchings amounted to some 3.2 million gross registered tons (grt). Of this, British yards were responsible for 1.4 million tons gross and Japanese yards for 0.2 million tons gross. By 1977 the positions of the UK and Japan were effectively reversed, and of the 25 million tons gross completed, Japanese yards were responsible for 11.7 million tons gross or 43 per cent and the UK for 1 million tons gross, or 4 per cent (Channon, 1980, p. 150).

And the reason? 'In large part the decline in the market share held by the British Industry was caused by its failure to expand capacity while other industries had substantially developed theirs' (*ibid*.). This 'failure to expand capacity' has a familiar ring. Consider the recent case of coal as shown in table 7.8.

The NCB's market problem is simple. Every major nation, and every major oil company, reacted to the 1973 oil crisis by investing in coal. The bureaucratic inefficiency of the NCB meant that everybody else got their extra coal on stream before the NCB: world coal production went up by a third between 1970 and 1982. Then came the international recession, when growth in the demand for energy slackened just as the increased coal capacity was reaching the markets. This caused a temporary excess of coal and drove down the price on the international market – just when the NCB got its new capacity coming on stream. The NCB's reaction is caution and retreat: cut more existing capacity, exactly the same response of British and Clyde shipbuilders in the 1950s and 1960s.

But don't you have to find a market for what you produce? Yes, just like other producers, but other producers realise that the market downturn is temporary. Even the cautious Mr MacGregor has been

Economic strategies of NCB management

Table 7.8 *Output of leading producers of steam coal (millions of tonnes)*

Country	1982	1970	% change
USA	701	550	+ 27
China	620	360	+ 72
USSR	555	474	+ 17
Poland	189	140	+ 35
S. Africa	139	55	+153
India	134	74	+ 81
UK	121	145	− 17
Australia	102	50	+104

Source: Eurostat.

quoted on foreseeing UK production rising to 125m tonnes to meet demand in the mid-1990s (*Economist*, 1984a). The current problem is how can we manage to bring on stream new capacity in the 1980s as well as preserve our existing capacity, and thus be in a position to meet the market upturn after the recession? If we don't, then coal will go the way of other British industries which have been 'rationalised'. It will lose out to the better equipped foreign competitors who will have the spare capacity to meet future demands; and it will have higher unit costs in an extremely capital-intensive industry, where volume of production is necessary to recoup the overheads of plant and machinery.

Further evidence can be offered regarding the irrationality of capacity reduction as a solution to what is ultimately a selling problem. A major reason for the seeming shortfall in demand for NCB coal in the early 1980s was the disappointing sales to industry. Practically the whole shortfall between forecasted demand in the *Plan for Coal* and what materialised can be accounted for by the sharply reduced sales to the British Steel Corporation (BSC), which itself had undergone massive rationalisation and reduction of capacity. One capacity feeds another. The real problem facing the NCB is to find a strategy which will get it over the 'hump' of the 1980s without destroying productive capacity which will put it out of the game in the 1990s.

We now turn our attention to offering some interim solutions, or 'best available' methods of dealing with this problem, especially with regard to maintaining the Scottish collieries.

150

The case for deep-mined coal

Table 7.9 *Comparison of average prices of coal and oil used by electricity supply industry (expressed in pence per therm equivalent)*

Year	Coal	Oil diesel plant	Steam plant	Gas turbines
1965–6	1.82	2.64	1.82	–
1969–70	2.09	2.74	2.05	2.87
1973	2.96	3.98	2.82	4.47
1974	4.16	8.41	6.85	9.59
1980	14.21	26.65	21.01	22.12
1982	17.48	34.00	26.40	37.60

Source: Electricity Supply statistics.

Revenue and pricing

The reform of the pricing structure of the nationalised industries relating to coal is long overdue. At the present, prices of coal sold to its largest customer the SSEB/CEGB are held down below the equivalent oil price while electricity suppliers pass on a substantial sum each year to the government. The government then lends the NCB the capital for its investment at a high level of interest on (usually) fixed interest loans. The differential in average prices of fuels used by SSEB/CEGB expressed in equivalent units of energy from 1973 to 1982 are listed in table 7.9.

In Scotland different prices exist for coal outputs, and even between pits for similar products. To take Monktonhall, for example, where 98 per cent of the output goes to the SSEB, the price was £41.80 per tonne from 1 November 1982, raised by 3.8 per cent on 1 November 1983 to £43.40 per tonne. Barony pit from January 1983 sold 76 per cent of its output to the SSEB at £42.50 per tonne, with 8 per cent to the domestic market at £56 a tonne, and 16 per cent to industry at £53 a tonne. Longannet's (a complex of several pits) prices were increased in 1983 to over £43 a tonne. Thus, if an industrial buyer requires coal, the payment will be in the region of £10 per tonne above the price charged to the SSEB by the NCB. As the Treasury admitted to the House of Commons Energy Committee (1984), the CEGB/SSEB/NCB arrangements 'had the direct effect of reducing the NCB's revenue and thus of increasing the level of deficit support'. A further complication involves mixing coals from different pits to produce inputs for blast furnace coke ovens and for electricity generation. It has been suggested to us that the allocation of income to pits in Scotland when using mixed coal has been in part an

151

arbitrary arrangement. Overall modifications to the pricing policies would transform the net proceeds position of the Scottish (and UK) pits. We therefore propose a change in the price structure of coal which will allow the NCB to cover its genuine operating costs and meet its capital requirements. This can be achieved by (1) altering the transfer pricing arrangement between the two nationalised energy groups, NCB and electricity boards, to divert the excessive profits of electricity derived from coal back into maintaining coal capacity; (2) altering the capital debt structure of the NCB to something similar to that of the BSC or British Airways, with a proportion of debt transferred into public dividend capital, and sensibly deferring the payment of a return on the capital invested in the new pits till the 1990s when higher prices will be available on international markets.

One immediate objection to this course of action is that it will mean higher UK energy prices. But we are not advocating that the final consumer of electricity pays higher prices. Energy is a combined coal–electricity generation complex. What we are saying is that the price of the key input into electricity generation, namely coal, has an administered price fixed in the public sector, and an end user price for the electricity also fixed in the public sector. We should alter the administered price of the coal input; that does not necessarily effect the end user price.

Altering the internal transfer price of coal from NCB to SSEB/CEGB will produce significant economic savings. The SSEB is building Torness at a cost of over £1bn despite a surplus of generating capacity at the moment. The electricity boards have, like the NCB, been criticised for 'appraisal optimism' but, unlike the NCB, they have been in a situation to fund their own schemes. An alteration of the transfer pricing will force the electricity boards to make better use of public investment capital and pay for necessary investment in the long-term future of a coal industry which we will need when the oil runs out.

The change in transfer pricing arrangements will also act as a check on governments artificially driving up the price of electricity. The present government has used the electricity boards as a syphon to drain off cash to help it reduce public spending and taxation. High energy prices are a form of tax. By limiting the artificial cash surplus accruing in the electricity boards we reduce the ability of a government to use this back-door method of distorting the efficient allocation of national resources. The SSEB and CEGB should also be forced to seek coal supplies of a low sulphur content as a first step in dealing with the acid-rain problem. Presumably low sulphur Scottish coal would then be in a position to command a premium price.

It might be argued that UK electricity prices are already high by

European standards, and that this is a disadvantage to industry. In 1981 the National Economic Development Council produced a major report on relative energy prices and UK international economic competitiveness. The report noted that in general French and German electricity prices were lower than those in the UK. French prices were 20–30 per cent lower, and German prices could be up to 25 per cent lower. But the NEDC made an important caveat: the lower European prices occurred at high-load factors: 'a particular problem in arriving at representative comparisons has been that the UK contains relatively few large, high load factor consumers' (p. 17). In other words, the decimated state of British industry, especially in steel and chemicals, leads to lower high-load factor demand which, as in any capital-intensive industry, means sales with higher than necessary unit costs. If we ran our industry, and hence our energy demand, at a European level, then, given the already existing coal and electricity capacity, unit costs would fall to European levels.

The NEDC report noted that 'UK steam coal is broadly competitive with imports', and that 'UK foundry coke is (ex-coke oven) some 30 per cent more expensive than the average for other countries', and 'more than 50 per cent dearer than in France' (*ibid.*, p. 15). However, the reason was not British inefficiency but the subsidies offered in other countries. The NEDC said 'we have the cheapest indigenously produced coal in the European Community ... Other countries ... subsidise their home production more heavily'. The NEDC recorded a French total aid package of £66 per tonne compared to £2 per tonne in the UK. This raises the question: why follow the Europeans down the road of subsidy? Why not follow the Japanese and import cheap foreign coal or even cheap oil from the glutted spot market? It seems to have brought the Japanese a cheap-energy/high-growth economy. Why not follow suit?

The Japanese were reaping the benefits not of 'cheap' coal but of systems economies of scale, that is, they were running their whole economy at a capacity level which generated cost reductions due to the scale of inter-industry purchases. The Japanese might have killed off most of their coal industry and bought cheap imports, but these were only cheap (given the transport costs involved) because vast amounts were imported. That only made sense because the Japanese created a huge protected steel industry to absorb the coal. That, in turn, only worked because the Japanese created a high-volume protected ship-building and car industry with big export markets. Thus each individual step was dependant on each succeeding one. To assess the economics of a large-scale industry in isolation and divorced from the interconnections with other industries gives a completely distorted picture of that industry's economics.

153

Economic strategies of NCB management

We can repeat the Japanese model, but from a different starting point. Rather than throw away the investment we have now made in coal/ electricity, we should build on it through a vigorous capacity expansion down stream of coal. For instance, and with some impact on current levels of unemployment, we should proceed with a major programme of public works including the Channel Tunnel/Bridge project with its huge demand for steel (and hence for coking coal). But, in order to get the scale of systems economies the Japanese enjoy, we will need to reinvigorate a European-wide market. However, this discussion of the Japanese model begs an important point. It is far from clear that imported coal is cheaper than the UK product. The Monopolies and Mergers Commission makes the following judgement: 'Historically NCB prices have been competitive with imported prices, but in 1979 and 1980 the strengthening of the pound made imported coal (priced in US dollars) an economic proposition and imports increased significantly' (MMC, 1983, para 4.57). A combination of the petro-pound, encouraged by the government to reduce inflation, and the growth in the international spot market for coal as a result of everybody else's new coal coming on stream before ours, opened up the UK to 'cheap' coal. But no sooner has the NCB retreated and cut back capacity than the dollar has soared and the price of foreign, and especially American, coal has gone back up again.

In short-run periods where world gluts of coal (relative to recessed industrial demand, that is) and exchange-rate fluctuations make UK coal seemingly 'uneconomic', there is still no rational economic case for capacity reduction that still involves the Exchequer in financial costs in excess of the short-run operating costs due to tax losses and welfare benefit payments. In the longer term, as the world economy recovers, demand for coal will rise (as it is now doing in Japan), taking up the price and making Britain's deep-mined coal the cheapest in Europe; and cheap enough to compete with non-European coal when you add transport costs or make allowances for quality.

Marketing and the European Economic Community

Forecasting the actual increase in demand for coal from now to the year 2000 is fraught with difficulties. Nevertheless, there is unanimity among forecasters (including the NCB) that demand for coal will rise, and especially so in the later 1990s. Part of the problem of sales has been the weakness of NCB marketing. By 1979/80, out of a total NCB coal disposal of 125.1m tonnes only 10.7m went to industry and 7.2m to domestic users. With the fall in input to coke ovens from 17.8m tonnes in 1976/7 to 11.7m tonnes in 1979/80, industrial and domestic coal use in the

154

The case for deep-mined coal

UK (excluding electricity) was lower by 1980 than it was in 1974. In 1981 the government belatedly made provision for £50m in grants for the conversion of industrial oil-fired boilers to coal (later raised to £75m). The NCB managed to find additional industrial purchasers of coal for 1,040,000 tonnes from 1982 to 1984, though the total take from industry actually fell. The effects of the recession, and in particular the collapse of the UK steel industry and its knock-on effect on engineering suppliers, made the UK marketing position of UK coal much more difficult. In the short term, given the lack of adequate government support on the demand side within the UK, it is unlikely that domestic industrial coal demand will rise by more than 1m or 1½m tonnes a year in the 1980s. A similar point is applicable for the domestic market.

However, the government could take steps to boost industrial and domestic demand at relatively little cost of capacity reduction. First, it seems commercially short-sighted to finance large stocks of coal, i.e. to pay extra not to do anything with the coal you dig out of the ground. This has especial force in older mining areas like Wales and Scotland, where the cost of maintaining stocks is much higher than the national average (for example, over £5 per tonne in South Wales) (MMC, 1983, para 5.60). Would it not be worth contemplating a scheme which promoted special contracts for industrial supply whereby the coal price was cut by the corresponding stock cost, so that at least if you were forced to subsidise you were using the subsidy to shift coal rather than build stockpiles?

On the domestic side, would it not encourage long-term demands if you used coal stockpiles and price reductions to provide old-age pensioners with more solid fuel to burn? If the government feels that financial stringencies are such that public expenditure must be restricted, then using existing coal supplies, with their low marginal cost and serious implications for a rising PSBR if pits are closed, might provide a cheap boost for the OAPs' material support at little damage to public sector finance. Thus the immediate problem of generating a short-term market for coal to maintain capacity 'over the hump' is partially solved at little damage to existing markets or without recourse to major subsidy.

If the government could be persuaded to raise PSBR by a modest amount of, say, £2bn to £3bn per annum, which could have no serious impact on interest rates, then a programme of public works could be instituted to reduce unemployment, but aimed in such a way as to boost industrial demand and coal demand. To the extent that such a programme, perhaps linked to a general European reflation, boosted economic growth then there would be an overall rise in coal/energy usage.

Economic strategies of NCB management

In the absence of these developments, or indeed alongside them, the NCB must turn to exporting, and the potential provided through the remainder of this century by the expected increase in European coal demand. In 1976/7 the NCB exported only 1.5m tonnes and only 1.8m as late as 1977/8. In 1980/1 this rose to 4.7m, and to 9.4m in 1981/2. Thereafter it fell back and was down to 6.8m tonnes in 1983/4. The net benefit to the UK of these export figures has been undermined because the CEGB decided to import steam coal under long-term contracts, and the NCB closed some excellent low-sulphur coking seams (including those flooded at Cardowan and Polkemmet). In 1983/4 the UK was a net exporter of only 1.7m tonnes of coal. The EEC is in a stage of transition over the common agricultural policy, Spanish and Portuguese entry and the size of the Community's budget. This is precisely the time for Britain to propose a common coal policy. The essence would be preferential treatment for EEC coal producers over non-EEC producers, such as South Africa with its obvious advantage of cheap labour. A common coal policy along the lines we suggest would provide an adequate vend for Polmaise coal and give much needed work to the railways, the docks and UK shipping.

We have to note the declared intention of the government to develop nuclear power stations at a time when the UK (and Scotland) has over-capacity of generating power. Building nuclear power stations is very expensive and we have as yet no more than a vague idea of the likely long-term costs, possible rates of closure through accidents, scale of compensation and so on. Modern coal-fired power stations are also much more efficient – the top ones in this country range from 33 to 38 per cent in overall thermal efficiency. The nuclear power stations average only 27.3 per cent (1982/3), a level left behind years ago by technical advances in coal-fired stations. The government's insistence on rushing ahead with Sizewell 'B' and Torness has been criticised by the Parliamentary Energy Committee, which has questioned the need for such a large programme of replacement coal and oil-fired stations by nuclear plant and expressed the view that 'not enough was being done to reduce capacity requirements by more effective conservation programmes and speedier conversion of oil-fired stations to dual coal–oil firing'. This would involve substantial long-term savings on the capital costs of unneeded capacity expansion.

An action programme for Scottish coal

Can Scottish deep-mined coal be saved as an industry in the 1980s? We have seen what closing it down will cost the Exchequer in financial terms. But maintaining the industry because to do otherwise is too expensive is

The case for deep-mined coal

hardly a long-term strategy. The immediate problem is to find a secure basis for the Scottish pits till the improved market conditions of the 1990s. The reformed pricing and accounting in the coal industry which we outlined above will be a beginning. Further than this, the SSEB and CEGB should be forced to seek coal supplies of a low sulphur content as a first step in dealing with the acid-rain problem. Low-sulphur Scottish coal would therefore command not just a market but a premium price. Such a price would improve Scottish Area revenues and act as an incentive on the SSEB/CEGB to seek ways to control acid-rain pollution with a real economic saving to society.

The industrial market for Scottish coal is very weak. De-industrialisation has hit demand very hard. In 1974 industrial coal consumption in Scotland was 697,000 tonnes. By 1982 it had fallen to 397,000 tonnes, with large customer losses in steel, food processing and the paper and printing trades. But there is a glimmer of hope in this. In the weak economic upturn of 1977/8 Scottish industrial coal consumption rose, only to fall again with the second oil crisis and the new world recession. In other words, when upturn last occurred there was evidence that industrial coal demand improved. Anything that encourages an improvement in general industrial expansion, especially a programme of major public works, should help boost Scottish industrial demand. It goes without saying that Ravenscraig must be retained.

We might suggest in this case that reconsideration is again given to the Scottish–Irish electricity grid connection under the Irish Sea, which would help absorb the SSEB's excess generating capacity and invigorate its coal demand. Scotland exports large quantities of coal to Ireland, and this project is proposed tentatively and not to threaten those exports in the short term. Though Scottish coal production has fallen considerably with the NCB's capacity-reduction programme, actual imports of coal coming into Scotland have increased in recent years. This indicates a soft underbelly of a market that Scottish coal could fight its way into (see table 7.10).

Scotland remains geographically well placed for exporting; there are already significant exports to Ireland. But the Scandinavian countries are rising coal importers. In 1983/4 the NCB as a whole exported 2,682,000 tonnes of coal and 477,000 tonnes of coke to Denmark, Finland, Norway and Sweden. This is a market which should be exploited to the full. And as for domestic users, the uniquely high concentration of council houses in Scotland, especially with their related dampness problems, offers an opportunity for the Scottish Area NCB to launch joint heating conversion programmes with Scottish local authorities. The improvement of the housing stock is long overdue and could form part of the modest capital

Table 7.10 *Scottish deep-mined coal production and coal imports*

	1977	1978	1979	1980	1981	1982
Saleable deep-mined coal ('000 tonnes)	8,674	8,309	8,172	8,213	7,502	6,918
Imports (including rest of UK) ('000 tonnes)	759	775	1,285	1,247	1,191	1,156
Imports as % of production	8.75	9.33	15.72	15.18	15.86	16.71

Source: Scottish Abstract of Statistics, 1984, table 12.14.

works programme already suggested.

Finally, the main customer of the Scottish Area must remain the SSEB. Part of the Scottish NCB's problems stem from the excess generating capacity which the SSEB has created and seems bent on further increasing. The role of the SSEB, and problems inherent in other nationalised industries (such as BSC Ravenscraig on which the output of Polkemmet depends) raises the necessity of achieving a greater co-ordination of nationalised industry management and planning. One suggestion has been made that the NCB and the BSC might be brought under a common management. Certainly we believe that consideration should be given to co-ordinating the future planning, investment, marketing and pricing of coal, steel, rail, electricity and – in Scotland – shipbuilding because they are so interdependent. It may be that such a co-ordination could take place on a Scottish as well as a national level. This is the essence of the Japanese planned approach to high-capacity utilisation: guaranteed demand at each industrial stage.

Postscript

This report presented the economic and financial case for the maintainance of the deep coal-mining industry in Scotland as it stood in 1984, based on the National Coal Board (NCB) accounts available at the time of writing for the year to March 1984, and presented a strong endorsement of a sustained level of investment to maintain this capacity for the foreseeable future. It was completed in December 1984 and published on 4 January 1985. The report, with others, helped overturn the strident statements made on the profits and losses of the coal-mining industry by the government, both for the UK and for Scotland.

After the completion of this report the authors were invited to

The case for deep-mined coal

examine the situation of the coal-mining industries in the European Economic Community and presented a further report in November 1985 (Kerevan and Saville, 1985). In the spring of 1985 the NCB reversed their decision to close Polmaise, in part because they decided that there was now a greater market potential for this type of low-sulphur product, and further investment is to take place in the colliery to extend its life.

In the original version, chapters were used to divide the text, for this publication it has been divided by subheadings. *The Economic Case* is reproduced here with some editorial compression and some omissions where the material duplicates that in other contributions to this volume, but it is largely left as in the original.

REFERENCES

Britton, A. (1983), *Employment, Output and Inflation: The National Institute Model of the British Economy*, London: Heinemann.

Central Statistical Office (1983), *Input-Output Tables for the United Kingdom 1979*, London: HMSO.

(1984), *National Income and Expenditure Tables of the United Kingdom*, London: HMSO.

Channon, D. F. (1980), 'British Shipbuilders', in Stopford, J. M., D. F. Channon and J. Constable (eds.), *Cases in Strategic Management*, Chichester: Wiley.

Commission on Energy and the Environment (1981), *Coal and the Environment*, London: HMSO.

Cooper, D., J. Bird and W. Sharp (1985), *Report of the Public Inquiry into the Proposed Closure of Polkemmet Colliery, Whitburn*, Linlithgow: West Lothian District Council.

The Economist (1984a), 'Training for the Long Fight', 16 June, p. 19.

(1984b), 'What Goal for Coal', 15 December, p. 31.

Henderson, D. F. (1984), *Scottish Input-Output Tables for 1979*, Edinburgh: Industry Department for Scotland, 5 vols.

House of Commons Select Committee on Energy (1984), *Electricity and Gas Prices*, First Report, vol. 1, London: HMSO.

House of Lords Select Committee on the European Communities (1983), *European Coal Policy*, London: HMSO.

Kerevan, G. and R. Saville, with D. Percival (1985), *The Case for Retaining a European Coal Industry*, Brussels: British Labour Group and the Socialist Group of the European Parliament.

Monopolies and Mergers Commission (1981), *Report on the Central Electricity Generating Board*, London: HMSO.

(1983), *National Coal Board: A Report on Efficiency and Costs in the Develop-*

ment, *Production and Supply of Coal by the National Coal Board*, 2 vols., Cmnd, 8920, London: HMSO.

National Coal Board (1974), *Plan For Coal*, London: NCB.

(1984), *Annual Report and Accounts 1983/4*, London: NCB.

National Economic Development Council (1981), *Report of the NEDC Energy Task Force*, no. 15, London: NEDC.

Regional Trends and Accounts for Scotland 1981 (1983), Edinburgh: Industry Department for Scotland.

Schultz, W. (1984), 'The Supply Potential of the International Steam Coal Market', *Columbia Journal of World Business*, vol. 19, no. 1.

Scotsman (1984), 'Six Scots Pits Face Axe, Says STUC', 30 November.

The Scottish Office (1984), *Scottish Economic Bulletin No. 29*, Edinburgh: HMSO.

Serpell, Sir D. (1983), *Railway Finances: Report of a Committee Chaired by Sir David Serpell*, London: Department of Transport, HMSO.

Smith, P. and Harrison, D. (1984), 'Jobs and the Scottish NCB', Glasgow: Scottish Trades Union Congress.

8

Aberystwyth report on coal

T. CUTLER, C. HASLAM,
J. WILLIAMS and K. WILLIAMS

Introduction

In the course of the long coal strike there was much discussion of the
kinds of calculation which should govern pit closures. It was suggested
and generally accepted that the NCB's private calculations of profit and
loss should not provide a basis for pit closure. David Metcalf and Gavyn
Davies (see chapter 2) in particular have analysed the problem in terms
of the social and real resource costs.

The approach of the present chapter is both narrower and wider. It is
narrower in that the first two sections are largely concerned with the
NCB's own forms of private calculation on such matters as operating unit
costs or the appraisal of major new investment projects. It is wider in that
the last two sections are concerned with the long-run energy choice
between coal and nuclear power. We would insist that the narrow
calculations about coal should be set in this larger context.

On the NCB's calculations and miscalculations, we have examined the
NCB's own *Reports and Accounts*, together with the Monopolies and
Merger Commission's Report on the NCB (MMC, 1983). The latter
source was crucial because it gave outsiders like ourselves access to a
mass of information which would not otherwise have been available. We
would claim to have reinterpreted this evidence. We argue that the
NCB's investment strategy prolonged, if not created, the recent crisis
about closure; that the NCB's unit-cost figures are an inadequate basis
for the enterprise's own closure decisions; and that the NCB's appraisal
techniques have a persistent inbuilt bias which protects capital-intensive
projects and sacrifices labour-intensive undertakings.

On the question of energy choices, we are concerned that policy
decisions about pit closure are apparently going to be taken without any
reference to broader choices about energy sources in the long run. We
were surprised to find that the official projections on electricity demand

161

and supply presuppose a future that is overwhelmingly nuclear. That, of course, requires a run-down of the coal industry. On examining the evidence we find that the commitment to a nuclear future was based on highly dubious cost assumptions.

Why was there a crisis about closures in the coal industry?

The crisis was caused by the NCB management's investment strategy of massive investment in new capacity which, in a depressed market, required the closure of existing capacity.

The crisis in the coal industry is about closures and it began nearly seven years ago. In the late summer of 1980 the NCB decided that a programme of accelerated closures was necessary (MMC, 1983, vol. 1, p. 38), and this was then proposed to the NUM. In the face of opposition from the NUM the initiative for accelerated closures was withdrawn and the government provided increased funds to cover the deficits of the NCB. The issue of closures did not go away. In 1984 the NCB tried to push through faster closure and provoked the coal strike. In this section we will try to analyse the origins and nature of the crisis about pit closure.

There has been a variety of rather half-hearted attempts to hang the blame for the crisis in coal on the work force. The miners did well in their pay settlements of the 1970s and regained a leading place in the manual earnings league-table. Labour productivity rose only modestly. Some commentators have thus made much of the point that wage costs per tonne apparently increased by 3 per cent p.a. in real terms in the years 1976/7 to 1980/1 (*ibid.*, p. 106). At the same time it should be empha-sised that the share of wage in total operating costs was declining: 51 per cent in 1976/7, 48 per cent in 1981/2, and 43 per cent in 1983/4. We wish to propose an alternative explanation of the industry's troubles which has been almost entirely neglected. That alternative explanation blames management for persisting with an investment strategy which creates large amounts of new capacity when the market for coal is weak.

To understand the origins of the crisis it is necessary to go back to the mid-1970s. A major programme of investment in new capacity and new pits was started under the 1974 *Plan for Coal* when the industry was planning for expansion. *Plan for Coal* forecast an output of about 135m tonnes by 1985, which would have been at about the same level as in 1971 just before the disruptions of the two miners' strikes of the early 1970s. The target output could not, at the time, have seemed excessively optimistic. The four-fold increase in petroleum prices had radically shifted the competitive advantage in favour of coal; there were high hopes of sustained economic growth; and the steel industry was confidently embarking on a major expansionary policy. It was equally clear that any proposal to increase, or even maintain, coal output would necessarily involve substantial investment. The coal industry was run down since there had been little investment in the previous decade.

The target was 4m tonnes of new capacity per annum in the years up to 1985. Investment in new pits and new capacity at existing mines increased dramatically in the late 1970s and early 1980s. In 1976/7 expenditure on new pits accounted for just 4 per cent of total investment by the NCB. By 1981/2, with Selby under construction, new pits accounted for 21 per cent of all investment (*ibid.*, p. 181). In the early days of *Plan for Coal* the NCB was also spending large amounts on extending capacity at existing pits. Thus by 1981 a great deal of new capacity was coming into production. In 1981/2 the NCB had 16m tonnes of new capacity in production, mainly in the form of new capacity at existing pits. A further 26m tonnes of new capacity was under construction, with nearly half of that accounted for by the Selby super pit (*ibid.*, pp. 42–3). This increase in capacity created a crisis because it came on stream as the demand for coal fell away with the onset of a major slump after 1979. Supply exceeded demand and the excess supply went into stocks and coal exports at distress prices. NCB coal stocks rose from 14m towards 25m tonnes in the three years from March 1979 and exports rose to 9m tonnes. This caused a financial crisis which was worsened by the way in which the NCB's two largest customers (Central Electricity Generating Board (CEGB) and British Steel Corporation (BSC)) took advantage of the situation and extracted concessions on price from the NCB.

From late 1979 through the early months of 1980 the crisis worsened and the NCB took stock of its position. As the MMC Report records in sober civil-service prose, 'in the autumn of 1980 it was realised that supply was likely to exceed demand by between 5 and 10m tonnes per annum over the period 1981–2 to 1985–6' (*ibid.*, p. 98). What regulators could be used to restore the short-run balance between supply and demand which was now completely upset? As early as March 1980 the NCB had examined the options (*ibid.*, p. 82) and concluded the only regulator available was 'the orderly closure of high-cost, short life capacity' (*ibid.*, p. 95). The NCB's return on the massive *Plan for Coal* investments would only come if the new capacity and new pits produced at full output. If new-capacity and new pits were brought into production in a situation of over-capacity then old-capacity and old pits would have to close. This point can be illustrated with one graphic example: the new super pit under construction at Selby would produce 10m tonnes per annum and this would require the closure of more than 30 small pits.

Economic strategies of NCB management

The NCB blamed some of its problems on the fact that closures of existing capacity had proceeded at a much slower rate than had been anticipated under the tripartite interim report of *Plan for Coal* (1974). There is some force in this. In fact, however, by 1981/2 the capacity taken out very closely matched the new capacity completed, which had always been the intention. In any case, it is clear that, after the large-scale closures of the 1960s, the 1.7m tonnes per annum from 1974 onwards represented the practical limit of what could be obtained on grounds of geological exhaustion and with the agreement of the work force. It is significant that 53 out of the 58 closures between 1974 and mid-1982 were by agreement (*ibid.*, p. 172). The criterion of geological exhaustion will always allow significant closures when roughly one-third of the NCB's pits are classified as 'short life' with known reserves for less than ten years. Moreover, it is important to recall that closures did not cease after the failure of the NCB to accelerate them in 1981. The NUM has continued its policy of accepting them through a reasonable interpretation of exhaustion and geological difficulty. Thus, in 1983/4, 15 closures and 7 mergers were effected and of these 22 schemes, which cut output by 4m tonnes, all but 5 were negotiated locally (NCB *Report* 1983/4, p. 2). The problem since the onset of the crisis in 1980/1 has been that, because of over-capacity, the Coal Board's management wants to take more closures than can be obtained on grounds of exhaustion and with the agreement of the work force.

We recognise that management was placed in an awful dilemma at the outset of the crisis in 1980/1. As new capacity was brought in, the short-term balance between supply and demand was completely wrong because an expected growth in consumption turned into an unexpected fall. All this was fundamentally a matter of misfortune rather than mismanagement. The expansion strategy had seemed reasonable. It came unstuck because of a fall in demand which would have been difficult to foresee. The major contributing factors were the decline in the demand from the steel industry following the rapid collapse and reversal of its expansion plans; the onset of the worst economic slump since 1929; and the unexpectedly widespread impact of fuel conservation after the renewed round of oil price rises in 1979. It is also true that the NCB management's expansion plans had always been imprudent. The NCB's investment appraisal techniques included no allowance for risks arising out of market factors such as a fall in price. As the MMC observed, such a test 'might have exercised a restraint on investment and might therefore have reduced the extent of the present excess capacity' (*ibid.*, p. 201).

The Board may have been imprudent, but we accept that there was little it could have done to avert the original crisis. But, at this point in

164

time, nearly seven years have passed since the onset of the crisis. We would argue that the continuation and intensification of the crisis in 1984 and 1985 can largely be attributed to NCB management's persistence with its investment strategy since 1980. In other nationalised industries which make losses and sell into weak markets, the expansionist plans of the 1970s have been rejected and there have been substantial cuts in their investment programmes; the Ryder Report (1975) on British Leyland is now of interest only to historians. But the NCB's *Report* for 1983/4 boasts that £6,500m has now been invested under the *Plan for Coal* (1974); half the original programme has been completed mainly in the form of additional capacity at existing mines and 'the balance is under construction, or approved, for completion during the 1980s'. The imbalance between supply and demand is as acute as ever because the management continues to invest in new capacity. The pressure of new capacity has actually intensified. According to the NCB's 1983/4 *Annual Report* (p. 1), 20m tonnes of new capacity are now in production and a further 22m tonnes are under construction. In 1985 closure remained an issue because there was still a vast additional supply overhanging the market while demand remained weak.

Why, then, has the NCB continued to concentrate its investment on securing additional capacity? Mostly it arises from a positive determination to do so. In its Development Plan for 1990 produced in mid-1981, the NCB stressed its intention to maintain long-term investment, and the Board roundly told the Monopolies Commission that the use of the investment programme to regulate the balance between supply and demand 'must not be contemplated' (*ibid.*, pp. 47, 95). That the Board has followed this policy through is clearly demonstrated by the high proportion of capital expenditure going to major new projects (48 per cent in 1982/3 and 57 per cent in 1983/4). That it intends to continue this stance is indicated by the projections to 1990 (when 39 per cent of capital expenditure is planned to go on new pits alone and a further 12 per cent on other major projects) (NCB *Annual Report*, 1983/4, p. 3).

The NCB defended its investment strategy by arguing that adjustment was not possible. There was little flexibility. Once begun it would be very costly to break contracts or stop schemes. There is obviously some force in this but, as will be shown, the inflexibility is overstated. Another source of justification arises from the NCB's stated expectation of a likely increase in demand after 1990, though much of this rests on an assumption of the power-station demand remaining at, or a little above, current levels (MMC, 1983, vol. 1, pp. 68, 98). Against this we would argue first that the NCB *should* have made some adjustment in its investment strategy, and secondly that it could have done so.

Economic strategies of NCB management

On the first point, the Monopolies Commission certainly felt that some adjustment was prudent: 'the NCB should henceforth adopt a much more cautious approach to investment intended to increase or maintain capacity'. They also pointed out that its procedures favoured output-related projects against cost-reducing projects and urged that the balance should be redressed (*ibid.*, pp. 95, 209). The stress on new capacity was particularly risky because it rested on market assumptions, especially on rising real selling prices, which could well be falsified (*ibid.*, pp. 95, 189–92). Moreover, a significant change in the government's method of financing such projects has greatly enhanced the risk. The government used to indicate not only the amount provided for capital expenditure in the current year, but also the level to which the NCB could commit itself for the two following years. The disappearance of these forward limits has intensified the risk attached to long-term projects. (The surprising thing is not that this government has imposed such a constraint, but that it has seemingly tolerated (if not encouraged) a loss-making nationalised undertaking to concentrate on expensive investment in new capacity.)

On the second point, it is clear that part of the investment in new capacity could not be sensibly halted. The major commitment at Selby was largely irreversible. That is not, however, the end of the story. The capital expenditure plan for the decade to 1990 showed that even for the first four years £450m – or over 60 per cent – of the proposed expenditure on major new projects was still unapproved (*ibid.*, p. 182, table 9.2). Still more would have been uncommitted. The Board's medium-term investment programme is up-dated annually (to cover the current year and the next five years) and would certainly have offered considerable possibilities for reallocation (*ibid.*, p. 43). An obvious case concerned the major new mine project, apart from Selby. The Ashfordsby new mine did not receive planning approval till May 1983, and was not approved by the Secretary of State until January 1984 and, crucially, the main earthworks and mining contracts were not expected to be let before the end of 1984 (NCB *Report*, 1983–4, p. 13).

The NCB's investment policy has intensified the crisis by maintaining the maximum pressure from new capacity on a weak market. It is this which seems to create the necessity for accelerated closures – that is, closures beyond the considerable numbers which would have gone through the established procedures. The NCB would claim that the strategy was justified because the financial imperatives demanded the development of high-output, low-cost, new capacity. The desirability of high-output pits is not beyond question if only because they will reduce flexibility. But what has not been challenged, but should be, is that this new capacity is so obviously low-cost. In any case, as we shall argue in the

166

next section, relative cost levels will not determine which pits close as the NCB tries to resolve the problem of excess capacity.

Which pits will close?

The labour-intensive / low output per manshift pits in the geographically peripheral coalfields of South Wales, Scotland and Durham will close.

When challenged on the cost figures, NCB spokesmen reply that pit-closure decisions are complex and many considerations are taken into account. As well as cost per tonne, geological reserves, type of coal produced and backward linkages to particular customers are all taken into account. This was the line taken in the South Wales NCB reply to Andrew Glyn's pamphlet (see chapter 4) and similar arguments were used in the Board's reply to criticism in *Accountancy* (1985) (see chapter 5). By implication, closure is a mystery which academic outsiders could not hope to understand. Against this, we will argue that the mechanisms underlying closure can be explained. More specifically, when it is a question of reducing the losses incurred by the NCB, closure must be concentrated in the labour-intensive pits in the geographically peripheral coalfields. Ironically, this strategy of retreat does not guarantee the NCB's return to profitability because, as we shall show, the profitability of the central high-investment pits is highly sensitive to unfavourable geology and high interest rates.

When large loss-making nationalised enterprises retreat, there is a characteristic pattern in their closure decisions. The pattern is clear in steel and cars. British Steel Corporation (BSC) closed Corby, Consett and Shotton and maintained Llanwern, Port Talbot and Ravenscraig. British Leyland closed Canley, Speke and Solihull and maintained Longbridge and Cowley. In both cases, the central high-investment plants were safeguarded while the smaller works and the branch factories were closed. Even though some of the closed works in steel were low-cost producers, that did not protect them from closure. We are all familiar with these effects. What we must now do is to try and understand the mechanisms underlying them. Why do enterprises protect the high-investment centre and sacrifice the periphery?

If we examine the case of coal, the answer is clear. It is not the level of costs at different sites, but differences in the composition of costs which are crucial in determining the strategy of retreat. To begin with, the central high-investment pits must be defended because their fixed costs are high. Unless loaded with throughput, their operating costs go through the roof and they become high-cost, unprofitable pits. Consider,

Economic strategies of NCB management

for example, the extreme case of Selby, whose operating costs are projected as £22.02 per tonne at an output level of 10m tonnes per annum (MMC, 1983, vol. 1, p. 228). Most of these costs are effectively fixed irrespective of output; as BSC found out, in a highly capital-intensive operation the modest share of labour in operating costs can only be taken out easily by closing everything down. If management quotad down Selby's output to 5m tonnes, then its operating costs alone would approach £40 per tonne.

If Selby's operating costs are to be contained, other pits must close. And here the distinction between avoidable and unavoidable costs becomes important. The NCB's losses can only be contained by taking out avoidable costs. The capital in the high-investment pits is a sunk cost – depreciation payments on it continue even after closure. The capital costs can only be avoided by an asset write-off such as the government granted the Coal Board in 1973. On the other hand, labour is a variable cost which management can take out by sacking workers. The prospects of savings here are considerable when wage charges still account for nearly half of the NCB's operating costs: in 1981/2 they accounted for 48 per cent of operating costs (*ibid.*, p. 14). It is of course true that closure does not take out all the wage charges when some costs, such as those of the voluntary early retirement scheme, will still have to be met. But, on almost any assumptions, closing pits will take out wage costs.

If the aim is to take out wage costs, differences in labour intensity between pits are quite crucial. Pits with a low output per manshift (OMS) have a higher labour intensity per tonne of coal produced. Other things being equal, therefore, closing low output per manshift pits takes out avoidable wage costs faster. From this point of view, low OMS is clearly the best single predictor of closure. The pits which are most at risk are the 70 or so pits which in 1981/2 had output per manshift of below 2 tonnes (MMC, 1983, vol. 2, appendix 3.7). As table 8.1 shows, most of the low OMS pits are concentrated in just 3 of the coalfields – the peripheral coalfields of South Wales, Scotland and Durham account for 65 per cent of these pits

Moreover, further closures amongst the low OMS pits in the peripheral coalfields would only represent a continuation of existing trends. From the beginning of 1974 to the end of the first quarter of 1982/3, 58 pits were closed and 34 of these closures were in the three peripheral coalfields; in Derby, Nottingham and the Midlands just 8 pits were closed (MMC, 1983, vol. 1, p. 175). If further closures were pressed through on the basis of taking out all the pits with OMS below two tonnes, the Scots and Durham coalfields would be halved in size and the South Wales coalfield would be virtually eliminated.

Aberystwyth report on coal

Table 8.1 *OMS of coalfields*

OMS	South Wales	Scotland	Durham	Other coalfields
Below 1.0 tonne	6	0	0	1
1.0 to 1.5 tonnes	15	3	5	3
1.5 to 2.0 tonnes	6	5	5	21

Source: MMC (1983), app. 3–5.

Connoisseurs of the 'strange but true' kind of coincidence may notice that our group of 70 low OMS pits included almost exactly the same pits as the other group of 70 pits which on the NCB unit-cost calculation lose more than £10 per tonne. Of the 70 pits apparently losing more than £10 in 1981, 59 had an OMS below 2 tonnes per manshift (MMC, 1983, vol. 2, appendix 3.8). There is a good reason for this. The NCB's unit-cost calculation on existing pits does not properly charge capital costs to each pit, but it does fully charge labour costs. In this case the apparently unprofitable and high-cost pits will of course be the labour-intensive pits with low OMS. Having operated a profit-and-loss accounting system for existing mines which confounds physically high output with economic efficiency, the NCB is able to turn round and demand the closure of labour-intensive pits on the bogus grounds that they are high-cost. Against this, we must insist that the question of uneconomic pits in the peripheral coalfields has very little to do with proven high costs of production: it is the composition of their costs which puts these pits at risk.

So far we have explained why a retreating NCB management will prefer to close the pits with low OMS. This is a real tragedy. If it had not been for the expansionist strategy of the NCB, which leaves more than 20m tonnes of new capacity hanging over the market, many of the peripheral pits would have reasonably bright futures. To begin with, the pits now at risk of closure are by no means all geologically exhausted. Of the 70 pits which made apparent losses of more than £10 per tonne, nearly half (33) were classified as 'long-life pits' whose known reserves would last more than ten years at present rates of working. The apparently loss-making pits are however small pits by current industry standards: of the 70 apparent loss-makers no fewer than 49 pits had an output of under 300,000 tonnes per annum. The only other distinguishing characteristic is low OMS, which could be explained either by adverse geology or by under-investment and technically inappropriate investment. This last possibility must be examined when low physical output in

Economic strategies of NCB management

British industry is so often the result of under-investment or misinvestment.

To be fair to the NCB, there is no evidence that any coalfield has been starved of investment; in South Wales, with 33 collieries in 1981/2, 14 pits had obtained major investment projects costing over £1m under *Plan for Coal* (*ibid.*, appendix 3.14). On the other hand, there is evidence that investment has been concentrated at individual pits which appear more profitable under the NCB's unit-cost form of calculation: 57 per cent of the NCB's capital expenditure over the period 1977/82 went to pits which in 1981/2 had made operating surpluses in at least three of the previous five years. On a pit-by-pit level, given the NCB's accounting framework, operating profits and losses do appear to be a matter of self-fulfilling prophecies: apparently profitable pits get investments which under the unit-cost calculation are almost bound to improve profitability.

There is one final irony in all this. The NCB will try to control losses by taking out the labour-intensive pits. But this does not guarantee the profitability of the NCB, because the economics of high-investment pits are unstable and their profitability is precarious. The crudest calculations show that coal from some of the new mines does not look very cheap in relation to current selling prices or the costs of production at existing mines. Selby coal will cost £32.70 per tonne (including interest charge) and the whole output will have to be sold to the CEGB which will not want to pay much more. If the ambitious output targets are not met, costs will rapidly increase. Furthermore, in 1981/2, on the NCB's unit-cost calculation basis, no fewer than 24 existing collieries were apparently producing at a cost of £30 per tonne or less (including historic cost depreciation and excluding interest). Given the deficiencies of the unit-cost form of calculation, it is not possible to get very much further with this line of argument. It is, however, possible to examine the profitability of the new capacity in a net present value (NPV) framework and the results of this exercise are quite remarkable.

It is sometimes argued that the NPV form of analysis discourages large-scale strategic investments because use of a discount factor diminishes the value of distant returns from major projects. The NCB has heroically redressed this imbalance by rigging the investment appraisal rules so that its NPV form of calculation favours large-scale investment in new mines. To begin with, cash flows from new mines are calculated over much longer periods than the 15 years maximum allowed at existing mines; in a new mine, cash flow is projected over the life of the seam, which in the Thorne appraisal was estimated at 47 years (MMC, 1983, vol. 1, p. 191). Furthermore, the incremental output from new mines is valued on a very much more favourable basis than output from existing mines, which is valued at distress stock or export prices up to 1990; in a new mine the distress price assumptions are relaxed and a second 'projection on real prices' is made, which in the Thorne appraisal allowed the NCB to assume that coal prices would increase in real terms at 2 per cent per annum (*ibid.*, p. 201).

Even after rigging the NPV rules in favour of new mines, the NCB can only show that these mines are profitable by making optimistic assumptions about favourable geological conditions and low rates of interest. Consider, for example, the case of Selby, where the NCB has invested £1,400m in new capacity. The NCB's own calculation shows a substantial positive net present value of £322m which appears to justify the project. But this depends on key assumptions about geology and interest rates; Selby is assumed to reach its target output of 10m tonnes and it is assumed that the cash flow can be discounted at an 8 per cent rate. But the NCB's major projects usually fail to reach target output; a sample of such projects showed their output was on average 10 per cent below 'stage II estimates' (*ibid.*, p. 205), and the deficit may well be larger in Selby where geological difficulties have already been encountered. The discount rate of 8 per cent is also unreasonably low, given present interest rates. As we explain in the appendix, we therefore constructed a computer program on which we simulated the effects of higher discount rates and reduced net cash flows resulting from lower output. Even modest increases in the discount rate and reductions in output have a dramatic effect. When we increased the discount rate from 8 to 10 per cent and reduced output from 10m to 9m tonnes, the NPV went negative. On this form of calculation, the Selby project should have been rejected as unprofitable.

Our conclusion is that the capital-intensive pits have knife-edge economics; their profits are easily wiped out by unfavourable geology or high rates of interest. At the very best, this kind of mining is a high-risk option. It is also precarious because it reduces management flexibility in response to changing market demands or opportunities. It is for this uncertain future that the NCB will sacrifice the labour-intensive, low OMS pits on the geographically peripheral coalfields. The one issue which we have not tackled so far is how many of these low OMS pits must close. In the short term this depends on the physical pressure of new capacity and the financial pressure of external financial limits on a loss-making NCB. Both these pressures could be relaxed by a government which halted the investment programme and tolerated operating losses. The Thatcher government will of course take up neither of these options. More than political spite is at stake here. As we will argue in the next section, in the medium and longer term the government plans to go nuclear, so the demand for coal will be limited and many pit closures are required.

How large an industry?

The size of the industry in the medium and long term depends on government decisions about coal's importance in electricity generation.

We now turn from the short-run crisis of over-capacity to the issue of how this crisis will be resolved in the long run. In the short run the number of peripheral pits closed will be influenced by the extent of the NCB's financial losses. But that financial consideration will not be decisive in the medium and long term. Therefore, it is foolish to suppose that if miners accept wage cuts they can have a larger coal industry and more secure long-term employment. That is an academic fairy tale. In the long term, the number of peripheral pits closed depends on the physical size of the market which the government makes available to the NCB. When over 70 per cent of our present coal output goes to the power stations, the size of market available to the NCB will depend on government decisions about how electricity will be generated in the 1990s and beyond.

The reality is that the NCB has become increasingly dependent on sales to the CEGB for consumption in power stations. This trend, illustrated in table 8.2, reflects the decline of traditional coal markets (domestic sales, sales to the gas and steel industry etc.), and the heavy reliance of the CEGB on coal-fired stations in the generation of electricity. In 1983, for example, just under three-quarters of UK electricity was generated in coal-fired stations as against 16 per cent in nuclear-powered and 7 per cent in oil-fired stations. So, the question of whether there really is a 'secure long-term future' for coal is vitally related to the role which coal is expected to play in the generation of electricity.

In emphasising this fundamental point we are establishing a connection between the future of coal and the more general question of long-term energy policy. Both the NCB and the government have been careful to disconnect these issues. As a result they have been able to convey the impression that if the 'uneconomic' pits are purged then the future for coal is bright. Peter Walker followed this line in his speech to the Conservative Party conference where he spoke of 'an expanding future' (*Financial Times*, 10 October 1984). Equally, in the NCB *Report* for 1983/4, Ian MacGregor stated that 'The NCB are capable of becoming a low-cost supplier of energy and the policies we are adopting ... will ensure that this industry has a secure long-term future.' From our

Table 8.2 *Percentage of consumption of NCB coal by market*

	1947	1965/6	1975/6	1981/2
Power stations	14.6	38	62	73
Coke ovens/gasworks	23	24.2	15.1	10
Domestic	19.8	15.3	9.3	7.3
Other	42.6	22.5	12.6	9.7

Source: calculated from MMC (1983).

perspective the future of coal hardly looks so bright.

The Department of Energy's 1982 *Proof of Evidence* for the Sizewell B inquiry is the one publicly available document which is an authoritative source on energy demand in the United Kingdom into the next century and how that demand will be met. A series of eight energy scenarios are presented, based on varying assumptions concerning energy prices, growth in GDP and the growth rate of manufacturing industry. In electricity generation, the choice is essentially one between coal and nuclear power. Table 8.3 shows that, whatever scenario is followed, the dominant role in electricity generation is taken by nuclear power stations. In a nutshell, by 2010, what is envisaged is a *complete reversal* of the roles currently played by coal and nuclear-powered stations.

If coal's percentage share of the electricity market falls in all the scenarios, the impact of this on the coal industry varies according to the size of total electricity demand, which is not the same in the different scenarios. Case Z is the most plausible of the Department of Energy's scenarios and the one which the department itself favours; this scenario assumes ½ per cent per annum growth in GDP, low industrial growth and high energy prices. The end result, on this basis, is that coal demand for electricity generating purposes in 2010 is 37.7m tonnes. The significance of this figure can be seen from the fact that in 1982/3 power stations consumed 86.2m tonnes. So, by 2010 there would be a fall of just under *50m tonnes* or just over 40 per cent of NCB output at 1982/3 levels.

If the government chooses the nuclear option the implications for coal are really dramatic. However, by accident or design, the issue is avoided in the Department of Energy's *Proof of Evidence*. In the scenario we have considered, even though Britain goes nuclear by 2010, a substantial coal industry is still required. Coal output will fall nearly 50 per cent from current (pre-strike) output levels, but in case Z there will still be a total UK demand for coal of 80m tonnes in 2010. This result is achieved by sleight of hand. The Department of Energy projects a highly problem-

Economic strategies of NCB management

Table 8.3 *Percentage of coal, nuclear and 'residual' shares of generating capacity*

Scenario	Coal	Nuclear	Residual
A	17.6	85	(2.6)
B	16	83	1
C	10	88	2
D (=Case Z)	13	76	11
E	17	83	0
F	15	83	2
G	22	66	12
H	12	71	17

Source: Dept. of Energy (1982).

atical increase in other 'fill in' demand which will partially offset what it expects to be a much more certain fall in demand for electricity generation purposes; between 2000 and 2010, the share of power-station demand in total demand for coal is projected to fall from nearly two-thirds (63 per cent) to less than one-half (47 per cent). An increase in 'fill in' demand over the next 25 years would be flatly contrary to the whole post-war trend. As table 8.4 illustrates in volume terms, the only expanding domestic market for coal since nationalisation has been sales for electricity generating purposes. After a period of continuous decline, consumption in markets other than power stations amounted to just 31.5m tonnes in 1981/2. The Department of Energy projects an increase of 10.8m tonnes or 34 per cent by 2010.

In terms of domestic demand there would appear to be only one possible area in which expansion is possible, conversion of industrial boilers from oil or gas to coal. Some such shift is possible but would depend on the capital cost of conversion and requires a substantial fall in gas supplies. In the other non-power station markets, the story is the same. There may be some readjustment in favour of coal, but that readjustment is very unlikely to be on the scale required by the Department of Energy projections. We may thus generally conclude that the department's 80m-tonne overall output figure for 2010 is over-optimistic. We should perhaps assume that coal does no better than maintain current output levels in the 'fill in' markets. In this case, 'going nuclear' has dramatic long-term implications for the future size of the coal industry because overall output would be no higher than 70m tonnes. If the trend of decline in the 'fill in' markets continues, overall

174

Aberystwyth report on coal

Table 8.4 *Coal sales to different markets (million tonnes)*

	1947	1960	1965/6	1975/7	1981/2
Power stations	27.5	52.7	69.9	75.8	85.3
Coke/gas	43.2	52.2	44.5	8.5	11.7
Domestic	37.2	36.1	28.2	11.4	8.5
Other	79.6	58.8	41.4	16.5	11.3

Source: MMC (1983).

demand could be well below 70m tonnes. Pit closures and job loss on a massive scale would be required.

Quite naturally, in the context of the recent strike, these points have not been emphasised by spokesmen for the NCB and the government. Generally, these issues are avoided by a careful choice of time horizon. A few years ago the NCB and the Department of Energy made bullish predictions about the demand for coal (MMC, 1983, vol. 1, p. 65). This was reinforced in June 1984, when Ian MacGregor stated that deep-mined production would rise to 125m tonnes over the next ten years (*Financial Times*, 15 June 1984). This statement was sharply criticised (rightly in our view) as being over-optimistic. What is more important, however, is to focus not on the output figure but on the time period in question. The bright prospect refers to the next ten years.

What is not emphasised and what has not been noticed is that, if the government chooses the nuclear option, coal demand will drop dramatically in a few years just after 2000. On the Department of Energy scenario, the phasing of the nuclear-power programme is such that the really large drop in coal demand is concentrated in the decade 2000 to 2010. This point is illustrated in table 8.5, which shows the projections, on case Z, for demand for coal in UK power stations and total UK primary demand for coal. All this is a direct result of the time-scale over which nuclear power is phased in. In 1980, nuclear (and hydro-electric) power accounted for 13 per cent of UK power-station fuelling. By 2000, on case Z, nuclear power accounts for 42 per cent of power-station fuelling and then jumps to a massive 67 per cent by 2010.

Our discussion so far has presented the energy issue as a matter of straightforward choice between domestic coal and nuclear. In our view this is legitimate because neither imports of foreign coal nor exports of our own coal will seriously affect the outcome. Peter Walker, in his speech to the 1984 Conservative Party conference, accepted that

Economic strategies of NCB management

Table 8.5 *Projected coal demand (million tonnes) from power stations and total coal demand*

	Case Z projections			
	1980 actual	1990	2000	2010
Coal demand (power stations)	89.7	72.7	63.5	37.7
Coal demand (UK total)	120.8	185.0	99.9	80.0

Source: Department of Energy (1982), p. A43.

imported coal is not a realistic option. This seems sensible. Expensive new port facilities would be required to bring in coal whose foreign sources of supply are uncertain and whose price depends on fluctuations in the exchange rates. More fundamentally, our balance-of-trade in manufactures has deteriorated steadily over the past 30 years and is now in deficit. With a huge balance-of-trade deficit in manufactures we will not be able to afford imported coal (or oil) when our own North Sea oil supplies dwindle and run out.

If domestic coal should be developed to ease the looming payments constraint, there is little prospect that domestic supplies will be cheap enough to find large export markets. It is sometimes argued that coal from super pits like Selby has considerable export potential. However, Selby coal will cost £32.70 per tonne (including interest) or $35.97 at an exchange rate of 1.10. If we add on roughly $10 for transport, this makes Selby coal considerably more expensive than the cheapest available; South African coal sells at $27 a tonne f.o.b. and $39 delivered to Rotterdam. Fluctuations in exchange rate, reductions in transport costs, or shifts in the energy policy of exporting countries could change the equation. But we would argue that no reliance should be placed on export markets to boost coal output.

The argument in this section opens up many issues. At an industry level it raises questions not only about the extent of closure but also about the long-run return on the NCB's massive investment in new capacity. It should also be clear by now that the crisis in coal is not simply a sectional industrial issue; through its linkage to energy policy, the resolution of that crisis affects all our futures. In our view it is a gross over-simplification to assume that the future market for coal depends on its economic competitiveness. The market in coal is an administered one and the future of that market depends on political decisions about when and how far electricity generation goes nuclear. It is sobering to find that, although there has been little public discussion and political debate, official government projections already imply a nuclear future which requires a massive run-down of coal. This policy might perhaps be justified if nuclear energy had proven cost advantage over coal in the generation of electricity. But, as we shall argue in the next section, nuclear energy has no cost advantage.

Is nuclear power cheaper?

The economic case for a nuclear future does not stand up to serious scrutiny and should not be accepted as a basis for major policy decisions.

We have demonstrated the extent to which a substantial nuclear-energy programme has a decimating effect on the coal industry in terms of both output and employment. One argument for such a programme is that it will lead to electricity being generated more cheaply and hence render UK industry more 'competitive'. One could raise many questions about such a position. However, here we will accept the premise and address the question, would a substantial nuclear programme result in cheaper electricity?

The CEGB has presented evidence which purports to demonstrate that the future costs of generating electricity via nuclear-powered stations will be markedly lower than if coal-powered stations were used. The relevant figures were put forward in the CEGB *Annual Report* for 1979/80 and they have been reproduced and discussed, in some detail, in both the MMC Report (1981) on the CEGB and in an important report of the House of Commons Select Committee on Energy (1981).

To understand the CEGB conclusions we need to give a brief account of the methods which they use to forecast the costs and benefits to be derived from investment in power stations. The CEGB use the familiar discounted cash flow (DCF) method to convert the cash values of future costs and savings into 'present values'. Under this method longer-term costs are expressed as lower 'present values' because of the reversed telescope effect of discounting. The method gives certain advantages to the case for nuclear powered stations. For example, there are large costs associated with the eventual decommissioning of nuclear stations, costs which do not arise at all when coal stations are decommissioned. This is thus an area in which nuclear stations apparently have a marked disadvantage. Under the DCF method, however, the present value of this cost becomes small because it is a cost incurred in the distant future

177

Economic strategies of NCB management

Table 8.6 *Net effective cost (NEC) of future stations at March 1980 price levels*

Capital charges at station and provision for decommissioning	Nuclear £/kW p.a.	p/kWh	Coal-fired £/kW p.a.	p/kWh
Interest during construction	77	1.39	36	0.76
Inclusive fuel costs	34	0.61	113	2.38
Other costs of operation	12	0.22	10	0.21
Generation costs	123	2.22	159	3.35
Less fuel saving from displacement of less efficient plant	148	2.68	143	3.02
NEC	−25	−0.46	+16	+0.33

Source: MMC (1981).

at the end of the station's life. Nuclear's cost disadvantage relative to coal is thus minimised.

The costs of a nuclear power station over its projected life can be divided into four categories: the capital cost (set out as an annual stream); decommissioning and allied costs; costs of fuel; and direct operating costs other than fuel, such as wages and salaries. The saving from a new projected power station includes benefits from displacement of less efficient plant. Under the CEGB's 'merit order' system, power stations are loaded and off-loaded in order of their respective costs of production, with output being concentrated in 'low-cost' stations (MMC, 1981, pp. 123–4). A new, more efficient, plant will push less efficient plants down the order of merit, thus saving on operating costs. The method thus compares the present value of costs under the four headings stipulated together with any benefits from displacement of less efficient plant.

The result of this analysis is the net present cost for each station over its lifetime (its net effective cost or NEC). The outcome, on this basis, of the CEGB's comparison of coal and nuclear stations is given in table 8.6. It is expressed in pounds per kilowatt/annum and pence per kilowatt/hour to

178

adjust for the fact that different stations will have different generating capacities (MMC, 1981, p. 68).

The lowest NEC represents the most attractive alternative. The negative figure for nuclear stations means that not only would a nuclear programme generate more benefits than additional coal-fired stations but it would be worth scrapping *existing* coal stations and replacing them with nuclear stations. As table 8.6 shows, this is because savings in fuel and operating costs on nuclear stations are expected to outweigh all the construction costs of the stations concerned. If we wish to examine this conclusion critically rather than accept it at face value, we must look at the key assumptions made by the CEGB. These relate to four broad areas. An assumption must be made concerning the capital costs of the stations involved. Nuclear stations are at least twice as expensive as coal-fired stations in capital-cost terms. Clearly, any major movement in the relative capital costs of the two types of station will affect their NECs.

A second key factor is construction time. The calculations assume an expected time by which the power station will be completed. This is significant because any delay in construction will affect relative NECs for two reasons. Extra capital costs and interest charges will directly rise the NEC while the saving derived from displacing less efficient plant will also be delayed.

The third key area is fuel costs. As can be seen from table 8.6, this is the one area where nuclear stations are hypothesised to do better than coal-fired stations. Clearly, however, any change in nuclear fuel prices relative to coal or coal to nuclear will affect the relative NEC position.

Finally, there is a whole series of assumptions concerning hypothetical plant performance and these fall into two main categories. The first kind of assumption concerns whether a plant performs to its design rating and thus gives the expected level of output. Where this does not happen the plant is said to be 'de-rated' and the extent to which the plant performs below its designed capacity is expressed in percentage terms; for example, 70 per cent of design rating = 30 per cent de-rating. The second major kind of assumption about plant performance concerns 'availability'. This is defined in the Select Committee on Energy Report as, 'the proportion of the year . . . during which a power plant is available for use at its rated capacity' (*ibid.*, p. 32). Each of these plant-performance variables will necessarily affect the final NEC outcome. Where a plant is operated below designed MWe capacity then necessarily capital costs are spread over a lower output, thus giving a higher cost per kW figure. Equally, to the extent that a plant is not 'available' for part of the year, then savings from substituting the more efficient plant are lost.

Economic strategies of NCB management

Table 8.7 *CEGB development review combined sensitivity analysis*

	£/kW per annum		
	AGR	PWR	Coal
Basic mean NEC	−26	−40	+18
Difference from basic mean NEC:			
1. Derating by 20% (nuclear)	+16	+12	
2. Lateness 6 years (nuclear)	+33	+33	
3. Lateness 2 years (coal)			+4
4. Annual availability minus 8 percentage points (nuclear)	+12	+12	
5. Nuclear fuel plus 0.13p/kWh	+7	+7	
Revised mean NEC	+42	+24	+22

Source: MMC (1981).

The CEGB's NEC calculation makes assumptions about all these factors, and any of these assumptions may turn out to be more or less incorrect in the light of experience. To evaluate the impact of incorrect assumptions it is sensible to estimate the sensitivity of the NEC outcome to various possible differences between assumption and out-turn. Table 8.7 presents the CEGB's own sensitivity analysis for two types of future nuclear station and for future coal-fired stations. AGRs (advanced gas-cooled reactors) are the second generation of nuclear reactors in the UK (following the original 'Magnox' types). PWRs (pressurised water reactors) are the most common reactor type on a world scale and the reactor now favoured by the CEGB for the prospective UK nuclear programme.

The first line of table 8.7 shows the starting point, the basic mean NEC giving a significant advantage to either of the nuclear-station types. If, however, the five possibilities envisaged in the table materialised, then the result is that both types of nuclear station end up with a mean NEC inferior to that of the coal-fired stations.

If we ask how likely is this kind of outcome, then we must turn to *past* experience of constructing and operating nuclear power stations in the UK and the USA. As we have no experience of PWRs in this country, the analysis must first be restricted to AGRs. In table 8.7 one can see that a combination of six years lateness for nuclear stations and two years for

180

coal stations results in a deterioration in the relative position of nuclear stations by £29 per kilowatt per annum. In fact the AGR programme (like the CEGB exercise) assumes a six-year period for construction, but AGR stations have been on average *seven years and one month overdue*. In contrast, the average construction time overrun for coal-fired stations has been *two years and three months* (*ibid.*, p. 84). In other words, the sensitivity assumption about nuclear stations being six years late while coal stations are two years late fairly reflects past experience.

As far as rating is concerned, the MMC report on the CEGB (1981) points out that the 1979/80 Development Review assumed that the first four AGRs would attain 80 per cent of their design rating. This corresponds to the 20 per cent *de-rating* referred to in table 8.7. However, the MMC indicates that this is optimistic: 'Very considerable uncertainties about their (AGRs) output persist and consideration has been given in the 1979–80 Development Review to the contingency that only *50 per cent* rating is achieved overall by the four stations' (MMC, 1981, p. 66).

As far as fuel costs are concerned, an increase of 0.13p per kilowatt hour in the cost of nuclear fuel would involve a £7 per kilowatt per annum deterioration in the AGR NEC. The assumption concerning nuclear fuel costs made by the CEGB was that fuel-cycle costs for AGRs should increase from 0.37p/kWh in 1986/7 to 0.47p/kWh at the year 2000 (at March 1979 prices). This represents a 1.7 per cent per annum price rise or an overall rise in real costs of 2 per cent over the period concerned. However, the CEGB's own figures show an increase of *90* per cent in *real terms* in total fuel-cycle costs in the 1975–80 period. On such a basis, fuel-cycle costs would, in just five years, rise by 0.33p/kWh, over two and a half times the 0.13p referred to in the sensitivity figure. In the restrained words of the Select Committee: 'it may therefore be optimistic for the Board to assume, for the purposes of the NEC, an increase of "somewhat under 2 per cent per annum" in real terms ... for total nuclear fuel costs up to 2000 ...' (House of Commons Select Committee on Energy, 1981, p. 39). At the same time, the calculations assume a real increase in coal prices of 2 per cent p.a. although current contracts provide the CEGB with coal at no increase in real prices.

So far there is insufficient evidence from operating AGRs to know how unrealistic the CEGB availability figure is. However, the past building experience, the recent trends in nuclear fuel costs and the Board's own assumptions concerning rating all strongly suggest the superiority of the coal-fired stations over AGRs. It may be thought that these arguments are largely irrelevant because the CEGB intends to use the US-developed PWR rather than the British-developed AGR in the proposed

181

Economic strategies of NCB management

Table 8.8 *PWR nuclear station achievement in the US 1982 and 1984 (reactors over 1,000 MWe)*[1]

	1984		1982
Over 60% cumulative load factor[2]			
	MWe		*MWe*
Sequoyah	1,183	Cook 1	1,093
Cook 1	1,093	Cook 2	1,136
Subtotal	3,406		2,229
Under 60% cumulative load factor			
Zion 2	1,085	Zion 1	1,085
San Onofre	1,181	Trojan	1,178
McGuire 1	1,220	Sequoyah 1	1,183
McGuire 2	1,220	Salem 1	1,135
Salem 1	1,135	Zion 2	1,085
Trojan	1,178	Indian Pt 3	1,000
Sequoyah 1	1,183		
Zion 1	1,085		
Indian Pt 3	1,000		
Salem 2	1,158		
Subtotal	11,445		6,666
Total MWe	14,851		8,895

Source: *Nuclear Engineering International* (1982, 1984).
[1] Nuclear station achievement (*Nuclear Engineering International*, 1982, 1984).
[2] Cumulative load factor is the complete load-factor history of the reactor.

next generation of UK nuclear power plants. PWR should – hypothetically, at least – achieve superior results to AGR. Table 8.7 indicates a lower NEC for PWR as against AGR. The advantage is deemed to derive particularly from expected lower capital costs (see, e.g. House of Commons Select Committee on Energy, 1981, p. 51).

What can be said in evaluating such claims? To begin with we can get an idea of the likely performance of PWRs in the UK by examining the US experience. The PWR reactor planned for Sizewell would have an output of over 1,000 MWe gross. In table 8.8 we make the relevant comparison and show cumulative load-factor performance for US PWRs over 1,000 MWe. From this table we can see that the US PWR reactor performance was very poor. In 1984 three-quarters of all PWRs operated below a 60 per cent cumulative load factor and the average was a miserable 48 per cent. The CEGB optimistically expects a 64 per cent load factor. On the basis of American experience, if the UK were to build 10–15 reactors, 3 out of every 4 would not meet this performance standard.

If performance levels are inferior, the disadvantage of PWR is reinforced, because the supposed capital savings from a PWR programme are chimerical. Some supporters of the PWR have argued that, since it is the most common reactor type on a world scale, this could have the effect of reducing the capital costs of the British programme: part of the CEGB's case for adopting the PWR for Sizewell B is that it will give Britain access to a technology which has been accepted by 20 nations so far (Fishlock 1983). What is implied is that the PWR is an off-the-shelf 'mass produced' reactor type and this will allow 'economies of scale' in reactor production.

This is clearly not the case, because any PWR reactor for Sizewell B and subsequent stations needs to be redesigned to meet UK safety standards: 'Sizewell will have design features not yet in operation on the Westinghouse PWR to reduce radiation dose to plant operators' (Fishlock, 1983). PWRs are the ultimate kind of highly engineered capital equipment. With designers working at the limits of knowledge and materials technology, unanticipated problems arise in the process of construction and use. The design of PWRs has continually changed for this reason. Economies of scale have never materialised because it has not been possible to develop and produce a standard reference design. This has been pointed out by such critics of nuclear power as Charles Komanoff (1981), but the same point has been made in a recent issue of *Atom* (the magazine of the United Kingdom Atomic Energy Authority), which is generally regarded as the 'house magazine' of the nuclear industry: 'Over the past 15 years America has been engaged in codifying regulatory requirements. In many instances we in the industry were the originators of such codes through standards setting procedures. Too often those groups had inadequate input from field operators. Tolerances were set by designers who over-specified. Furthermore, regulators pressured for tighter standards … The result has often been to make great difficulties for operators in the field … The heavy stream of new specifications has been very difficult to apply in practice in the middle of construction' (C. Walske, 1984). Furthermore, as the poor performance of US PWRs indicates, design changes have not engendered improvements in performance. This point is made by Thomas in a paper submitted to the Sizewell inquiry on behalf of the Electricity Consumer Council: 'In analysing the performance of nuclear plant a number of authors have attempted to quantify the difference between and within generations. Generally the results have not unequivocally shown the expected pattern of improved performance between and within generations' (Thomas, n.d.).

Against this background, we would argue that series ordering will bring minimal benefits for unit capital-cost reduction. On the contrary, if Britain joins the PWR club, we would expect capital costs to escalate as new problems emerge and design is continuously modified on efficiency and safety grounds. Series production will become job-lot construction. The House of Commons Energy Committee concluded that 'the cost reduction from factory manufacture of the main PWR components is greatest when specialised plant capable of supplying parts for several reactors a year can be fully loaded' (House of Commons Select Committee on Energy, 1981, p. 37). We would argue that past experience indicates that this condition has not, cannot, and will not be met.

PWR reactors are now far and away the world's most common reactor type and that in itself creates problems. The October 1984 supplement of *Nuclear Engineering International* shows that PWRs made up 59 per cent of operating reactors at the end of 1983, 69 per cent of reactors under construction and 74 per cent of planned reactors. PWR is a variant or sub-type of the LWR (light water reactor), and 300 reactors of the latter type will be operating world-wide by the end of 1985. In this situation, Cave (1980, p. 14) calculates that the chance of a core melt-down accident somewhere in the world before 1990 is about 1 in 5, unless some substantial improvement in LWR safety can be achieved. The odds on catastrophe can be disputed but it is still clear that the more PWRs the greater the likelihood of an accident somewhere in the world. Were such an accident to occur, even outside the UK, there would be immediate pressure on the CEGB to modify designs and/or close down reactors in service. This would be hugely expensive.

British supporters of PWR believe that it will overcome the problems and difficulties which beset the earlier AGR programme. However, US operating experience has been disappointing, the case for 'economies of scale' cannot be sustained, and a serious accident anywhere in the world would push up costs. The economic case for a preponderantly nuclear future is manifestly not made. But it is on this case that a hugely reduced future size for the coal industry, involving still further closures, is made to rest.

Conclusion

If the crisis in coal is resolved through massive closures then we all lose. Most obviously the miners lose because, whatever the government and the NCB promise, we do not believe that large-scale closures can be made without compulsory redundancy. This is particularly so because the present work force in mining is a young one; the mining work-force average age is just 38 years (NCB *Annual Report*, 1983–4). Sacked miners will go into the dole queue and many of them will probably never work again. The problem here is not simply high unemployment rates in the country as a whole and more especially in the peripheral coalfields; re-employment prospects for redundant mineworkers are bleak because of changes in the employment profile over the past twenty years. In that period our economy has lost more than 3 million manufacturing jobs, which were mainly jobs for male unskilled or industry-specific skilled workers. Most of these workers can take little comfort from the fact that part-time female employment in ill-paid service trades has expanded by 2 million over the past twenty years.

It is not necessary to sack miners if we reject a nuclear future. Assume, to put the strongest case, that no new nuclear reactors are built and, when they come to the end of their useful life, existing nuclear power stations are replaced with coal-fired power stations. In this case we could look forward to a power-station demand for 110m tonnes of coal on the Department of Energy's case Z in 2010. When the few remaining nuclear power stations were retired shortly after 2010, power-station demand would then rise to 120m tonnes. If the productive future can be made secure in the long run, financial losses at the NCB would have to be accepted in the short and medium term. It is worth pointing out that these overall operating losses have not been huge if we balance profits of £530m in the period 1975–81 against operating losses of £500m in the period 1982–4. Many of the Board's problems have been caused by the peculiar way in which the NCB is financed. Effectively, the NCB is financed by loans from the government and on many of these loans it pays high rates of interest; for example, on loans from the Secretary of State since 1973 the Board pays an average rate of interest of 12.5 per cent.

An acceptance of operating losses would not alter the fact that over the next decade, when the management's investment strategy has produced over-capacity, the Board will have to make hard decisions about taking capacity out and bringing capacity in. Over this time period, the case for the small traditional pits does not rest simply on the social justice argument that, when the management's investment strategy has failed, it

185

is socially unjust to make the miners suffer. As we have argued, there are good economic reasons to suppose that the Board's concentration on super pits is economically irrational. The technical and geological problems of this type of mining have probably been underestimated and costs of production at super pits will not be low. Quite apart from this, the concentration of output at a few large pits means that super pits are inherently a high-risk option.

As the over-capacity problem eases, the future operating losses at the NCB need not be huge if coal is priced realistically. This would involve accepting the fundamental point that, for geological reasons, domestic coal will never be a cheap energy option. Even so, the arguments for domestic coal are compelling. Given the weakness of our national manufacturing sector and our growing balance-of-trade deficit in manufactures, we will not be able to afford large imports of foreign coal (or oil) when our own North Sea oil runs out. The choice then is between domestic coal and nuclear energy. Our argument is that we should choose coal because, quite apart from the environmental considerations, nuclear power is almost certainly likely to be more expensive than coal-fired power. Most other European countries will not have the luxury of a choice between coal or nuclear power, because they do not have large domestic coal reserves. We are concerned that, when Britain has the choice, the Thatcher government will choose the wrong option.

In this context, we are concerned about the irreversibility of closure at pits which are not geologically exhausted. Factories can be mothballed and then reopened without difficulty; pits which are closed cannot be reopened. When the pits are closed, there are massive reinvestment costs associated with getting back into coal. In this situation the government could argue that there is no alternative to the nuclear future. In effect, therefore, the larger the number of closures in the short run, the more our energy options for 2000 and beyond are closed. The number of pits which close will depend on many considerations, not least the extent of the defeat which the miners suffer. But at an ideological level, the number of pits which close will partly depend on the government's success in promoting the notion that there are 'uneconomic pits' whose closure would be economically beneficial. We have written this report to question the assumptions underlying this argument and to promote a more informed discussion of the broader issues which are relevant. Naturally, we believe that our arguments about the economics of coal and nuclear power are correct, but we will in the end be satisfied if we succeed in opening out a debate which has become shamefully narrow.

Aberystwyth report on coal

Postscript

The original Aberystwyth 'Report on Coal' was published in February 1985. It was produced independently by a team who had worked together before and developed a distinctive approach to the problems of British manufacturing and the broader national crisis. The coal report is one result of a team project of research into the current British crisis and its development over the past thirty years. Apart from research papers on industrial policy and on the industries of coal, steel and cars, the work produced so far includes two substantial books: *Why Are the British Bad at Manufacturing?* (K. Williams *et al.*, 1983), *Keynes, Beveridge and Beyond* (T. Cutler *et al.*, 1986) and *The Breakdown of Austin Rover* (K. Williams *et al.*, 1987).

From this perspective, the Aberystwyth team insisted that the NCB management's investment strategy had created and sustained a crisis of over-capacity. They were also the first researchers to raise fundamental questions about whether the management's concentration on capital-intensive super pits was economically rational. On the issue of final demand for coal and the implications of going nuclear, the Aberystwyth team drew attention to the significance of the Department of Energy's *Proof of Evidence* to the Sizewell inquiry.

This is a revised version of the original report. First, a major section arguing that the colliery accounts biassed results towards newer capital-intensive pits and against older labour-intensive ones, through omitting capital charges, has been excluded. This is partly because similar points are made elsewhere in the book. Secondly, the final section on the costs of generating electricity from nuclear power has been extended and incorporates some new material which reinforces the original conclusion that nuclear is unlikely to be cheaper. The basic argument of the original report remains unchanged.

Appendix
Net present value and the Selby super pit

To begin with, we undertook an exercise in reconstruction and interpolation based on our limited information about the NCB's NPV calculation on Selby (MMC, 1983, vol. 1, pp. 228–9). The NCB project a NPV for the Selby pit of £322m on the basis of an output level of 10m tonnes. We know total capital expenditure so far is £1,351m, which we have rounded up to £1,400m. In addition, we are told that the operating profit is £9.00 per tonne on operating costs of £22.02. In the first instance the problem is that we are not directly given a net cash flow figure. To obtain a net cash flow figure, we added a depreciation per tonne of £6.00 onto the (pre-interest) profit per tonne figure of £9.00. This would give a net cash flow of £15.00 per tonne. The depreciation provision is prudent because £6.00 per tonne on 10m tonnes will add up to an annual charge of £60m, which amounts to a heavy burden on the capital expenditure.

The next step was to show that our speculation about depreciation charges was consistent with the results obtained by the NCB in calculating cash flow over the assumed 37-year life of the project. We tested two cases using a £6 depreciation charge and net cash flow of £15 per tonne as well as a depreciation charge of £5 and net cash flow of £14 per tonne (table 8.9). The resulting net present values fell rather neatly either side of the NCB case. Our calculations are based on current prices with the net cash flow per tonne of coal remaining constant over the 37-years time horizon. In our view, if the NCB did not do this, it should have done so.

With the aid of our reconstruction of the Selby calculation, we can now explore the sensitivity of the NCB's results to changes in the assumptions about the interest rate and output levels. We explored separately and jointly the implications of a 10 to 14 per cent discount rate and output reductions of 10 per cent to 9m tonnes and 20 per cent to 8m tonnes. As output share falls of 10 per cent below target are normal (*ibid.*, p. 205) on

Table 8.9 *NPV of Selby*

	NPV	Discount rate (%)	Years
NCB case	£322m	8	37
Reconstruction			
(A) £15 per tonne	£369	8	37
(B) £14 per tonne	£249	8	37

Table 8.10 *Selby NPV with various discount rates and output levels*

	NPV £m	Years	Discount rate (%)	Reduction (in net cash flow %)
The NCB results	322	37	8	–
Case 1				
(reconstruction)	369	37	8	–
Variations on case 1, viz.				
Case 2	55	37	10	–
Case 3	(169)	37	12	–
Case 4	(337)	37	14	–
Case 5	190	37	8	10
Case 6	13	37	8	20
Case 7	90	37	10	10

big projects, the 20 per cent reduction in output envisaged in case 6 (table 8.10) is not unreasonable. As will be seen, this kind of output shortfall more or less wipes out all the present value. Even if output shortfalls are contained at 10 per cent below target, the results are not very reassuring. The key point here is that, with output 10 per cent below target, a modest rise of discount rate from 8 to 10 per cent is quite disastrous. As case 7 shows, these two effects together result in a substantial negative net present value.

Economic strategies of NCB management

REFERENCES

Berry, A. J., T. Capps, D. J. Cooper, T. M. Hopper and E. A. Lowe (1985), 'NCB Accounts – A Mine of Mis-information', *Accountancy*, January, pp. 10–12 (reproduced in chapter 5).

Berry, A. J., T. Capps, D. J. Cooper, P. Ferguson, T. M. Hopper and E. A. Lowe (1985), 'Management Control in an Area of the NCB', *Accounting Organisations and Society*, vol. 10, pp. 3–28.

BPP (1981), See House of Commons Select Committee on Energy.

Cave, L. (1980), 'Towards the Forgiving Reactor', *Nuclear Engineering International*, December, pp. 14–16.

Central Electricity Generating Board (1982), *Proof of Evidence to the Sizewell B Enquiry*, London: CEGB.

Cutler, T., K. Williams and J. Williams (1986), *Keynes, Beveridge and Beyond*, London: Routledge and Kegan Paul.

Department of Energy (1974), *Plan for Coal*, London: HMSO.

(1982), *Proof of Evidence to the Sizewell B Enquiry*, London: Department of Energy.

Elkington, J. (1984), *Suntraps*, Harmondsworth: Penguin.

Financial Times (various dates).

Fishlock, D. (1983), 'Nuclear Power', *Financial Times*, 19 January.

Glyn, A. (1985), *The Economic Case Against Pit Closures*, Sheffield: NUM (reproduced in chapter 4).

House of Commons Select Committee on Energy (1981), *Government Statement on the New Nuclear Programme*, BPP 1981, HC 114, i.

Jeffrey, J. W. (1982), 'The Real Cost of Nuclear Energy in the UK', *Energy Policy*, June, pp. 76–100.

Komanoff, C. (1981), 'Comparative Costs of Nuclear and Coal-Fired Stations; Cost Escalation at Nuclear and Coal Plants', House of Commons Select Committee on Energy, 1980–1, *The Government's Nuclear Power Proposals*, HC 114, iv.

Mackerron, G. (1983), 'A Case not Proven', *New Scientist*, 13 January.

Metcalf, D. and G. Davies (1984), *Pit Closures – the Economic Issues*, London: London Weekend Television (reproduced in chapter 2).

Monopolies and Mergers Commission (1981), *Central Electricity Generating Board*, London: HMSO.

(1983), *National Coal Board: A Report on Efficiency and Costs in the Development, Production and Supply of Coal by the NCB*, 2 vols., Cmnd. 8920, London: HMSO.

National Coal Board, *Annual Report and Accounts, 1974–5 to 1983–4*, London: HMSO.

Nuclear Engineering International (1982, 1984), 'Nuclear Station Achievement', October 1982, pp. 54–5.

Ryder Committee (1975), *British Leyland, the Next Decade*, London: HMSO.

Thomas, S. (n.d.), 'The Genealogy of Westinghouse Plant', Electricity Consumer Council, ECC/P/ADD(1), London: ECC.

Walske, C. (1984), 'A Perspective on Nuclear Power in the USA', *Atom Magazine*, no. 337, pp. 7–10.

Williams, K., J. Williams and C. Haslam (1987), *The Breakdown of Austin Rover*, London: Berg.

Williams, K., J. Williams and D. Thomas (1983), *Why Are the British Bad at Manufacturing?*, London: Routledge and Kegan Paul.

PART III

Coal in context

9

Economic background to the coal dispute

P. W. ROBINSON

Introduction

This chapter attempts to explain the economic forces behind the decline of the coal industry. The main findings (presented in the order in which the argument is developed) are:

1. Coal output has been declining throughout this century. This decline accelerated in the 1950s and 1960s when coal was faced with competition from oil.

2. The decline was arrested by the oil-price increases of the 1970s, which have allowed coal to establish and maintain a price advantage over alternative fuels. Despite this, coal has not increased its market share over the past decade.

3. Because of energy conservation in response to the price increases of the 1970s, total energy demand has fallen over the past ten years.

4. With coal holding a stable share of a static market, the output projections for the industry drawn up in the 1970s including those in the 1974 *Plan for Coal* are now totally outdated.

5. Even if total energy demand were to expand, there would not necessarily be increased demand for British coal, which is more expensive to produce at the margin than alternative sources of supply (from the US, South Africa and Australia).

6. Home-produced coal enjoys some natural protection from overseas competition because of high transport costs. In addition there is a tax on fuel oil and informal restrictions on imports. These partially insulate the domestic price of coal from changes in the world price.

7. The cost of producing coal has risen substantially in real terms since 1973/4, despite a major investment programme. Productivity has risen slightly faster than the national average, but wages and non-wage costs have risen very much faster.

The original version first appeared in *Economic Outlook*, October 1984.

Coal in context

8. The upward pressure on costs has come partly from the mineworkers' climb from twelfth to first or second place in the wages league; and partly from the failure to close non-economic pits fast enough.
9. This pressure on costs meant that by 1981/2 less than half of the industry's total output was produced at profitable pits, which employed only 65,000 mineworkers.
10. There is a large tranche of marginally uneconomic pits which may be unprofitable one year but profitable another, and there is a strong case for keeping such pits open.
11. The number of pits which are profitable at the margin is very sensitive to movements in costs. If mineworkers' wages had risen only in line with the national average for manufacturing over the period 1973/4 to 1981/2, the number of jobs in profitable pits would have been 95,000 rather than 65,000.
12. The subsidy per man in the most inefficient pit in 1981/2 was of the order of £14,000. The subsidy per man in the marginal pit at break-even point for the industry as a whole was nearly £5,000.
13. Under a cash limit system every pound spent on subsidising miners is a pound less available to spend elsewhere. Subsidising coal miners is a costly way of preserving jobs compared with alternatives.

The price of coal and the size of the coal market

Since 1973 the dollar price of oil has risen ten-fold – a five-fold increase in real terms. Costs have risen very much less rapidly, and the oil industry is extremely profitable, with producers earning large rents. Coal is a close substitute for oil (notably in the electricity-generating industry), so a rise in oil prices increases the demand for coal. In theory therefore the oil shock should have raised coal prices and profits, and led subsequently to an expansion of the industry as new higher-cost sources of supply were brought on stream. What we observe in the UK is the stark contrast to this theoretical prediction: a declining industry which continues to make substantial losses. How has this state of affairs come about?

The short answer, which again we know from elementary theory, is that either the price of coal has not increased as rapidly as the oil price and/or the cost of producing coal has increased more rapidly. In fact both of these things have happened.

Figure 9.1 shows the behaviour of oil and coal prices since 1967. Before the oil-price shocks of the early 1970s the two prices moved fairly closely in line. Since then there has been a tendency for coal prices to move up with oil prices, but over the past ten years coal has been some 30–40 per cent cheaper than oil.

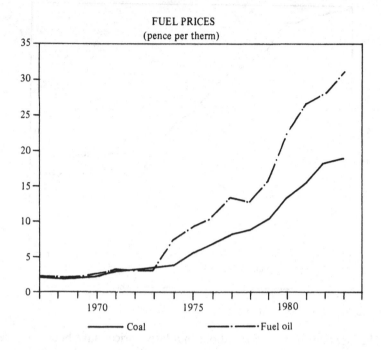

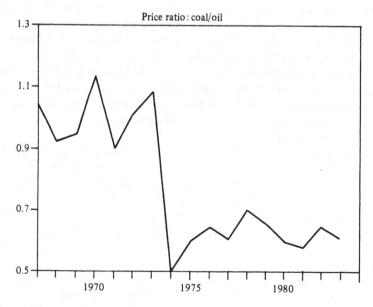

Fig. 9.1 Comparative fuel prices: coal/oil.

197

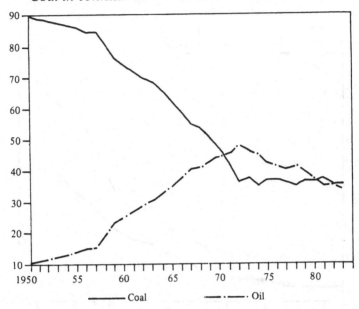

Fig. 9.2 Shares of UK energy market, coal/oil (%).

The fact that such large variations in relative prices have been possible illustrates a very important point about the energy industry. The response to any change in relative prices is slow. This is because consumption of energy generally requires capital equipment which cannot be changed straight away. If the price of coffee rises, consumers can drink more tea the very next day. But if oil goes up in price, those with oil-fired central heating (or power stations) cannot in general switch to gas or coal overnight. We should not infer from this however that the long-run price elasticity of demand for different forms of energy is low. If the relative price difference is expected to persist, users will gradually switch in large numbers.

The long-term substitutability of different fuels is illustrated by the post-war history of the energy industry. At the end of the war coal accounted for over 90 per cent of total energy use in the UK. By 1972 that share had declined to only 36 per cent. As long as the price of coal and oil were closely matched, coal lost market share at a rapid and accelerating rate (fig. 9.2). This is hardly surprising. Compared with oil, coal is bulky, difficult to transport and poses severe waste-disposal problems. At the same price per calorie any user would prefer oil. Over time many did in fact switch. And coal's problems were compounded from the late 1960s onwards by competition from North Sea gas, which offered many of the advantages of oil plus greater security of supply.

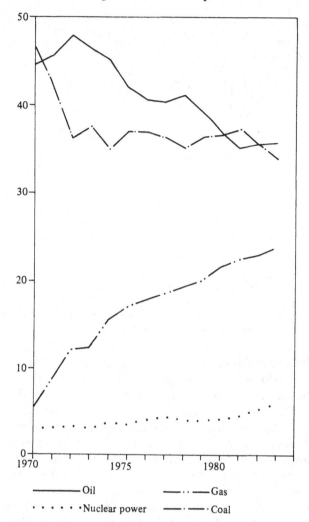

Economic background to the dispute

Fig. 9.3 Shares of UK energy market, oil, gas, nuclear energy and coal.

The steady conversion to oil came to an end with the first oil crisis. The sharp rise in oil prices permitted the coal industry to find a price at which users are broadly indifferent between coal and oil. With a price advantage of around 30–40 per cent, the coal industry has arrested the catastrophic fall in its market share. However it has not *increased* its share since 1974. The markets lost by oil have been replaced by gas (mainly) and nuclear energy (fig. 9.3). Clearly the oil price rise has not permitted a previously healthy coal industry to make super-normal profits. It has rescued a chronically uncompetitive industry from a state of terminal decline.

Coal in context

Fig. 9.4 Total production of coal in Great Britain (*Digest of UK Energy Statistics*, Ministry of Power Statistical Digests).

Figure 9.4 places this decline in historical perspective. There is nothing new about pit closures. Coal output has been falling intermittently for most of the century and particularly steeply and continuously since the mid-1950s. The period of stable output in the 1970s stands out in sharp contrast against this historical background. But, as fig. 9.5 shows, there is an even sharper contrast between the post-war decline in coal demand and the projections of future demand on which official policy has been based since the mid-1970s (Dept of Energy, 1974). What was the basis for such optimism?

Demand for coal depends on total demand for energy, and the share of that market taken by coal – which depends in turn on its relative price. Because of the long lead times which are a feature of the industry – it takes many years to prospect for oil, dig a new coal mine or construct a power station – energy experts spend much time endeavouring to forecast energy demand 10–15 years ahead. As we have seen in public inquiries (Vale of Belvoir, Sizewell (Dept of Energy, 1982)) the case for a new coal mine or a new nuclear power station stands or falls on the size of the energy market in the 1990s, and on the prices and demand elasticities for different fuels. (Dept of Energy, 1981.)

Over the period since 1974 evidence has accumulated to suggest that the *long-run* price elasticity of demand for energy is much higher than the

200

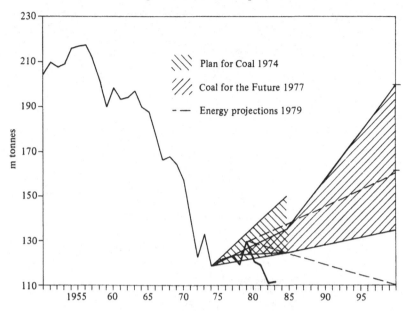

Fig. 9.5 Coal output.

short-run elasticity. We have already noted that the substitution of one kind of energy for another is a long process, requiring capital expenditure, so that the response to price changes is slow. Precisely the same arguments apply to energy as a whole. We can make do with less energy and still enjoy a high standard of living, but the adjustment process takes time. We can insulate our houses, design more fuel-efficient cars, move closer to our places of work, give up 'industrial' products in favour of services. None of this happens overnight, but if the price signals are strong and persistent (as they have been), these changes inexorably occur. The demand for energy is extremely price inelastic in the short run, but the experience of the last ten years has shown that the longer-run price elasticity is nevertheless quite high. Capital equipment reaching the end of its productive life is being replaced today with more energy-efficient equipment in response to price changes that occurred ten years ago; and many of the effects of the second oil-price shock have still to be felt (Manners, 1976; 1981).

The point is illustrated by fig. 9.6, which shows the behaviour of the energy ratio in the UK since 1950. The energy ratio relates total consumption of energy to gross domestic product and this ratio has been falling steadily over the post-war period. Up to 1973 this simply meant that energy demand, though rising, grew less rapidly than GDP. Since

Coal in context

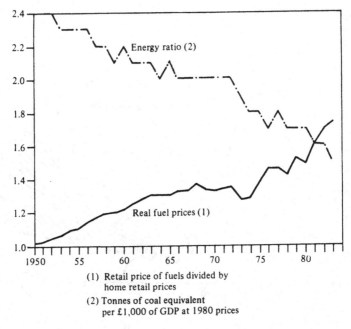

(1) Retail price of fuels divided by
home retail prices
(2) Tonnes of coal equivalent
per £1,000 of GDP at 1980 prices

Fig. 9.6 Real fuel prices and energy ratio.

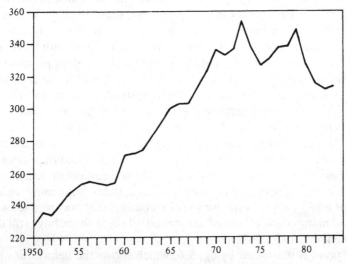

Fig. 9.7 UK energy consumption (tonnes of coal equivalent).

202

then output growth has been slower and the decline in the energy ratio more rapid. Consequently we have seen an absolute fall in total energy consumption in this country – as fig. 9.7 shows.

This brief excursion through the recent history of the energy industry, and the position of coal within it, enables us to answer the question raised at the outset, namely why is coal not a profitable and expanding industry? Part of the answer is that although there has been a considerable improvement in coal's competitiveness vis-à-vis oil since the first oil crisis, the starting point in the early 1970s was so uncompetitive that the improvement was insufficient to carry coal into an era of expansion. The other half of the answer lies in the demand for energy as a whole, which has proved much lower than was anticipated. Since 1973 we have witnessed the exercise of consumer sovereignty. There is a normal downward-sloping demand curve for energy. A monopoly supplier can fix the price at any chosen level, but he does not thereby repeal the laws of supply and demand. The consumer will determine the quantity sold at any given price. When the price of energy went up, demand fell.

The adjustment to higher energy prices is slow and probably far from complete. The resumption of growth in the economy since the 1980–1 recession has barely stabilised the demand for energy, which fell sharply during the recession. There is little reason to expect a substantial increase in energy demand in future, as the effects of resumed growth will be largely offset by the continuing drive towards economy in energy use that has been brought about by the steep rise in real energy prices of the past decade. If total energy demand is stable, there is little prospect that the coal industry, which at present relative prices cannot increase its market share, will see a growing demand for its products. There can be no doubt that the plans to expand the coal industry in the aftermath of the energy price shocks of the 1970s – including the *Plan for Coal* (1974) – are now totally outdated.

The costs of producing coal

Although the coal industry was not able to match the rise in the oil price in the 1970s, coal prices nevertheless rose sharply. Between 1972/3 and 1981/2 the price of deep-mined coal rose from just under £7 per tonne to over £35 per tonne. Allowing for the rapid inflation over that period, this represented an increase in real terms of 54 per cent. However, even with this increase in prices the Coal Board continued to make a loss on its deep-mining operations. The reason is that costs also rose substantially in real terms. And although costs increased less rapidly than prices, the

Coal in context

Table 9.1 *NCB deep mines, unit operating costs and revenues*
(£/tonne at 1980 prices)

	1972/3	1981/2	% change
Revenue	20.3	31.2	54
Costs:			
Labour	11.8	17.6	49
Depreciation	1.3	1.9	44
Other*	9.1	15.1	65
Total	22.2	34.6	55

* Overheads, materials, repairs, power, heat and light. *Excludes* interest charges.
Source: MMC (1983), vol. 2, p. 25, appendix 3.3.

improvement was insufficient to eliminate the large losses that were being made in the early 1970s.

Table 9.1, which is calculated from data given in the Monopolies and Mergers Commission (henceforth MMC) report on the National Coal Board (1983), illustrates the problem. Since 1970 miners' wages have moved from below the average manufacturing wage to substantially above it (fig. 9.8), taking them from twelfth position in the earnings league to first or second place. Although mining productivity also grew faster than in manufacturing between 1972/3 and 1980/1, real unit costs in mining increased by 49 per cent compared with only 2 per cent in manufacturing. Had mining wages grown in line with manufacturing wages over that period the industry would have been in surplus by 1981/2.

However, table 9.1 shows that wages were not the only problem – not even the major problem. Other costs rose even faster. This highlights a particular problem of the coal industry, which is that costs have a built-in tendency to rise. The older the mine the further is the seam of coal from the pithead and the greater are the geological difficulties and costs of extraction. For any particular mine costs are rising all the time. This means that the industry as a whole can only remain profitable by closing down high-cost capacity and opening new lower-cost mines.

One problem in the 1970s was that there had been inadequate investment in the 1960s, so an insufficient number of new coal faces were brought into operation. But it also seems probable that an insufficient number of old pits were closed down. Pit closures present many problems. One little recognised technical difficulty is that the cost of

Economic background to the dispute

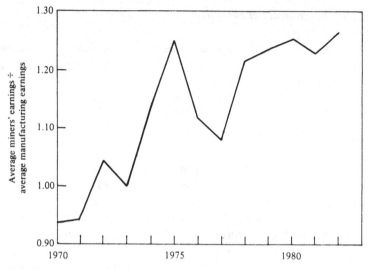

Fig. 9.8 Earnings in coal industry relative to manufacturing.

extracting coal in a particular pit can vary sharply over time – an annual variance of 15 per cent is the norm for the industry. Under these circumstances it would clearly be wrong to close a pit just because it makes a loss in one particular year. Against a background of over-optimistic demand forecasts, the temptation to give a loss-making pit another chance must have been strong – especially as closure always imposes severe disruption for the workers and families involved. But, whatever the reason, it is clear (with hindsight) that the failure to close uneconomic pits sufficiently quickly has been an important factor in the industry's chronic problems.

To keep the industry competitive it is necessary not just to close old pits but also to invest in existing and new pits. If management blames the unions for resisting closures, the miners in their turn blame management for inadequate or ill-chosen investment. It is extremely difficult to judge from aggregate figures whether investment in coal has been adequate, but table 9.2 shows that investment per man has been greater in the mining industry than in manufacturing industry as a whole, and has risen more rapidly. This investment has not always produced the returns expected of it, partly because output (and hence productivity) in the new and more efficient mines has been held back because of general over-supply. Pit closures would thus lead to productivity gains in the newer pits and better returns on past investment.

The problems that are created when uneconomic pits are left in operation too long are revealed starkly in fig. 9.9, which shows the supply

Coal in context

Table 9.2 *Investment per employee*
(£/man at 1980 prices)

	Coal industry	Manufacturing industry
1974/5	1,158	597
1975/6	1,744	618
1976/7	1,901	666
1977/8	2,087	747
1978/9	2,608	811
1979/80	3,203	856
1980/1	3,387	857
1981/2	3,311	932

Sources: MMC (1983), appendix 3.14, p. 64 and *National Income Blue Book*.

curve for the industry in 1981/2. The curve is constructed from data on individual pits from the MMC Report, ranked in order of cost. It shows how the output of the industry can be increased by moving up the supply curve, bringing into production successively higher-cost pits to the point at which the (marginal avoidable) cost of the marginal pit is just equal to the price of its output. As fig. 9.9 shows, there is a large tail of pits where costs are far in excess of any likely return.

The role of imports

In fig. 9.9 there is a horizontal line which represents the price at which coal can be sold. Why a horizontal line rather than a downward-sloping demand curve? Because the UK coal industry can be considered as one relatively small supplier of coal to the world coal market. Under the classical assumption of perfect competition the market price cannot be affected by the action of a small producer, who simply takes the price as given and regulates his output accordingly.

This text-book model is a reasonable approximation to the facts (though some important qualifications emerge below). But if this is an accurate representation of the position of the British coal industry, it follows that all the expansionist plans of the 1970s, drawn up in the wake of the oil-price hikes, contained not one but two fundamental flaws: not only has the demand for energy in general and coal in particular proved more price-sensitive than was assumed; but also the benefit to UK producers is far less than was assumed. The rise in price has not only reduced total demand, it has also increased competing supplies. As the

Economic background to the dispute

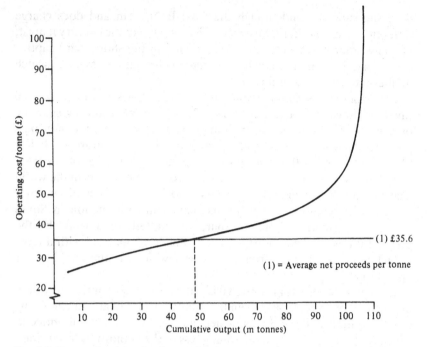

Fig. 9.9 Deep-mined production: unit operating costs against cumulative output, 1981/2 (MMC from NCB information).

price of coal has risen, the industry has expanded – but it is the low-cost producers in the United States, Australia and South Africa who have benefited, not the high-cost marginal British producers (Turner, 1984).

This description is an over-simplification, because of yet another important special characteristic of the coal industry: transport costs – especially over land – are a substantial proportion of the total cost of a tonne of coal delivered to its point of use. This means that it is impossible to say, in the abstract, whether or not imported coal is cheaper than domestically produced coal. It may be cheaper for a coastal power station to buy imported coal, but not cost effective for an inland power station – especially one located near a coal mine. Since over three-quarters of total coal output is used to generate electricity, the competitiveness of imports over the medium term depends crucially on where new power stations are located (Robinson and Marshall, 1983).

Although high import costs effectively give UK producers a local monopoly of supply in some parts of the country, the potential for coal imports does loosely link UK coal prices to the world price. For Thames-side power stations imports are always a viable alternative to domestic supplies, and though the Coal Board can and does charge different prices to different users in different parts of the country it must, like any other business, avoid offending its (in the short term) captive customers, who otherwise will make the investment necessary to switch to alternative sources of power.

The Monopolies Commission study (1983) shows the price of coal (average proceeds per tonne) in 1981/2 at £35.6, with sterling standing on average at 1.91 to the dollar. It might be imagined that the industry's prospects have subsequently improved dramatically as sterling fell below $1.20 in October of this year, pushing up the sterling price of imported coal. However, there have been a number of developments in the world coal market in the intervening years to offset the effect of currency movements. Additional capacity has come into production in South Africa and America: Polish output, interrupted for a while by the political unrest, is back on stream; and this has coincided with a large reduction in coal demand from France as new nuclear plant has become operational.

These developments illustrate vividly the huge uncertainties surrounding the prospects for coal. Given the industry's marginal cost curve, the level of output and employment depends on two factors: the price at which coal can be sold; and the willingness of the authorities to subsidise marginal high-cost production. At a given level of subsidy, the number of jobs in the industry depends ultimately on the sterling price of internationally traded coal. In the short term this is affected by currency movements, but in the longer term it is the cost of overseas production that determines job prospects for the miners. The world coal market is currently in glut and this, like the potential over-supply of oil which has intermittently made headlines recently, could be part of a wider pattern pointing to a long-term fall in energy demand and price.

UK industrialists frequently argue that they are handicapped, in competition with trading partners, by electricity costs that are higher than those prevailing abroad. The high cost of coal, the major primary energy source for electricity generation, is blamed. These claims are only partly justified, for it should be borne in mind that electricity costs are held down by the relatively high proportion of coal (which is cheaper than oil) used to generate electricity in this country compared with abroad. However, the UK coal industry is undoubtedly protected by the tax on fuel oil. And there is also evidence of informal official restraints on the Central Electricity Generating Board when they have tried to burn more imported coal. This kind of protection preserves jobs in the coal industry at the expense of jobs lost in manufacturing. And table 9.3 suggests that there is only a loose connection between world prices and

Economic background to the dispute

Table 9.3 *Average price of coal (£ per tonne)*

Year	Used by the electricity industry	Rotterdam spot price	% difference
1979	25.32	22.15	14.3
1980	31.84	23.33	36.4
1981	37.43	34.66	8.1
1982	40.21	34.57	16.3
1983	42.49	31.58	34.5

UK prices, with the consumer yet to feel the benefit of the fall in world coal prices that has occurred since 1982.

The case for subsidy

The Coal Board is at present making a loss. To any economist who believes in the role played by markets in allocating resources between competing claims this is an important signal which suggests that the coal industry ought to contract. The resources absorbed by the marginal loss-making pits can be put to better use making or doing things that people will buy *without* being subsidised.

However, the issue is not as simple as this. There are many instances of democratically elected governments subsidising loss-making operations for many years. What are the arguments for doing this? And do they apply in the case of coal?

Agriculture is subsidised around the world. One historical reason has been to ensure security of supply in case of war. Another has been the supposed amenity value of agricultural land. A third has been the problem of variable supply conditions. Maintaining agricultural production capacity such that there is always enough food (even under the worst possible conditions) means that on average there will be too much food produced. The subsidy paid to the marginal producers in good years can be regarded as an insurance against starvation in bad years.

Coal-mining resembles agriculture in having variable costs of production from one year to another. Given this variability, it is not sensible to close a pit just because it makes a loss in one year. A loss-making pit this year may be profitable next. There is a strong case for keeping the most efficient tranche of loss-making pits in production in any given year if there is a reasonable chance that they will make a profit in future. But it is obvious that the coal industry has no amenity value, while subsidising domestic production does nothing to increase security of supply.

Although the variability of costs and revenues is a good argument for keeping open pits at the margin of profitability, it is not these pits which are at the centre of the present debate. The Coal Board wishes to close a number of pits which are making substantial losses. The case for closing these pits is, in strict accounting terms, overwhelming. But it is by no means obvious that a wider public interest is served by closure. If public spending is not cash-limited, it is worth closing the pits if the costs incurred do not exceed the benefits. The costs are not limited to the lost income and production of the miners themselves. Miners' wages are spent in the local community, generating additional income and employment. When these multiplier effects are taken into account, the increase in unemployment resulting from pit closures is likely to be greater than the number of jobs lost in the pits themselves.

Against these wider costs must be set benefits, of which the chief (stressed by market economists) is the alternative output produced by resources freed from the uneconomic pits. However, these benefits cannot be taken for granted. Most of the marginal coal mines are located in areas of industrial decline with high average rates of unemployment. Moreover, most mining communities are extremely cohesive and offer a quality of life to the inhabitants which is not easily obtained elsewhere. Miners who become unemployed have little chance of finding alternative employment in their own communities and may choose to remain unemployed in their home town rather than seek work outside.

Given these social realities, it must be recognised that the benefits of closing pits, in terms of alternative output, will be slow to appear. Moreover, as miners drift away from their communities they will incur additional social costs. The infrastructure in mining communities (housing, schools, roads, hospitals) will be under-utilised, with corresponding pockets of congestion in the areas to which the miners move. The cost of adapting the social infrastructure to the new pattern of employment should be set against the benefits obtained from the extra output.

If a given marginal pit is kept open none of these social costs is incurred. Moreover the pit will continue to produce a known quantity of coal with a definite market value. These are two large items to throw into the balance against the prospective benefits from closure – a stream of alternative output which may be very slow to materialise. These conclusions suggest that a pit would have to be *very* uneconomic before a full social cost-benefit analysis would show it to be worth closing (Davies and Metcalf, chapter 2).

Economic background to the dispute

The case against subsidy

No economist, however great his faith in market processes, can dismiss these arguments lightly. However there are powerful counter-arguments. Those who resist closure of uneconomic pits because of the disruption involved must admit that these disruption costs will be incurred eventually, if only through geological exhaustion. Putting off closure reduces the present value of these costs, but this has to be weighed against the (often sharply rising) costs of keeping an increasingly uneconomic pit open.

Secondly, the value of the marginal tonne of coal produced by an uneconomic pit is extremely hard to assess. At the limit it may have to be stockpiled or dumped on the export market, and is worth very much less than the market value of an 'average' tonne of coal. At present it certainly replaces an extra tonne of coal that could be produced at much lower cost from one of the efficient pits, which have been running at less than full capacity. This argument suggests that the loss of output from closing marginal pits would be much smaller than on conventional cost-benefit calculations.

Thirdly, it is extremely difficult to apply cost-benefit analysis to major economic, social and technological changes, where the benefits are typically spread very thinly over whole societies, and endure for many years, while the costs fall heavily on comparatively few people and for a relatively short period of time. A cost-benefit analysis of the introduction of the railways, taking into account the likely disruptions to existing communities and to the coach trade, could well have shown the enterprise to be unviable on social grounds. Or, to take a more contemporary example, many of the redundancies that occurred in the manufacturing recession of 1980/1 could have been avoided by public subsidies justified on cost-benefit grounds. There can be no question that a society which resists change because of its high social costs will in the short run be a more comfortable place to live in. But in the long run it risks becoming a backwater.

Fourthly, given the extreme difficulty of agreeing on the appropriate criteria for cost-benefit studies (length of time horizon, appropriate discount rate) and the equally great difficulty of actually evaluating all the costs and benefits (about which no two economists, notoriously, would ever agree), the rough justice of the market place has an undeniable attraction.

Finally, if a case for subsidising mining employment can be made, then it can be generalised to all other threatened industries, in the private or the public sector. Mineworkers would have to take their turn, and given

211

the high cost of keeping a marginal pit open they would not be at the front of the queue.

This last argument acquires particular force if the cost-benefit framework of analysis is abandoned in favour of an overall limit on public spending (which may be justified on other grounds, e.g. the need for lower taxes to improve incentives or for lower public borrowing to control inflation and reduce interest rates). In these circumstances the (opportunity) cost of subsidising miners is the cash that is not available to spend elsewhere, for example in subsidising jobs in the private sector or creating jobs in the National Health Service or in education. Within this framework, subsidising inefficient collieries, viewed as a job-creation scheme, is not at all cost-effective: the subsidy per man in the least efficient pit in 1981/2 was £14,000. For this amount of money it would have been possible to meet the full salary cost of an extra two jobs at the average wage or to preserve more jobs in less capital-intensive industries by subsidising marginal employees.

The marginal costs and savings of closing uneconomic pits

This brief consideration of the case for subsidy shows how the debate about pit closures quickly raises larger issues which are beyond the scope of this chapter. The dispute assumed enormous political importance precisely because it raised those issues. But in the end the closure of pits will be crucially determined by the *marginal* costs of keeping those pits open or of closing them. Too much of the debate has so far been conducted in terms of broad aggregates – the total cost of subsidising the Coal Board, the average price of coal, and the average cost of producing it. But these averages are not what will, in the end, determine pit closures.

At the margin the government faces a choice between subsidising the Coal Board to keep miners at work in uneconomic pits or subsidising the miners directly through the unemployment benefit. Obviously any consideration of the marginal costs and savings which arise from pit closures must be based on the appropriate measure of cost. Part of the Coal Board's overall loss is attributable to sunk costs, notably interest charges, which have to be paid whether or not a particular pit is closed. Any proper assessment of the savings from closing a particular pit should ignore such costs. Thus if a pit is profitable, taking into account only the *avoidable* costs incurred by keeping it in operation (wages and salaries, power, heat and light, necessary maintenance), it should be kept open, even if it appears *unprofitable* when made to bear its share of the unavoidable costs of the industry as a whole (Glyn, 1984).

Economic background to the dispute

Table 9.4 *Colliery operating costs*

	Output ('000 tonnes)	Output per shift (tonnes)	Employment	Loss (£/tonne)	Total loss (£m)	Subsidy per job (£)
Least efficient pit	62	0.64	470	104.8	6.5	13.825
Typical loss-making pit	261	1.77	715	10.2	2.7	3.723

Fortunately there is in the MMC Report (1983, appendix 3.3–3.5) data on colliery operating costs which comes close to this definition of avoidable costs. Drawing on this data it is possible to construct a cost curve for the industry based on marginal avoidable costs. The idea can be explained most easily in terms of a concrete example. In 1981/2 according to the MMC (1983) the least efficient pit produced 62,000 tonnes of coal and made a loss of £104.8 per tonne. The total loss was thus nearly £6.5 million. The pit employed some 450 people, so the cost of keeping those men in work was nearly £14,000 per job (table 9.4). Clearly at these rates of subsidy it is sensible to close the pit, since the money saved is far greater than any possible combination of unemployment pay and lost taxes.

Consider on the other hand a marginal colliery, where total losses in 1981/2 were £2.7m, with an implied subsidy of £3,760 per man to keep over 700 miners in employment. If the colliery were closed the government would save some £3,760 per man in subsidies. But it would also lose the revenue from taxes and social security on the miners' income, and it would have to pay unemployment benefit and/or supplementary benefits to the miners as long as they stayed out of work. Any government concerned to control *total* public spending would have to think twice about closing such a pit even though the Coal Board might need to do so in order to hit its external financial limits.

What is clear from the example of the two pits shown in table 9.4 is that the variations in subsidy from pit to pit is so large that any debate about the future of 'the industry' conducted in terms of national averages is liable to be highly misleading. Each pit has to be treated on its merits and any discussion of 'the industry' has to centre on its marginal cost curve.

This can be drawn from data on individual pits, as fig. 9.9 showed, but fig. 9.10 does not help in the present debate since it shows profits or subsidies in £ per tonne. Since the crucial issue is employment and the required *subsidy per man*, the data used to construct fig. 9.9 have been

213

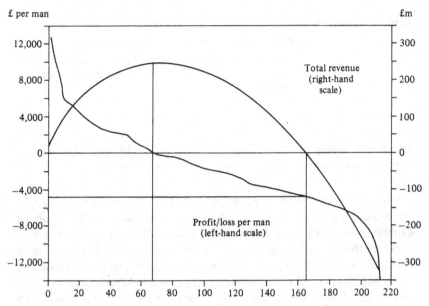

Fig. 9.10 Mining employment and subsidy.

transformed to produce a demand curve for labour in the coal industry. This is plotted in fig. 9.10, which shows, on the vertical axis, the cost per job of subsidising miners in different pits in 1981/2, ranging from the most economic (where the cost was negative – i.e. the pit was profitable) to the least economic, where the cost was as much as £14,000 per job. The horizontal axis shows the number of jobs, so that we can read off from the chart the employment available at each level of subsidy. The zero line shows what total employment would be if all pits were required to make a profit.

The merit of fig. 9.10 is that it enables us to quantify the costs of employing workers in the coal industry *at the margin*. It reveals the interesting fact that in 1981/2 the number of miners employed in deep-mines collieries that were actually profitable was only 67,000. However, the chart also shows that the losses made on the next tranche of collieries were relatively small. Given the variation in costs from year to year it is probably worth keeping many of these collieries open. The figure shows that, by using the surplus from the profitable collieries to subsidise the losses made by the most efficient of the unprofitable ones, the Coal Board could in 1981/2 have employed 165,000 miners without requiring any outside subsidy. But note that even if the industry had been cut back to this break-even point of 165,000 jobs, the subsidy to workers in the marginal colliery was £4,745 per man in 1981/2. In other words, even if the mining industry as a whole is not receiving any subsidy – the cross-subsidy within the industry is very large – some very efficient pits are subsidising some very inefficient ones. This point is presumably not lost on the miners of Nottinghamshire, where a high proportion of the profitable pits are located.

A particular feature of fig. 9.10 is that the slope of the job curve is relatively flat on either side of the zero line. This implies that a relatively small change in profitability (and hence in the required subsidy per job) has a large influence on employment. Since profitability is itself the difference between two much larger figures for costs and revenues, any change in costs has a proportionately much larger effect on profit.

Table 9.5 illustrates the point with a calculation of the effect on the required subsidy per tonne of holding mining wage increases over the period 1973/4 to 1981/2 in line with the national average. The reduction in wage costs by 1981/2 would have been some 14 per cent and the reduction in total costs around 7 per cent. The effect is to reduce the net subsidy required from £3.89 per tonne to £1.14 per tonne. There is thus a very large percentage change in subsidy per tonne, which also translates into a large reduction in the implied subsidy per worker of the order of £1,500 per man. A reduction in costs of this order would have had a dramatic effect on the number of pits which were profitable at the margin, increasing the number of jobs requiring no subsidy by some 28,000. In other words, a reduction in real wages of 14 per cent would have increased the level of profitable employment by over 40 per cent.

From an up-to-date version of fig. 9.10 (which could presumably be constructed by the Coal Board), it would be possible to carry out two kinds of calculations. One, as illustrated above, relates employment to wage restraint and shows that a considerable increase in the number of profitable jobs could be secured by (for example) a freeze on real wages over the next few years. The other compares the level of subsidy in existing pits with the Public Sector Borrowing Requirement (PSBR) costs of closing those pits. These costs include redundancy and social security payments and lost taxes and, like the subsidies, vary enormously from pit to pit. Social security benefits depend on the family situation of the miners; redundancy payments depend on how long they have been in the industry. There is a time dimension which raises all the usual difficulties about the appropriate horizon and rate of discount. The speed with which redundant mineworkers become re-employed will vary from area to area. These problems make it difficult to produce meaningful figures, even illustrative ones, for the cash costs of closing an 'average' pit. But such calculations could be carried out for individual pits and it is hard to see how any national solution to the dispute can be found without such information.

Coal in context

Table 9.5 *Effect on coal cost (£/tonne in 1981/2) of wage restraint*

	Actual	Lower wages	% difference
Net proceeds	35.59	35.59	
Operating costs:			
Wages, etc.	20.10	17.34	−13.7
Other	19.38	19.38	−
Total	39.48	36.72	−7.0
Required subsidy	3.89	1.14	−70.7

Conclusions

The aim of this chapter has been to clarify the issues, not to propose solutions. If there is a single moral it is that the coal dispute was not (and should not have been allowed to become) a national dispute. Pit closures are a micro-economic issue which should be settled by marginal analysis on a case-by-case basis. Such an analysis might provide some justification for subsidies within the framework of the government's Medium Term Financial Strategy. But the marginal approach also shows that wage restraint could be an important factor in increasing the number of profitable (and hence secure) jobs within the industry.

Postscript: the coal industry after OPEC III

Immediately after the year-long coal strike the prospects for the industry appeared remarkably bright. Normal production was resumed more quickly than expected. The fall in the exchange rate, especially against the dollar, had greatly lessened the threat from cheap imported coal. The number of miners employed in deep mines was quickly reduced from 180,000 to 140,000, and the closure of uneconomic pits enabled production in the new super pits to be stepped up. The resulting sharp rise in productivity meant that the underlying position of the industry was close to break-even, and at the coal prices prevailing last year could even have made a modest profit.

The fall in the price of oil plunged the industry into a new crisis. To preserve coal's market share, its price must follow oil prices downwards, which will drastically reduce the amount of coal that can be profitably produced in this country, with obvious implications for employment. In

Economic background to the dispute

this Postscript we present some new calculations, which show the scale of the required reductions, and consider the policy implications. We conclude that there is no case for constraining coal prices to remain above true market-clearing levels, since this amounts to a concealed tax on users of coal (and hence users of electricity) which would hamper the employment-creating growth of manufacturing industry. There is, however, a strong case for allowing the coal industry to increase its borrowing to cover the deficits that result from keeping higher-cost pits in production in order to reduce future dependence on imported oil.

Relative prices and market share

The UK sterling oil price was fairly steady at around £20 per barrel in the period 1982–5 and coal prices have also been fairly constant over that period. Since December 1985 the price of oil on world markets has fallen from $26 per barrel to well under $15, with some trades occurring on the spot market at less than $10 per barrel. Under these circumstances the price of the major fuels which compete with oil must also – eventually – fall.

The fall is not immediate because (as explained above) buyers (and especially the really large buyers) cannot in general switch quickly from one source of energy to another. A power station can take up to 15 years from conception to completion, so the choice between a new coal- or oil-fired station must depend on the relative prices of coal and oil in the year 2000 and for many years (the life of the station) thereafter. The fact that today's oil price is well below the coal price is not a compelling reason to switch from coal to oil, and the fact that the coal price has fallen far less than oil shows that demand for coal is holding up well and users are not (yet) switching.

These considerations suggest that the market share of different fuels will change fairly slowly in response to price movements. Figure 9.1 shows that such changes nevertheless occur, and fig. 9.2 suggests strongly that they are price related. As we have explained, coal steadily lost market share as long as it was priced at parity with oil on a pence-per-therm basis, because it is a distinctly inferior fuel from the user's point of view. For this reason the Coal Board has, since the mid-1970s, priced its coal so as to maintain a price advantage of around 35–40 per cent compared with oil, and has with that policy succeeded in holding its market share. However, the dramatic fall in the price of oil threatens to push the coal–oil price ratio well above the levels prevailing in the 1960s. If the present ratio is maintained, the Coal Board must expect to start losing market share again, at the rate of about three percentage points per year. On that basis the industry would have shrunk to nothing before the year 2000.

These facts have not escaped the Central Electricity Generating Board, which is currently negotiating a reduction in the price of coal. The CEGB's position is strengthened by its experience in using oil-fired generating stations during the coal strike. These stations, though uneconomical with oil at $25 per barrel, are commercially viable at present prices. The CEGB can thus, unusually, threaten an *immediate* and *massive* switch from coal to oil unless prices come down. Given the strength of their position (and the enticing prospect of lower electricity prices, which is helping to win them government support), it seems likely that prices will soon start to come down.

The consequences of a lower coal price

If the price of coal does fall, what are the consequences for the industry? To assess this we have to look at the cost curve. Figure 9.11 shows our estimate of the industry cost curve in 1986/7, constructed using the methodology explained in this chapter and chapter 6. It takes account of the latest information on closures, but ignores the *geological* deterioration in productivity (as exhaustion approaches) that must have occurred since 1981 in some pits that are still open. It also ignores the discovery of new seams in existing pits that may have boosted productivity. The curve may therefore be inaccurate in detail, but as an overall picture of the UK supply curve for coal it is unlikely to be seriously misleading and almost certainly underestimates costs in the less productive pits.

A crucial element in the calculation is the behaviour of productivity for the industry as a whole. In recent years output has fluctuated in the range 2.3–2.4 tonnes per manshift, but since the end of the strike accelerated closure of uneconomic pits has enabled the Coal Board to step up the output from the more efficient pits. There has also been an across-the-board improvement in performance as the miners have striven to make up, through productivity bonuses, some of their earnings lost during the strike. The result is a sharp increase in productivity, and if progress is maintained the average for 1986/7 could be in excess of 3.0 tonnes per manshift. We have used that figure in the calculations shown in the diagrams. (We also show below the consequences of making alternative assumptions.)

An important feature of fig. 9.11 is that the supply curve for coal is, over the critical range, very gently sloping – in other words there are a large number of pits with a similar cost structure close to the margin of profitability. This means that comparatively small changes in the price of

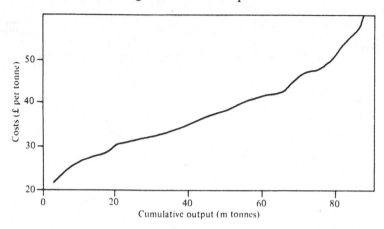

Fig. 9.11 The supply curve for UK coal.

coal make a large difference to the number of pits that are profitable. This has important implications for the debate on closures. It implies that a comparatively small fall in the price of coal can threaten a relatively large number of jobs in the pits that are close to the margin. But it also means that a comparatively small amount of subsidy or borrowing could secure a relatively large number of jobs. As explained above and in chapter 6, it is possible, given the available information on costs, prices and employment in each pit, to calculate the implied cost per job of keeping loss-making pits open, and hence the cumulative subsidy to the industry associated with any level of employment. The results of these calculations are shown in fig. 9.12, which has been computed on the basis of an average coal price of £35 (see table 9.6 for wage and productivity assumptions). Figure 9.12 takes into account, as fig. 9.11 did not, variations in the quality, and hence the selling price, of coal from pit to pit. The graph suggests that at the assumed wage, price and productivity levels prevailing this year, the industry will have to shrink from its current level of 140,000 men to only 110,000 in order to break even. If it is required that every pit be profitable, then there will be only 53,000 jobs in the industry.

These estimates are surrounded with enormous uncertainty – uncertainty about official intentions (all pits break even or the industry breaks even), uncertainty about productivity performance and, above all, uncertainty about the coal price. To illustrate these uncertainties we have carried out two simulations to show how the industry might have looked in 1984 under two alternative productivity assumptions, and a further three simulations to illustrate prospects for the current year

219

Coal in context

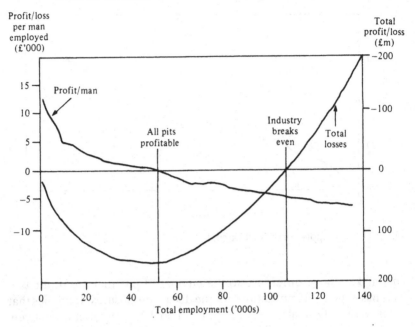

Fig. 9.12 Profits and employment.

under three different price assumptions. The results of this exercise are shown in table 9.6.

In 1985/6 productivity was still strike affected, rising sharply during the year from below pre-strike levels to the new (much higher) post-strike norm. At the same time expectations about future coal prices were being progressively revised downwards. The figures nevertheless bring out very clearly the extent to which the industry has benefited from an improved productivity performance. With coal prices at £45 per tonne and productivity at 3 tonnes per manshift our calculations suggest that the future of the industry was more secure than for many years. This is borne out by recent reports that the South Wales area, for example, achieved a 45 per cent jump in productivity, and recorded a net profit in March, the first time it had done so since 1972.

The other side of the productivity improvements has been further reductions in employment, which had shrunk to 139,000 by the end of the 1985/6 financial year. If the coal price remained at last year's exceptional levels, there would be employment for many of these miners in profit-making pits, provided the recent productivity gains were maintained. If by contrast productivity fell back to pre-strike levels, there would be jobs for only 86,000 men in profitable pits – though the high coal price might make it possible for the industry as a whole to reach profitability at

Table 9.6 *The coal industry: prices, wages, and employment*

	Coal price £/tonne	Productivity tonnes/manshift	Wages £/week	Coal output (m tonnes)			Employment ('000s)[4]		
				All pits profitable	Industry break-even	Actual	All pits profitable	Industry break-even	Actual
1981/2	35.6	2.43	156.4	45	92	109	66	165	218
1984/5[1]	41.7	2.43	173.0	40	80	96	59	138	174
1985/6[2]	45.0	2.43	191.0	55	99		86	185	139
	45.0	3.00	191.0	87	–		151	–	
1986/7[3]	40.0	3.00	206.0	55	103		86	197	
	35.0	3.00	206.0	37	68		53	110	
	30.0	3.00	206.0	9	25		11	34	

[1] Estimates of underlying levels. Actuals are strike-affected.
[2] Average conceals sharp changes through the year, with coal prices falling and productivity rising.
[3] Coal prices in likely range. Productivity assumption conservative.
[4] Estimates of profitable employment are generally overstated, because calculations ignore geological deterioration.

221

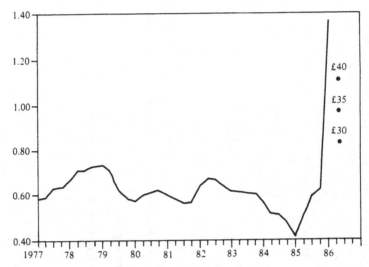

Fig. 9.13 Price ratio: coal to oil (pence per therm). Estimates assume oil price at present levels and coal prices as shown (£ per tonne).

existing manning levels. In fact it is highly unlikely that coal prices will remain much longer at their present levels, given the fall in the price of oil. The 50 per cent fall in the price of oil has as yet had surprisingly little effect on the price of coal, even in the spot market, and its relative price compared with oil is now at a historic and clearly unsustainable peak, as fig. 9.13 shows. But as long as low oil prices persist, the question is not whether the coal price will fall, but how soon and by how much.

We have considered the effects on the industry of a (conservative) fall in the coal price to £30–40 per tonne, which still leaves the relative price of coal at a historic high. Table 9.6 shows that even this effectively removes any hope of bringing the industry to the point where the current work force all have secure jobs in profitable pits. With the price at the top of the illustrative range the number employed in profitable pits shrinks to 86,000. As the coal price falls below £38, the industry as a whole moves into deficit, raising the prospect of a new wave of pit closures in order to break even. At £35 the required closures match those which provoked the 1984/5 strike. If the price falls to £30 then profitable production is really only possible in a few of the new super pits and the industry shrinks to a small rump of some 30,000 miners, producing only a quarter of today's potential output.

Economic background to the dispute

The policy response

These gloomy predictions depend on the wage and productivity assumptions spelled out in table 9.6. If there were no increase in wages (unlikely) or a much greater increase in productivity (quite possible), then the level of profitable employment and output would be greater. But the scale of the probable fall in the coal price is unlikely to be offset by wage restraint or productivity improvements. So, if oil continues to trade at around $10–15 per barrel, the coal industry and its political masters face the following choices:

Strategy 1: Sell coal at current high price. This would enable the industry to stay, in the short term, at around its present size without a government subsidy. There would, however, be a concealed subsidy from energy users, mainly paid in the form of high electricity bills. And as long as the disparity between coal and oil prices persists, energy users would convert to oil. If oil prices remain low this would slowly but surely strangle the industry.

Strategy 2: Sell coal at competitive prices. With no incentive to convert to oil, domestic demand for coal would be maintained. But the industry would make a loss if it remained at its present size. This would imply a choice between a further round of pit closures – which might be bitterly regretted if the oil price subsequently recovered – and borrowing to keep open capacity which is currently uneconomic. This could be regarded as an investment, which would reap a return if and when oil prices rose again. Like all investments it would be kept under constant review and could be discontinued if ever the cost became excessive in relation to the prospective return.

In the present climate it seems likely that strategy 1 will be chosen. The government wants to eliminate the subsidy to the coal industry. The Coal Board would prefer the independence which it would then enjoy. It is not yet certain that oil prices will be low for ever, so that users will be slow to convert to oil even if coal prices remain high. These are good reasons for taking what is in any case the line of least resistance and hoping that the problem of low oil prices will disappear before too much damage is done. The disadvantage of strategy 1 is that in the short term it places an arbitrary burden on coal users, handicapping energy-intensive industries which ought to flourish and create new jobs in a cheaper-energy world. In the longer term it condemns the industry to inexorable decline if oil prices do not rise again.

There is a good case for keeping open pits which are not profitable at present energy prices as an insurance against much higher energy prices in future. This will mean a loss for the Coal Board, but as long as the industry is obliged to charge a competitive price for its product (for example by allowing the CEGB to use cheap imported coal or oil as they wish), this does not distort the energy market. The External Financing Limits of the Coal Board ought to be extended to allow them to finance such a loss, which serves simply, at an explicit and transparent cost, to keep output and employment of the UK coal industry at a higher level than it would otherwise be. If the assumption that this will produce savings at some future date when energy prices rise again becomes patently unrealistic, the borrowing will become hard to finance, and can be discontinued.

For these reasons strategy 2 would be in the long-term interests both of the industry and the country at large, but its adoption would require jettisoning much ideological baggage, both by the Coal Board and by the government. The outcome is likely, as so often, to be determined more by political expediency than economic rationality. The losers will be those who produce and consume coal.

REFERENCES

Davies, G. and D. Metcalf (1984), *Pit Closures: Some Economics*, 'Weekend World'. London Weekend Television (reproduced in chapter 2).
Department of Energy (1974), *Plan for Coal*, London: HMSO.
   (1982), *Proof of Evidence from the Sizewell 'B' Public Enquiry*, London: HMSO.
Glyn, A. (1984), *Economic Aspects of the Coal Industry Dispute*, Sheffield: NUM (see chapter 4).
Manners, G. (1976), 'The Changing Energy Situation in Britain', *Geography*, vol. 61, part 4, pp. 221–31.
   (1981), *Coal in Britain*, London: George Allen and Unwin.
Monopolies and Mergers Commission (1981), *Central Electricity Generating Board*, London: HMSO.
   (1983), *National Coal Board: A Report on Efficiency and Costs in the Development, Production and Supply of Coal by the NCB*, 2 vols. Cmnd. 8920, London: HMSO.
Robinson, C. and E. Marshall (1983), 'What Future for British Coal Policy?' *Surrey Energy Economics Discussion Paper*, no. 14.
Turner, L. (1984), *Coal's Contribution to UK Self-Sufficiency*, Aldershot: Gower.

10

Nuclear power and the coal industry

S. FOTHERGILL

Introduction

Some two-thirds of the coal produced in the UK is consumed by power stations, and this proportion has been rising steadily throughout the post-war period. The consequence is that the future of the coal industry is inextricably bound up with the future of the electricity supply industry.

Over the next few years the electricity industry faces a number of strategic decisions. By far the most important of these concerns the scale and speed of implementation of any future nuclear power programme. The construction and operation of power stations of any kind involves vast sums of public money and has major knock-on consequences for other industries and for the economy as a whole. In the case of nuclear power, the main knock-on effect is on the coal industry, because to a large extent coal and nuclear power are in direct competition as sources for electricity generation. Furthermore, decisions taken now about power-station capacity have extremely long-lasting effects and constrain choices and decisions 20, 30 and even 50 years hence. A large power station typically takes ten years from the planning stage to commissioning, and delays have meant that some stations take much longer. It is then likely to remain on the electricity grid for perhaps a further 40 or 50 years. Thus at least some of the major changes that are occurring now in the electricity industry are the result of decisions taken 20 years ago. A case in point is the commissioning in 1985 of three large nuclear power stations (Dungeness B, Hartlepool and Heysham I), ordered originally by Harold Wilson's Labour government in the mid-1960s. As these stations build up to full power, they are mostly displacing power stations burning coal. Towards the end of the 1980s two further nuclear stations will open (Heysham II and Torness); these were ordered when Tony Benn was Energy Secretary in the late 1970s. They too will displace coal.

The aim of this chapter is to examine the effects of the nuclear-power

225

programme on the demand for coal. The main interrelationships are quantified to the extent that is possible given the available data and uncertainty inherent in energy economics. Too much reliance should not be placed on individual figures; they are intended to indicate only the broad order of magnitude of the costs, benefits and effects. The chapter falls into two halves. The first compares the generating costs of coal-fired and nuclear power stations. The second estimates the likely effect on the demand for coal for alternative nuclear programmes, depending on different assumptions about the growth of the national economy.

Nuclear and coal generation costs

Nuclear power raises a wide range of social, political and safety issues, but the purpose here is to look just at the purely economic, accounting costs. For several years the Central Electricity Generating Board (CEGB) has argued that nuclear power is cheaper than all alternative sources of power, a view elaborated at length at the inquiry into the proposed Sizewell B nuclear power station. Indeed, the CEGB has argued that nuclear power is so cheap that it is worth building new nuclear power stations even if this leads to the premature retirement of existing, serviceable coal and oil stations.

As the Monopolies and Mergers Commission (1981) pointed out, the CEGB's enthusiasm for nuclear power was at least in part based on defective accounting methods. From an accounting point of view there are two sets of costs involved in a power station: the capital cost (and any associated interest charges) of building it, and the operating costs (mainly fuel) of running it. This distinction is especially relevant to a comparison between coal and nuclear power. Nuclear power stations are extremely expensive to build but relatively cheap to run; coal stations are less expensive to build but much more expensive to run. In an inflationary period, this raises accounting problems about how to weight capital costs incurred in one period against running costs incurred in a later period. The CEGB used to get round the problem by simply looking at the amounts of money actually spent, without allowing for inflation – a procedure known as 'historic cost accounting'. The effect, in a period of inflation, is that the capital costs incurred some years ago look small in relation to the operating costs. This made nuclear power, with its high capital costs and low running costs, look very attractive.

But this sort of accounting makes no sense. The problem is that by mixing different years' prices in this way the real value of the resources that went into building the power station are being underestimated compared to the running costs. A further problem is that, when the funds set aside for depreciation are based on historic capital costs, they are inadequate to replace the power station when it finally wears out. In the 1980s the accountancy profession has therefore moved over to a new method – 'current cost accounting' – which measures previous years' capital expenditure in today's prices. The relevance of this discussion to a comparison of coal and nuclear power is that since the CEGB has now adopted current cost accounting there is no longer an automatic bias in favour of nuclear power. The CEGB still says that nuclear power is cheaper, but the margin is not so overwhelming.

But just how much cheaper is nuclear power, if at all? This question can be answered by comparing the economics of three generations of nuclear power stations with their coal-fired counterparts – using current cost accounting, of course. First, however, it is useful to clarify one point. Whatever the overall costs of nuclear power, once a nuclear station has been built it is always economic to run it to the limits of its availability, in preference to even the most efficient coal-fired station. This is because the operating costs, primarily fuel, are considerably lower than for coal or oil stations. This is not the same, however, as saying that on balance nuclear power is cheaper; this requires both operating costs and fixed costs (the cost of construction) to be taken into account.

Magnox v. 1960s coal

The first generation of British nuclear power stations, generally known as the 'Magnox' stations, were commissioned between 1962 and 1971. Eight were built for the CEGB, and one for the South of Scotland Electricity Board (SSEB). With one exception (Wylfa) their generating capacity is small by comparison with the coal-fired stations built in the 1960s.

Table 10.1 compares the generating costs of the CEGB's eight Magnox stations with those of the twelve large coal-fired power stations commissioned by the CEGB between 1965 and 1974. These are the CEGB's own published figures (CEGB, 1985) and are revisions of earlier estimates (CEGB, 1983). They show the average generating costs, at constant prices, over the whole of the lives of the power stations up to March 1984. The cost of electricity from a power station is sensitive to its 'load factor',[1] the normal measure of operating performance, in that a higher load factor means that fixed costs are spread over a large volume of electricity. However, throughout this period these stations were used to the limits of their availability to provide power all day every day – what the industry calls 'base-load' electricity – so the load factors and the costings in table 10.1 represent the best performance that the stations could achieve. The capital charges, the sum set aside to repay the cost of

Coal in context

Table 10.1 *Estimated generating costs: Magnox v. 1960s coal-fired stations (pence per kilowatt/hour at March 1984 prices)*

	Magnox	1960s coal
Capital charges	1.37	0.46
Fuel	0.89	1.71
Other operating costs	0.34	0.21
Total cost	2.60	2.38

Source: CEGB (1985)

building the power stations, are calculated on a current cost accounting basis. They include allowances for interest during construction, anticipated costs of closure and demolition, and the 5 per cent real rate of return the government requires on nationalised industry investments. The fuel costs for the Magnox stations include allowances for the reprocessing and disposal of spent nuclear fuel. The other operating costs are mainly labour and maintenance.

Taking all the costs together, the coal-fired stations provide cheaper electricity than the Magnox stations, though the margin is not overwhelming. This is consistent with earlier estimates produced by MacKerron (1982) for the Electricity Consumers' Council and supports the argument by others, such as Sweet (1982) and the Committee for the Study of the Economics of Nuclear Electricity (1982), that nuclear power does not have an advantage if the costings are done on a proper basis. The averages shown here do however disguise a spread of costs for individual stations. The most successful of the Magnox stations – those with above-average load factors, or with lower capital charges because of lower construction costs – probably provide electricity as cheaply as their coal-fired counterparts; the worst are undoubtedly much more expensive.

These 'lifetime-to-date' estimates present a similar picture to the estimates for 1983/4, the most recent year for which CEGB figures are available: the coal stations had a cost advantage of 0.22 pence per kilowatt/hour during this single year. But in defence of the Magnox stations the CEGB anticipates that over the whole of their lives (that is up to the 1990s or beyond) they will provide power as cheaply as coal stations of the same vintage. This is partly because the CEGB assumes a

Nuclear power and the coal industry

large increase in real terms (that is, faster than inflation) in the price of coal, and partly because they assume that towards the end of their lives the coal stations will no longer be used to provide base-load power, so their fixed costs will be spread over a smaller volume of electricity. Against this view, it should be noted that there has been a persistent tendency for the cost of nuclear fuel to rise in real terms, whereas during the past two or three years and for the foreseeable future the price of coal has been stable or has fallen in real terms.

AGR v. 1970s coal

The second-generation British nuclear power stations are the advanced gas-cooled reactors, or AGRs. Initially four were ordered for the CEGB (Hinkley Point B, Dungeness B, Hartlepool and Heysham I) and one for the SSEB (Hunterston B). Construction of these started in the middle and late 1960s. Hinkley Point B and Hunterston B were finished in the late 1970s, but the remaining three were affected by spectacular delays and are only now being commissioned. Two further AGRs were ordered in the late 1970s, Heysham II (for CEGB) and Torness (for SSEB). These are due for completion in the late 1980s, and their construction is on schedule. The AGRs are much larger than the Magnox stations and they therefore make a much more important impact on the overall configuration of power-station capacity and electricity supply.

Table 10.2 shows a comparison between Hinkley Point B and the first phase of Drax, a coal-fired station completed at about the same time. The figures again come from the CEGB and have been calculated in the same way as in the comparison between the Magnox and coal stations. In other words, they refer to the generating costs over the whole of the power stations' lives up to March 1984, and they include an allowance for a 5 per cent real rate of return on the capital cost. Both stations are used to provide base-load electricity, so their load factors are the maximum achievable. The capital charges are higher for Hinkley Point B; the fuel costs are higher for Drax I. However, on balance the comparison again shows a modest cost advantage for the coal station.

Over the single year 1983/4 the picture is a little different. Because Hinkley Point B achieved a very good load factor during this year its generating costs were significantly lower (1.98 pence per kilowatt/hour compared with 2.42 for Drax I). Over the whole of the power stations' lives, the CEGB also anticipates a small advantage for Hinkley Point B. The same comments, though, apply to the CEGB's lifetime estimates as to the comparison between Magnox and the 1960s coal stations: they are based on assumptions that make coal-fired power stations appear much

Coal in context

Table 10.2 *Estimated generating costs: AGR v. 1970s coal-fired station pence per kilowatt/hour at March 1984 prices)*

	AGR (Hinkley Point B)	1970s coal (Drax I)
Capital charges	1.37	0.47
Fuel	0.93	1.81
Other operating costs	0.34	0.18
Total cost	2.64	2.46

Source: CEGB (1985).

more expensive in the future. Also, at least three of the remaining AGRs (the ones so long delayed) are likely to generate electricity more expensively than Hinkley Point B because their capital costs have been so much greater.

PWR v. modern coal

The CEGB now plans to abandon the AGR in favour of the pressurised water reactor (PWR), an American design. The proposed Sizewell B nuclear power station would be the first in Britain to use the PWR. An assessment of the comparative economics of Sizewell B and a modern coal-fired equivalent (basically using the proven technology of Drax II) is facilitated by the substantial volume of evidence presented at the Sizewell inquiry, particularly by the CEGB. However, it would be quite wrong to use the CEGB's figures without some important modifications.

Taking the Sizewell PWR first, there are two areas where the CEGB is probably being too optimistic. The first of these concerns the capital cost. The CEGB has no experience of building PWRs, so the best guide is probably the American experience. This suggests that a Westinghouse PWR, of the sort proposed at Sizewell, costs 2.3 times more than a US coal plant, in terms of dollars per kilowatt (Komanoff, 1981, 1982). The CEGB, in contrast, projects a capital-cost ratio of only 1.6. Since the CEGB has recent experience of building coal-fired stations, it is likely that the capital cost estimates of a coal station are reliable and the capital cost of the PWR has been underestimated. The second area of optimism in the CEGB estimates concerns the PWR's load factor, estimated to be 64 per cent. Comparisons with the 4-loop Westinghouse reactors (of the

230

same design as Sizewell B) in the United States suggest a 'settled-down' load factor of 58 per cent (Komanoff, 1982).

So far as a modern coal-fired power station is concerned, the assumption that requires modification concerns coal prices. The CEGB assumes that the price of coal will rise by 1.7 per cent a year in real terms until the end of the century and 2 per cent a year in real terms thereafter. Not surprisingly, this has the effect of making coal appear an expensive source of power, especially by the second and third decades of the next century. This assumption about an escalating real price of coal was widely criticised at the Sizewell inquiry, and is at odds with recent events. For example, in 1983 the CEGB and NCB reached a joint understanding that the price of coal should fall in real terms, at least until October 1987. The *Medium Term Development Plan* of the electricity supply industry (Electricity Council, 1985) assumes the price of fossil fuel will remain constant in real terms until 1991/2, the furthest year ahead for which it makes an estimate. In addition, the price of coal on the world market, which the CEGB assumes will rise sharply and eventually pull up UK coal prices, remains depressed.

In table 10.3, which compares the costs of a PWR and a modern coal-fired station, the CEGB's assumptions have therefore been varied. The first column of figures shows the PWR's costs on CEGB assumptions. The second column presents revised estimates which bring the capital cost and load factor into line with US experience. The figures for the coal station assume coal prices that are stable in real terms (column 4) or increasing by 0.85 per cent p.a. (column 3), half the increase assumed by the CEGB. The table shows the annual operating costs in about the year 2000. A new nuclear or coal-fired station would not be completed until the mid-1990s, and would take a year or two to settle down, so by the year 2000 the stations would still be new and would be supplying base-load electricity to the grid. The figures for the PWR are for Sizewell, which is designed to produce 1,100 MW. For technical reasons a new coal-fired power station would be larger (probably 1,875 MW), so the comparison is made with a 'notional' coal station of the same capacity as Sizewell B, and the costs have been scaled down proportionately. This table also presents the information differently from tables 10.1 and 10.2. Here the total costs are shown in £m. This introduces a small complication, because although the power stations have the same capacity they would produce differing quantities of electricity because of differing load factors. The CEGB anticipates a 72 per cent load factor for a coal station, compared with 64 per cent for the PWR, so a coal station would save additional fuel (mainly coal) at other power stations. Likewise, if there is a shortfall in PWR performance, in line with US experience, more fuel

231

Coal in context

Table 10.3 *Estimated annual costs of a PWR and a modern coal-fired power station, c. year 2000 (£m, March 1985 prices)*

	PWR		Coal-fired station	
	CEGB estimates	Alternative estimates	Coal prices +0.85% p.a.	Coal prices stable
Fuel	43	39	179	153
Other operating costs	12	12	13	13
Capital charges	121	171	72	72
Fuel at other stations	0	15	−34	−31
Total cost	176	237	230	207

Source: adapted from Fothergill, Gudgin and Mason (1983).

will have to be burned in other power stations. The fuel savings and losses elsewhere in the CEGB system are therefore included in table 10.3.

The table shows that, as with earlier nuclear power stations, the costs of a PWR are mainly capital charges, whilst the costs of a coal station are mainly fuel. The balance of advantage, taking all costs together, depends very much on the assumptions that are used. On CEGB assumptions the PWR will be cheaper; on alternative assumptions it is more expensive. Since the estimated range for the PWR is £176–237 million, and for the coal station £207–230 million, there really isn't much to choose between the two on cost grounds alone. In fairness to the CEGB, though, one aspect of these costings should be highlighted. The figures relate to a fairly early period in the power stations' lives; a PWR might reasonably be expected to be operating until 2030, and a coal station a little longer. If coal prices do rise significantly and steadily in real terms, as the CEGB anticipates, then in the later years of the power stations' lives the coal station will look increasingly uneconomic.

However, there are also economic considerations in the choice of power-station design that extend beyond the CEGB's balance sheet. In particular, coal and nuclear power stations have different implications for employment, not so much at the power stations themselves but for the industries and firms supplying the power stations. These have been examined by Fothergill, Gudgin and Mason (1983). Table 10.4 shows the estimated effects on employment of operating a coal-fired power station instead of a PWR, in about the year 2000.

Nuclear power and the coal industry

Table 10.4 *Estimated effects on employment of operating a modern coal-fired power station instead of a PWR, c. year 2000*

	Job gains	Job losses
Coal industry	6,400	
Railways	300	
Nuclear fuel production		300
Electricity industry	100	
Suppliers	2,400	
Rest of economy		1,500
Net effect	9,200	1,800

Source: Fothergill, Gudgin and Mason (1983).

The largest employment gain would be in the coal industry. A PWR such as the one proposed at Sizewell displaces roughly 2.7m tonnes a year of coal consumed by the CEGB. Thus, if a coal-fired power station were built instead, this extra coal would need to be produced (unless it were simply diverted from other potential markets). Mining this coal is estimated to require 6,400 workers. The precise magnitude of this job gain depends on trends in miners' productivity and on exactly which pits produce the coal. Here it is assumed the coal would come from relatively low productivity, marginal pits.

The other major job gain from operating a coal station instead of a PWR would be in firms supplying the coal industry. Very roughly, every five jobs in coal-mining support a further two jobs in related industries. There would also be a small job gain on the railways, for whom the movement of coal is a major part of the freight business. Offsetting these gains, it is estimated that there would be a small job loss in the rest of the economy, arising mainly because the higher capital charges associated with a PWR would not be available to finance further power-station construction, or (if reclaimed from the CEGB by the Exchequer) to finance tax cuts. On balance, however, operating a coal-fired power station rather than a PWR would create more jobs than it would destroy.

Why nuclear power?

So is nuclear power cheaper than coal? The answer from the three comparisons – dealing with Magnox, the AGR and the PWR – is 'probably not'. The very best of the existing nuclear power stations may

233

generate electricity as cheaply as their coal-fired counterparts, but they are the exceptions rather than the rule. Nuclear power in the past has not been 'a good buy'. Looking to the future, if the CEGB's assumptions about Sizewell B prove correct, nuclear power may be cheaper, but the assumptions are highly dubious. And in addition a PWR offers the prospect of less employment, directly and indirectly, than a coal-fired power station. What can certainly be concluded is that nuclear power does not have the massive cost advantage that it was once thought to have, or that its ardent proponents still believe it has.

If nuclear power is not so much cheaper, this raises some interesting questions. Why have governments and the electricity supply industry been so enthusiastic for nuclear power in the past, and why does the CEGB still favour a major nuclear programme?

So far as the CEGB is concerned, the prominence of scientists and engineers at all levels has probably been influential. Many technologists have a faith in the potential of science and technical progress, to the neglect of wider economic, social and environmental considerations. Nuclear power is at the leading edge of technology, and therefore seen as good; coal-fired technology is rather traditional, even nineteenth-century, and therefore bad. Associated with these views is the feeling that nuclear power can always be made more economic next time round, even if it has not been terribly cheap in the past. The frequent changes in nuclear power station design, especially the changes from Magnox to AGR and then to PWR, fuel the view that future achievements can be more impressive than those of the past.

From the government's point of view there are probably a number of forces at work. The formidable strength of the nuclear lobby, backed by major industrial companies seeking contracts, is well documented (see for example Sweet, 1985). This lobby also works to persuade the higher echelons of the CEGB and SSEB. There are also strategic considerations which may override economic matters at the highest level. One is the need, especially on the part of Conservative governments, to weaken the bargaining power of the National Union of Mineworkers by providing a major alternative source of electricity generation to coal. During the 1984/5 miners' strike, for example, the nuclear power stations were operated flat out, some achieving unprecedented outputs, in order to reduce the electricity industry's use of coal. A second strategic consideration is that a by-product of spent nuclear fuel is plutonium, the material from which nuclear bombs are made. It is perhaps worth remembering, in this context, that Calder Hall (part of the Sellafield site operated by British Nuclear Fuels Ltd) was in 1956 hailed as 'the world's first nuclear power station', but in reality it has been operated to maximise the output of plutonium, not electricity. Chapelcross nuclear 'power station' in Scotland is run in the same way. After reprocessing, the spent fuel from the reactors run by the CEGB and SSEB also provides weapons-grade plutonium.

The point here is not to evaluate or comment upon these different arguments, but simply to note that the momentum behind the nuclear power programme is not just sustained by economic considerations. Indeed, on the basis of the evidence on comparative costs it appears to have been sustained in spite of the economic considerations.

Forecasts of electricity demand

So far we have discussed the relative costs and nuclear power. Now we move on to examine the quantities of coal that are likely to be demanded, depending on the scale of the nuclear programme.

The starting point must be the demand for electricity; this in turn depends closely on the level and structure of economic growth. The Department of Energy no longer publishes forecasts of economic growth or energy demand. However, as part of its submission to the Sizewell inquiry the CEGB prepared detailed forecasts of electricity demand that can form the basis of meaningful estimates (CEGB, 1982). The CEGB presented figures for electricity demand under four scenarios of national economic growth:

Scenario A   High growth in GDP (2.6 per cent p.a.) based on services
Scenario B   High growth in GDP (2.6 per cent p.a.) based on manufacturing
Scenario C   Medium growth in GDP (1.0 per cent p.a.)
Scenario E   Unstable low growth in GDP (−0.4 per cent p.a.)

Demand for electricity under each of these scenarios was calculated sector by sector, and took account of changing efficiencies in the use of energy and relative fuel prices. The four scenarios imply divergent requirements by 2010, ranging from 80m to 182m tonnes of coal equivalent, compared with 96m tonnes in 1983/4. Even for 1995, the projections range from 85m to 138m tonnes. These projections reveal the uncertainty inherent in energy forecasting. However, the CEGB admits that scenarios A, B and E are all extreme cases. The realistic range for energy demand is probably somewhat narrower. This chapter therefore uses three more conservative scenarios derived from the CEGB projections:

Coal in context

Scenario A/B

This is an average of the CEGB's scenarios A and B, and represents high growth (by recent standards) with some expansion in both services and manufacturing. It probably represents the best which a Labour government might hope to achieve if it were to stay in office for a long period and if its policies were to be successful in improving the performance of the UK economy. In this scenario the CEGB's projections for 1990 have been revised down a little, because economic growth has already slipped below the trend for scenario A/B and because a Labour government is unlikely before late 1987 or 1988.

Scenario C

This is the CEGB's own forecast, and the one which it considers most likely and therefore uses in its central estimates in evaluating Sizewell B. The Electricity Council's current forecasts for 1991/2 are a little below scenario C.

Scenario F

This implies that CEGB overall fuel requirements will remain stable at the 1983/4 level. This represents lower demand than scenario C, but rather higher than in the CEGB's scenario E. There is some support for the view that the CEGB's annual requirements will stay roughly the same. In the first four years of the 1970s they averaged 97.5m tonnes, but this slipped to an average of 95.3m tonnes in the first four years of the 1980s, despite a small growth in GDP in the intervening period. In addition, the Treasury is increasingly using electricity price rises to boost CEGB profits and thus raise more revenue for itself – a sort of 'back-door' taxation. Large electricity price rises dampen demand and encourage a switch to other fuels.

The projected overall fuel requirements of the CEGB under each of these scenarios are shown in table 10.5.

The nuclear power programme

What we need to establish is the share of CEGB fuel requirements that will be met by nuclear power. In 1983/4, nuclear power provided 9 per cent of the CEGB's capacity and 14 per cent of the electricity generated; coal stations provided 64 per cent of capacity and 81 per cent of electricity; oil-fired stations, expensive to run and thus operated only for short periods, provided most of the remainder.

236

Table 10.5 *Projected CEGB overall fuel requirements*
(million tonnes of coal equivalent per year)

	1983/4 actual	1990	1995	2000	2005	2010
Scenario A/B	96	113	130	140	148	155
Scenario C	96	105	112	115	117	119
Scenario F	96	96	96	96	96	96

Source: adapted from CEGB (1982).

Much of the nuclear capacity that will be operating during the next two to three decades is already installed or committed. The CEGB's existing Magnox and AGR stations provided power equivalent to 14m tonnes of coal in 1983/4. By 1990, with Hartlepool, Heysham I and Dungeness B fully operational and Heysham II coming on stream, the CEGB estimates that this will have risen to 19m tonnes. The existing nuclear power stations are also likely to remain operational for longer than was once supposed. In their evidence at the Sizewell inquiry, the CEGB gave them a design life of 25 years (except for Wylfa at 20 years), in which case the Magnox station would have to be decommissioned in the late 1980s and 1990s. However, because the running costs of nuclear stations are substantially below those of coal and oil stations, the CEGB has a financial incentive to keep them operational as long as possible, even if this requires capital expenditure to replace some components. Already the CEGB has revised the planned lives of the Magnox stations to 30 years and it would be surprising if this were not eventually to be extended again. In estimating the supply of electricity from nuclear power stations it is therefore prudent to assume that existing stations will have lives of 35 years. The Magnox stations, in other words, would mostly not be decommissioned until around the turn of the century or shortly after.

The first line in table 10.6 shows the energy supplied by the nuclear power stations already completed or under construction. It assumes no further nuclear construction after Heysham II (not even Sizewell B), a 35-year design life, and a modest load factor of 50 per cent for the last ten years of the power stations' lives. It also assumes that the nuclear stations continue to be used to the limits of their availability, to provide base-load electricity, because of their relatively low marginal costs. The figures show that even if there is no new nuclear construction, nuclear power would still meet a significant proportion of the CEGB's needs into the early part of the next century. In 2010, the quantity of electricity supplied

237

Coal in context

Table 10.6 *Alternative CEGB nuclear power programmes*
(million tonnes of coal equivalent per year)

	1983/4 actual	1990	1995	2000	2005	2010
No new nuclear	14	19	19	15	12	12
Minimal nuclear	14	19	22	29	26	26
Major nuclear	14	19	26	37	51	70

Source: adapted from CEGB (1982).

by nuclear stations would be only slightly less than in 1983/4. The CEGB does of course plan further nuclear power stations, beginning with Sizewell B. The electricity supply industry's (ESI) medium-term development plan states that 'if the result [of the Sizewell inquiry] is favourable then the ESI would wish to maximise economic benefit from the introduction of PWR technology by proceeding as rapidly as possible with a "minimum family" of 4 or 5 PWRs to a replicated design' (Electricity Council, 1985).

The 'minimal' nuclear programme, shown in the second line of table 10.6, assumes that a programme of five PWRs goes ahead, and that these are commissioned during the 1990s. Thereafter no further nuclear construction is assumed. The effect of this minimal programme is to double the power from nuclear stations, to 29m tonnes of coal equivalent in the year 2000. A high level would be sustained into the first decade of the next century, even as the Magnox stations were decommissioned. Nevertheless, the CEGB clearly has ambitions for a larger programme. It argues that it is economic to build PWRs even if this leads to the premature retirement of existing, serviceable coal- and oil-fired stations. The logic of this is that the only important constraints it would impose on a nuclear programme would be its ability to finance and construct the new stations. At the Sizewell inquiry the CEGB outlined a 'high nuclear background' against which it evaluated the PWR. This represented the programme with which it ideally would have liked to proceed. Under scenario C, it implies the commissioning of 12 PWRs by the year 2000, and a further 27 between 2000 and 2010. The CEGB also outlined a 'medium nuclear background', under which further nuclear construction would be limited to capacity need, building up nuclear capacity to an arbitrary minimum level of 40 per cent of total capacity. Under scenario C, this implies 9 PWRs by the year 2000, and an additional 14 during the following decade.

238

Nuclear power and the coal industry

The slippage in timing caused by the Sizewell inquiry means that the 'high nuclear background' is now unlikely, at least within the time-scale originally suggested. But on past form the CEGB and the government do not wait for capacity need to emerge before they order new nuclear stations. The 'medium nuclear background' may therefore err on the conservative side.

The 'major' nuclear programme, shown in the third line of table 10.6, assumes a programme mid-way between the CEGB's high and medium nuclear backgrounds under scenario C. This would involve the completion of 10 or 11 PWRs by 2000, and a total of 31 by 2010. Given the present preferences of the electricity supply industry and the government, such a programme must be regarded as realistic. It would lead to a massive increase in nuclear power, from 14m tonnes of coal equivalent in 1983/4 to 37m tonnes in 2000, and 70m tonnes in 2010.

Other sources of power

The remaining issue which needs to be clarified is the role of sources of electricity other than coal and nuclear power. These are mostly oil at present, renewables (tidal power, wind power etc.) in the early years of the next century, and international connections.

The CEGB's oil-fired stations are used only to meet peak demand, and this is likely to remain so because of the high price of oil. They do not represent a threat to the demand for coal, except in that they can be used to replace coal during exceptional circumstances such as in 1984 and 1985. No new oil-fired stations are likely. The CEGB takes the view that renewable energy sources may be technically and economically viable by the turn of the century, and would justify modest investment. Like nuclear power stations, renewable-energy installations would be cheap to run and would therefore be used to the limits of their availability.

International connections are set to play an increasing role. The CEGB and the French EDF are just completing a cross-channel link. The original intention was that it would take electricity in both directions to meet peak demands in the two countries (which occur at different times). However, the French have invested very heavily in nuclear power and because of the down-turn in economic growth they now find themselves with a massive surplus of generating capacity. Since this is mostly nuclear the marginal cost is low, and they have every incentive to sell electricity abroad at a highly competitive price. If the CEGB treats the cross-channel link as just another source of electricity, the inevitable consequence will be that it will be used to supply base-load electricity to the UK. The flow will be all one way.

Coal in context

The significance of the channel link should not be underestimated. At 2000 MW it is equivalent to almost two Sizewell Bs, and operated on base-load it could provide the same electrical power as nearly 8.5m tonnes a year of coal. If the link is used in this way, if it displaces coal burned by the CEGB, and if the coal is thus not produced, it could destroy around 12,000 mining jobs at present average productivity levels, or perhaps 25,000 mining jobs if the coal would have come from low-productivity, marginal pits.

It is likely that the channel link will indeed be used to supply base-load power to the UK, but not all the electricity will be at the expense of UK coal. The link will obviate the need to use some oil-fired stations, and it would in any case have saved some coal (by allowing the CEGB system to operate more efficiently) even if it had been used as originally planned. A plausible assumption is that it will displace some 6m tonnes of coal more than was originally anticipated, until perhaps the year 2000, after which the surplus of French generating capacity may not be so marked. The CEGB's figures, presented at Sizewell, on the use of sources other than coal and nuclear power, need modification to allow for this.

The CEGB's consumption of coal

We are now able to estimate the CEGB's future consumption of coal. Full details of the CEGB's estimated fuel usage, including sources other than coal and nuclear power, are presented in the appendix. Table 10.7 deals specifically with coal. This is a particularly important table because it demonstrates the interrelationship between coal and nuclear power.

The first conclusion to be drawn from table 10.7 is that in the short and medium term the CEGB's use of coal is largely unaffected by decisions about further nuclear power stations. At most, by 1995 the choice of nuclear strategy might make a difference of 5m tonnes to coal consumption, and in 1990 it would have no impact at all. The reason is simply that nuclear power stations take a long time to build, so even stations ordered in the near future would only just be being completed by the mid-1990s. The CEGB's nuclear capacity until then is fixed by decisions that have already been taken.

The second conclusion is that what does affect the CEGB's consumption of coal during the next ten years is the rate of economic growth. Assuming no new nuclear stations are ordered, the CEGB's consumption in 1995 could vary from 67m tonnes (under scenario F, low growth) to 93m tonnes (under scenario A/B, high growth).

The third conclusion, looking further ahead, is that there is a major conflict between coal and nuclear power. The choice of nuclear strategy

Nuclear power and the coal industry

Table 10.7 *Estimated CEGB demand for coal*
(million tonnes per year)

	1983/4 actual	1990	1995	2000	2005	2010
Scenario A/B						
No new nuclear	77	82	93	107	126	130
Minimal nuclear	77	82	92	96	116	122
Major nuclear	77	82	88	88	91	78
Scenario C						
No new nuclear	77	77	81	84	97	98
Minimal nuclear	77	77	79	75	87	89
Major nuclear	77	77	77	67	62	45
Scenario F						
No new nuclear	77	68	67	69	76	75
Minimal nuclear	77	68	66	59	66	66
Major nuclear	77	68	64	51	41	22

Source: author's estimates adapted from CEGB (1982).

could make up to 20m tonnes difference to the demand for coal by the year 2000, and 50m tonnes difference by 2010. These are enormous quantities, the latter equalling roughly half the entire present output of the UK coal industry.

Fourthly, there may be scope for modest increase in the CEGB's use of coal if the economy follows the growth trajectory implied by scenarios A/B or C, but only if the scale of any future nuclear programme is kept to a minimum. If a major programme of nuclear power-station construction goes ahead, even on these more optimistic assumptions about economic growth, the CEGB's use of coal would rise a little until the 1990s but then fall back to present levels (under scenario A/B) or be almost halved in fifteen years from the mid-1990s onwards (under scenario C).

Fifthly, if the CEGB's overall fuel requirements remain stagnant, as implied by scenario F, any nuclear power-station construction will lead to a reduction in the CEGB's existing consumption of coal. Indeed, even if there is a moratorium on nuclear power-station orders, the CEGB's consumption will slip by about 9m tonnes a year by the end of the decade simply because of the completion of existing nuclear stations. If stagnant CEGB fuel requirements are combined with a major nuclear programme, CEGB coal usage would plummet to almost 20m tonnes a year by 2010 – barely a quarter of the present consumption.

Coal in context

Table 10.8 *Principal SSEB power stations*

	Capacity MW	Type	Date of commissioning
Kincardine	400	Coal	1962
Hunterston A	300	Magnox	1964
Cockenzie	1,200	Coal	1967
Longannet	2,400	Coal	1970
Hunterston B	1,320	AGR	1976
Inverkip	1,980	Oil	1976
Torness	1,320	AGR	(1987)

Source: SSEB.

Scotland

The preceding analysis has concerned the CEGB, which supplies electricity in England and Wales. The SSEB, which supplies most of Scotland, is worth examining separately, partly because there is no evidence comparable with that provided by the CEGB for the Sizewell inquiry and partly because the SSEB system is smaller and simpler.

The dominant feature of the SSEB is its chronic over-capacity. The principal SSEB power stations are listed in table 10.8. They include a Magnox station (Hunterston A), an AGR (Hunterston B), and a further AGR (Torness) due for completion in 1987. When this station comes into operation the SSEB will have a capacity of 9,000 MW, compared with the highest recorded peak demand on the SSEB system of 4,730 MW. The three nuclear stations, with a combined capacity of 2,940 MW, will be adequate to supply almost the whole of Scotland's base-load electricity requirements, and will undoubtedly be used for this purpose, leaving the coal stations to supply only peak demand and to cover for breakdowns and planned maintenance at the nuclear stations. The Torness AGR will operate directly at the expense of the Scottish coal-fired stations, especially as the Inverkip oil-fired station is already mothballed. If its load factor lives up to expectations, it will displace about 3m tonnes a year of Scottish coal. This reduction in SSEB demand for coal in the late 1980s is not the result of decisions that are being taken now, it must be stressed, but is built in to decisions that have already been taken.

There is an alternative. This is that the SSEB sells its surplus electricity to the CEGB, and since Longannet is a relatively new, efficient coal-fired station this makes sense. But if the SSEB and CEGB do follow this course the consequence will be an equivalent reduction in the CEGB's own fuel requirements, mainly for coal. In effect, the construction of the Torness AGR creates a zero-sum game for the coal industry: if the same quantity of coal continues to be burned in the Scottish power stations, less will be burned in those south of the border. No allowance for this potential reduction in CEGB usage of coal has been included in the estimates shown earlier in table 10.7.

The crisis ahead

When the CEGB and SSEB demands for coal are combined, what becomes apparent is that nuclear power presents the coal industry with a crisis in 1987 or 1988, as well as a long-term threat. By then, Torness and the four English AGRs under construction will be in service, and the channel link will be supplying large quantities of French nuclear electricity. Also, any growth in the national economy cannot be expected to have raised the electricity industry's overall fuel requirements very much above present levels. The result, in all three scenarios of national economic growth, is that the consumption of power station coal will fall by 1988. Table 10.9 illustrates this point. Scenario C indicates a fall of 7m tonnes a year, to about 74m tonnes, but the reduction may be somewhat greater because scenario C is a little more optimistic than the Electricity Council's present medium-term forecast. If the demand for electricity does not grow as projected by scenario C or the Electricity Council, a reduction in coal-burn of up to 12m tonnes is likely by 1988.

The demand for coal for power station stocks will compound the problem. Following the end of the miners' strike, the CEGB and SSEB can be expected to rebuild their stocks to something approaching pre-strike levels, and during 1985 and 1986 this can be expected to inflate the demand for coal by as much as 10m tonnes a year. But by 1987 or 1988 the stocks will have been rebuilt, and this source of demand for coal will fall away. Looking ahead to 1988, therefore, the total fall in the demand for power station coal may be as much as 20m tonnes a year. Thereafter the consumption for power station coal can be expected to increase for a few years if there is growth in the national economy and in electricity demand, as no further nuclear stations would be completed until well into the 1990s. However, the likely fall in demand in the late 1980s represents nearly 20 per cent of the entire annual output of the coal industry.

Coal in context

Table 10.9 *Combined CEGB and SSEB consumption of coal (million tonnes)*

	1983/4 actual	1988 projected
Scenario A/B	81	77
Scenario C	81	74
Scenario F	81	69

Source: Author's estimates.

The scope for increasing coal consumption

It is clear that the scale of existing and possible future nuclear-power programmes impinge adversely on the demand for coal. But, for a given level of electricity demand and a given nuclear programme, what flexibility is there still for increasing the electricity supply industry's consumption of coal? The following four possibilities are worth considering.

Conversion from oil to coal

The first is the proposal, often put forward, to convert oil-fired stations to coal. The conversion of parts of the Isle of Grain power station has been considered by the CEGB but recently rejected as uneconomic, though it is technically quite feasible. From the point of view of the coal industry this option is not as attractive as it first appears. The problem is that it might save as much coal as oil. The oil-fired stations are at present regarded as too expensive to run except to meet peak demand, but a newly converted station burning coal would probably be as efficient as the existing big coal stations and thus would be used to supply base-load electricity. In doing so it would displace other power stations, most of which burn coal. Moreover, very little oil is burned anyway by the CEGB and SSEB. Under scenario C, with no further nuclear power stations, the CEGB anticipates burning only 3m tonnes of oil in 1990, 7m tonnes in 2000, and none at all by 2010. Not all oil-fired capacity is likely to be suitable for conversion to coal, so the potential for burning additional coal is strictly limited.

Operating lives of nuclear stations

A second possibility is the early closure of existing nuclear power stations. As explained earlier, for economic reasons the electricity supply industry will want to keep these operational for as long as possible. The

244

consumption of coal could be increased by ensuring that this does not happen, and that the stations are closed at the end of their original design lives. This might be politically defensible on safety and environmental grounds, especially as the Magnox stations fall well short of the engineering standards demanded of new nuclear power stations, and there may be unknown and unpredictable dangers in keeping them going so long. Again, however, the impact on coal consumption would be strictly limited. The stations affected would be the Magnox – the AGRs are designed to operate well into the next century – and they are relatively small. If they were closed from the late 1980s onwards, as originally planned, coal consumption would rise by only perhaps 3m tonnes a year in the 1990s, and if no coal-fired replacement were built at least part of the shortfall in electricity production would be met by existing oil-fired stations.

The more drastic policy of closing the nuclear stations before the end of their original design lives could not be implemented quickly. The problem is that their immediate closure would leave the CEGB and SSEB short of capacity to meet peak demand: the big AGRs in particular will comprise some 13 per cent of total generating capacity by the late 1980s. Sufficient alternative generating capacity would have to be completed first, and this could not be in service before the mid-1990s.

Demotion of nuclear stations

The third possibility for increasing coal consumption would be a demotion of the nuclear stations from their position as providers of base-load electricity. They could be closed all summer, just as many coal- and oil-fired stations are now, and brought into operation only to meet peak demand in winter. They would be replaced, on base-load, by existing coal-fired power stations. Potentially, this could cut the quantity of electricity supplied by nuclear power by perhaps 60 per cent, and allow a big increase in coal consumption – possibly 15m tonnes in the early 1990s. This policy could also be implemented more or less immediately, and even now would be associated with an increase in coal consumption of around 10m tonnes a year.

The trouble with this proposal is that it would overturn the main principle by which the CEGB and SSEB organise electricity generation, namely that the power stations with the lowest marginal costs are always run first. The principle was overturned during the miners' strike, when expensive oil-fired stations were used instead of the coal stations, so there is a precedent. But it is a costly one. During the miners' strike this strategy cost the CEGB an extra £2bn. Nuclear stations do have lower running costs than coal stations (though their overall costs are no lower,

245

as demonstrated earlier), so to switch them off in favour of coal would add to the CEGB and SSEB's costs.

Assuming a coal price of £40 per tonne, the cost of using an extra 15m tonnes a year would be £600m. Other running costs (e.g. labour, maintenance) would be incurred at the coal stations, but would be offset by equivalent savings at the nuclear stations, and there would be savings in nuclear fuel costs. Assuming fuel costs per unit at the nuclear stations are only 45 per cent of those of the older coal-fired stations that would replace them – an assumption in line with the CEGB's own figures on generating costs – savings of fuel would total £270m a year. The net cost to the CEGB and SSEB of demoting the nuclear stations would thus be roughly £330m a year.

Channel link

The fourth possibility for increasing coal consumption concerns the channel link. If this were used as originally intended rather than to supply base-load power, coal consumption would be increased by around 6m tonnes a year. Again this would add to the CEGB's costs, because the French are likely to sell their electricity at well below the running cost of British coal-fired stations.

The exact cost of not using the link to provide base-load electricity depends on coal prices at the margin to the CEGB and on the price of French electricity, both of which are uncertain. Assuming a coal price of £40 per tonne, the cost of using an additional 6m tonnes would be £240m, plus perhaps £10m in other running costs. Assuming a French electricity price equivalent to three-quarters of the fuel cost of British coal stations (which is still higher than the marginal cost of UK nuclear power), the CEGB would save £180m by buying less electricity from France. On balance the net cost to the CEGB of this proposal would thus be around £70m a year.

Benefits to the coal industry and the Exchequer

The last two of these proposals – the demotion of the nuclear stations and restriction in the use of the channel link – offer the prospect of substantial increases in coal consumption in the second half of the 1980s, totalling 21m tonnes a year. The net cost to the CEGB and SSEB, on the assumptions outlined above, would be £400m a year.

Glyn's estimates of the costs of colliery closure (chapter 4) shows the benefits of keeping 21m tonnes of deep-mined capacity in operation. If the pits which would otherwise close are those with the highest costs, the closure of this capacity would mean the loss of 62 pits and 58,000 miners'

Nuclear power and the coal industry

jobs. Glyn also shows, based on 1983/4 costs and revenue, that the closure of 21m tonnes of high-cost capacity would reduce NCB losses by £362m a year, but would cost the government £907m a year in additional unemployment benefit and other costs. On balance, therefore, the financial cost of these proposals to the public sector works out like this: the CEGB, SSEB and NCB's profits would be reduced by £762m a year (£400m+£362m); but the government would save £907m a year in unemployment benefit and related costs. The net gain to the public sector is £145m a year. All these figures are approximate, of course. What they illustrate, however, is that if there is the political will to plan the public sector as a whole, losses in one area can be more than offset by gains in another, and jobs can be protected. In this instance what is required is a political decision to override the traditional criteria by which the CEGB and SSEB operate their power stations. The proposals outlined above might protect nearly 60,000 miners' jobs, at no net cost to the Exchequer.

Conclusions

Four broad conclusions emerge from this chapter. First, taking both capital and running costs into consideration, nuclear power does not have a decisive cost advantage over coal as a source of electricity. In the past, most nuclear power stations have probably generated electricity more expensively than their coal-fired counterparts, and it remains highly questionable whether a new generation of nuclear power stations will perform any better. A coal-fired strategy need not therefore lead to higher electricity prices or be damaging to national efficiency and economic growth. Indeed, it may benefit the national economy and it will certainly protect more jobs.

Secondly, in the short and medium term – up to the mid-1980s – decisions about the future scale of the nuclear-power programme make little impact on the electricity-supply industry's demand for coal because of the very long lag between the ordering and completion of power stations. In so far as nuclear power impinges adversely on coal consumption during this period, especially during the coming two to three years, this is almost entirely because of decisions that have already been taken and power stations that are already under construction.

Thirdly, up to the mid-1990s the dominant influences on the consumption of power-station coal are the rate of growth of the national economy and the way the electricity industry's existing mix of coal and nuclear stations is operated. The faster the growth of the economy, the greater the demand for electricity and the greater the consumption of power-station coal. A demotion of the nuclear power stations from their present role as suppliers of base-load electricity, plus restrictions on the use of the channel link, would also lead to a swift and substantial increase in coal consumption which would protect miners' jobs at no net cost to the Exchequer.

Fourthly, in the long term there is a conflict between coal and nuclear power. The larger the nuclear programme, the smaller the electricity industry's consumption of coal. The ordering of further nuclear power stations is compatible with a significant increase in the demand for coal only if the national economy achieves a sustained high rate of growth and if the new nuclear programme is small in scale. A major nuclear programme of the sort preferred by the CEGB is incompatible with the growth of coal consumption, whatever the performance of the national economy, and if the economy grows only slowly, as during the last decade or so, a major programme would lead to a large reduction in coal consumption from the mid-1990s onwards. By 2010, the reduction in coal-burn would be so large that the coal industry as we know it today would effectively be destroyed.

A clear policy recommendation that emerges is that there should be an immediate moratorium on the ordering of new nuclear power stations. Except in the context of rapid national economic growth, anything more than a very small nuclear programme will remove the scope for increasing coal consumption. Moreover, at this point in time it is by no means clear that there will be more than a marginal increase in electricity demand, and thus in the utilities' fuel requirements, so there is a real risk that new nuclear power stations will lead to a reduction in the existing level of consumption of power-station coal. A moratorium on the ordering of nuclear power stations is an essential, strategic step to safeguard the long-term future of the coal industry.

But a moratorium does not solve the crisis, arising out of previous decisions about the nuclear programme, which the coal industry faces over the next few years. As explained, the only practical solution to this requires changes in the way existing coal and nuclear generating capacity is used. The strategic decisions of the CEGB and SSEB have major consequences for the coal industry, jobs and public spending, yet at present these decisions are taken on narrow commercial grounds without regard to the wider consequences. The government has a responsibility to ensure a co-ordinated use of energy resources, and to ensure that the decisions of one nationalised industry do not create dire problems for another, or for public finances. It should now exercise that responsibility to increase the use of coal at the expense of nuclear power, and to avoid the reduction in coal consumption that will otherwise inevitably occur.

Postscript

This chapter was written shortly after the miners' strike ended. It was originally prepared as a background paper for the NUM, and was subsequently published by the Coalfield Communities Campaign, a consortium of coalfield local authorities, as one of a series of working papers used to brief and lobby politicians and others. However, the chapter synthesises material and arguments that date from during and before the strike. In particular it draws on the author's work (with Graham Gudgin and Nigel Mason) in preparing the NUM's evidence to the Sizewell B nuclear power-station inquiry in 1983, and it also makes extensive use of the CEGB's evidence to that inquiry. Had the paper been written earlier, during the strike, its contents would not have been significantly different.

One item of substance has been changed since the original draft. In this version the comparisons between the Magnox, AGR and coal stations use CEGB data that became available in April 1985; the earlier version used figures that were revisions of those produced by MacKerron (1982). The new figures are more appropriate and reliable, but the essence of the argument in this part of the paper is not affected.

Appendix
Estimated CEGB fuel requirements
(million tonnes of coal equivalent per year)

	1983/4 actual	1990	1995	2000	2005	2010
		Scenario A/B				
No new nuclear						
Coal	77	82	93	107	126	130
Nuclear	14	19	19	15	12	12
Other	5	12	18	18	10	13
Total	96	113	130	140	148	155
Minimal nuclear						
Coal	77	82	92	96	116	122
Nuclear	14	19	22	29	26	26
Other	5	12	16	15	6	7
Total	96	113	130	140	148	155
Major nuclear						
Coal	77	82	88	88	91	78
Nuclear	14	19	26	37	51	70
Other	5	12	16	15	6	7
Total	96	113	130	140	148	155

Nuclear power and the coal industry

	1983/4 actual	1990	1995	2000	2005	2010
			Scenario C			
No new nuclear						
Coal	77	77	81	84	97	98
Nuclear	14	19	19	15	12	12
Other	5	9	12	16	8	9
Total	96	105	112	115	117	119
Minimal nuclear						
Coal	77	77	79	75	87	89
Nuclear	14	19	22	29	26	26
Other	5	9	11	11	4	4
Total	96	105	112	115	117	119
Major nuclear						
Coal	77	77	77	67	62	45
Nuclear	14	19	24	37	51	70
Other	5	9	11	11	4	4
Total	96	105	112	115	117	119
			Scenario F			
No new nuclear						
Coal	77	68	67	69	76	75
Nuclear	14	19	19	15	12	12
Other	5	9	10	12	8	9
Total	96	96	96	96	96	96
Minimal nuclear						
Coal	77	68	66	59	66	66
Nuclear	14	19	22	29	26	26
Other	5	9	8	8	4	4
Total	96	96	96	96	96	96
Major nuclear						
Coal	77	68	64	51	41	22
Nuclear	14	19	24	37	51	70
Other	5	9	8	8	4	4
Total	96	96	96	96	96	96

Coal in context

NOTE

Load factor is the electricity actually supplied by a power station over a year expressed as a percentage of the electricity that would have been supplied if the power station had operated at full power, 24 hours a day, for the whole year.

REFERENCES

Central Electricity Generating Board (1982), *Proof of Evidence to the Sizewell B Enquiry*, London: CEGB.
  (1983), *Analysis of Generation Costs*, London: CEGB.
  (1985), *Analysis of Generation Costs: 1983/4 Update*, London: CEGB.
Committee for the Study of the Economics of Nuclear Electricity (1982), *Nuclear Energy: The Real Costs*, Camelford: CSENE.
Electricity Council (1985), *Medium Term Development Plan 1985–92*.
Fothergill, S., G. Gudgin and N. Mason (1983), *The Economic Consequences of the Sizewell B Nuclear Power Station*, Department of Applied Economics, University of Cambridge.
Glyn, A. (1984), *The Economic Case Against Pit Closures*, Sheffield: NUM.
Komanoff, C. (1981), *Power Plant Cost Escalation*, New York: Komanoff Energy Associates.
  (1982), *The Westinghouse PWR in the United States: Cost and Performance History*, Paper presented at the Polytechnic of the South Bank, October 1982.
MacKerron, G. (1982), *Nuclear Power and the Economic Interests of Consumers*, Research Report, No. 6, London: Electricity Consumers' Council.
Monopolies and Mergers Commission (1981), *Central Electricity Generating Board*, London: HMSO.
Sweet, C. (1982), *The Costs of Nuclear Power*, Sheffield: Anti-Nuclear Campaign.
  (1985), 'Why Coal is Under Attack: Nuclear Powers in the Energy Establishment', in H. Beynon (ed.), *Digging Deeper*, London: Verso.

11

The restructuring of the British coal industry

A. BURNS, M. NEWBY and J. WINTERTON

Introduction

The crisis in the coal industry arose from a combination of a static market coupled with increased productivity. This productivity rise was achieved through concentration of the industry into larger units. Economies of scale have been achieved by linking existing pits together to create pit complexes (super pits) and by bringing new capacity on stream. New technology and changes in work organisation have been applied in these larger pits to reduce the manning levels and further increase their output. Both of these processes increase the output from the super pits and reduce the amount of coal needed from the other pits. This forms the background to the 1984 miners' strike over the closure of so-called 'uneconomic pits'.

Static UK demand for coal and the establishment of output targets in line with this demand translates productivity increases directly into job losses. The investment programme to increase productivity through reorganisation and new technology has been concentrated in what the NCB terms the 'central' coalfield (Yorkshire, Nottinghamshire and the rest of the East Midlands), which enjoys more favourable mining conditions. Areas like South Wales, where seams are heavily faulted, and Scotland, where seams are narrow and often steeply inclined, have not received the same attention.

Over the last ten years the NCB has introduced automation and has done this in a piecemeal fashion while denying the existence of an overall plan. In this way the strategy was obscured from the NUM until its existence was deduced from an analysis of papers written by NCB engineers in technical journals. Pits in the 'peripheral' areas face closure and suffer from a lack of investment, whereas miners in the 'central'

This is a revised and shortened version of an article which appeared in the *Cambridge Journal of Economics* (1985), vol. 9.

coalfield face job losses through automation and are experiencing adverse changes in work organisation. Because the overall NCB strategy was not perceived and because of these different area interests, the miners have responded differently in different areas. In South Wales there have been demands for greater investment to enable pits to reach the productivity levels of the 'central' coalfield, and job losses have been blamed on 'lack of investment', whereas in Yorkshire the problem is perceived more in terms of job losses arising out of the modernisation of existing collieries and the creation of super pits like Selby. These differences inhibited the development of an industry-wide strategy by the NUM as a response to NCB decisions.

Traditional mining involved hand-getting of coal by small groups of miners working their individual 'places'. Between the two world wars hand-getting was replaced by partially mechanised working of longwall faces, which entailed an extreme division of labour into three distinct shifts. Full mechanisation, with the introduction of the shearer loader between 1958 and 1968, brought significant gains in labour productivity. In seeking similar improvements through automation no new mining machinery has been developed, but NCB engineers have concentrated upon the organisation and control of production using existing mining techniques. The automation programme has been facilitated by the development of micro-electronics.

The Operational Research Executive (ORE) was established on nationalisation and played a major part in developing the longwall system of coal-getting. Ten years ago the NCB established a Central Planning Unit (CPU) alongside the ORE to deal with strategic issues for the industry; it consists of only six people, who draw on the services of other departments, in particular the ORE (Ormerod, 1983). The main function of the CPU has been to determine a twenty-year strategic plan for coal, based on the question 'Where can we invest in new capacity?' (*ibid.*). The other objectives of the CPU are to change the behaviour of the Coal Board from that of a bureaucracy to that of a '*rational actor*. Analyse the goals and objectives, setting out the options, calculating the cost and benefits of each option, and make the choice in order to give the maximum benefits according to agreed values, and to analyse and adapt to different value systems [*sic*]' (*ibid.*).

The CPU and the ORE developed the National Coal Board Strategic Model (Plackett *et al.*, 1982), which integrates market models with models of the NCB's production as a basis for planning. The mining model in essence constructs a supply curve for coal-giving cost versus tonnage, and gives this information broken down by pit, region or area;

the model is used to explore the cost implications of different types of capacity: 'political considerations also play a part' (*ibid.*).

The main analytical tool of the ORE and the CPU in developing their model has been systems theory (Beishon and Peters, 1972). When the systems approach was used to plan the introduction of power loading, the objectives included a form of work organisation that would promote group identity and autonomy; skill levels, job content and job control were all raised for face teams during this period (Trist and Bamforth, 1951). The automation phase, however, has seen a dramatic change in the kinds of objectives adopted by the NCB, with most of the 'human-relations' aspects playing a minor role in the design.

At the centre of the present dispute is a set of decisions taken by the NCB in the early seventies about its future organisation of coal mining. In this chapter we want to illustrate the way in which systems engineering has carried a set of objectives through into an actual design, and to show that the design is comprehensive in that it includes payment systems and work organisation as well as technical features. However, the particular design depends upon the specification of objectives; systems engineering can be used for rational economic planning and control and to incorporate objectives such as democracy into a design. Lastly, we want to draw out the way in which the NCB's approach led to the recent dispute and to look at the prospects for an effective union response.

Systems theory

There are two strands of systems theory, one developed in the West during the Second World War, and the other in the East out of Marxist economic theory and the needs of economic planning (Beer, 1974; Lange, 1970). Descriptions of the tools used in this kind of analysis can be found in Allen (1973, chapter 9), Lange (1969, 1970), and Beishon and Peters (1972).

Systems theory had been practised in a number of disciplines for many years without being formalised as a particular way of approaching complex problems: it is characterised by a holistic approach to problem areas, its emphasis on relating structure and function to goals or objectives, and by the prominence it gives to dynamics. The central problems in using systems theory are, however: (1) identifying the appropriate system boundary (plant, company, sector); and (2) explicitly determining the objectives. For example, the problems of a transport system can only be understood by examining road, rail and other forms of transport in an integrated manner. The objective of profitability for public transport would result in a very different system from one

255

designed to minimise road traffic in cities. Although the systems approach is found in economic analysis, most writers have been concerned with the dynamic behaviour of economies and with business cycles within given systems and not with the design of new systems. In most economic writings we see a rather mechanistic approach (Phillips, 1954) to working through the changes in the economic system and the emphasis on designing a system to meet objectives is largely lacking.

The change from systems theory to systems engineering represents a change of emphasis from analysis to design. Systems engineering entails defining goals or objectives for the system, translating these into objectives for sub-systems, and finally designing each element to meet its objectives. The power of this approach is that concrete realisations of the design are not sought until after this stage.

The major determinant of a design is thus the definition of the problem and the objectives to be met. The role of objectives is brought out starkly by the experience of Beer in developing an economic control system for Chile in 1970 with the needs of the people and an extension of democracy as objectives (Beer, 1975), and the experience of the miners who are suffering the application of systems theory to meet the objectives determined solely by the NCB.

Systems engineering in the coal industry

The NCB has adopted the systems approach and has specified its objectives clearly and explicitly; this provides an appropriate means of tackling the complexity of its operations. The complexity is dealt with by breaking the overall system into sub-systems, each with a clear specification of its objectives, inputs and outputs (in terms of labour, materials and information), and the type of control strategy to be used. The coal industry has passed through two of the three phases described by Babbage (1832): the *division of labour* into 'detail' tasks; *mechanisation*, the replacement of detail tasks by machines; and is now embarked on the third, of integrating the machinery into a single complex operation, that is *automation*. It is because the automation phase requires the integration of many tasks and the co-ordination of the activities of sub-systems that systems theory has been chosen as the appropriate tool.

An analysis of the use of systems engineering in the coal industry has been undertaken over the last five years by the Working Environment Research Group (WERG) based at the University of Bradford. A major report, *An Interim Assessment of MINOS* (Burns *et al.*, 1982) was prepared for, and presented to the NUM executive in December 1982, and has since been updated (Burns *et al.*, 1984b). Following the unsuccessful attempt at introducing face automation in the 1960s, it is clear that a major reassessment of the NCB's technical objectives was undertaken, and that this resulted in an increased cognisance being taken of the systems engineering approach. For example, Chandler, head of computer systems at the NCB's Mining Research and Development Establishment (MRDE), gave an early description of the proposed method of auto-mation (Chandler, 1978). This was one of a series of relevant papers published in the late 1970s when the existence of such a programme was being publicly denied (Hartley, 1979; Lefevre, 1977; Morris and Gray, 1977; Steiner and Hvidsten, 1978; Tregelles and Barham, 1979; Wolfen-den and Hartley, 1977). In the period 1981–3 trial systems had been devel-oped and evaluated (Cleary, 1981; Cooper, 1982; Fenelly, 1982; Horton, 1983; MRDE, 1981, 1983a, 1983b). Of recent publications, the Monopo-lies and Mergers Commission Report on the NCB (MMC, 1983) is the best illustration of the proposed future development of British coal-mining.

The NCB has determined the objectives of this automation phase of development without consulting the miners in any way. The objectives were derived from the historical problems of supervision (Goodrich, 1920; Heath, 1969) and a desire to repeat the productivity gains of the second phase of mechanisation. The systems approach directs the atten-tion of engineers not just to the machinery, but also to the whole structure of the industry and to the form of work organisation within the industry (Trist and Bamforth, 1951). The objectives that the Board chose were:

1. Increased labour productivity (Cooper, 1982; Horton, 1983).
2. Increased productivity of capital (Cooper, 1982; Horton, 1983).
3. Increased control over all aspects of the industry's operations (Chandler, 1978).

The first two objectives are clearly spelled out in papers by NCB engineers, and the size of the gains to be made were indicated by work-study findings that showed that coal-cutting machinery was running for only one-third of the potential cutting-time in an average shift. The Board identified the other two-thirds of the potential time as being equally split between 'lost time' (delays caused by the men) and 'operational and ancillary time' (delays caused by maintenance and repair). Thus the first two objectives were translated into:

1. A need to remove the 'lost time' by closer control of men.
2. A need to exert closer control over the machinery to remove 'operational and ancillary time'.

The strategy of control chosen was one which could be seen as redressing the balance and removing the miners' gains in terms of skill and work-place control that had been won or created in the second phase of mechanisation. Moreover, the Central Planning Unit was established

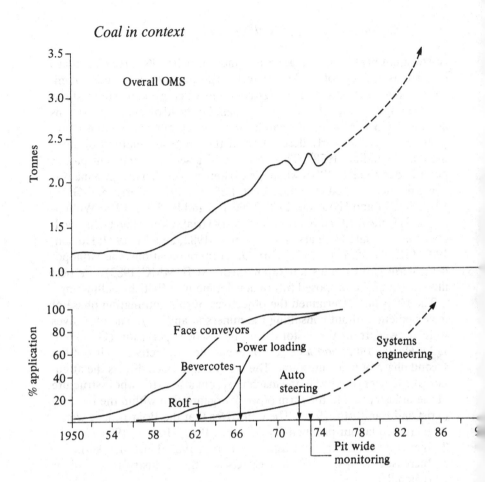

Fig. 11.1 Productivity growth.

in 1974, the year of the second major strike of the early seventies. Thus the NCB has chosen a control strategy designed to reduce human intervention: 'Normally and whenever possible, the control actions are taken automatically by the computer. When an operator needs to change the state of the plant he does so by using simple keyboard procedures' (Chandler, 1978).

Following the introduction of the Anderton shearer loader, production settled down to about 2.25 tonnes per manshift overall, and to about 7.75 tonnes per manshift at the face. Attempts to introduce stand-alone automation such as ROLF (remotely operated longwall face) and ELSIE (electronic signalling and indicating equipment) failed and the NCB undertook a review of the whole of its operations. Using a systems approach to mining, the NCB engineers concluded that no new techniques were required for winning, transportation, coal preparation, and driving roadways (MRDE, 1981), and identified the key problem as that of controlling all the equipment currently used in mining, both above and below ground. The NCB decided that the level of utilisation of the machinery was too low, machine downtime excessive, and machine reliability was inadequate. The gains expected from the application of systems engineering are shown in fig. 11.1, which also relates productivity growth to past technical changes. Recently there has been talk of overall output per manshift approaching 8 tonnes in the future (Dunn, 1984).

The systems approach focusses attention not on the detail of individual components but on the interaction of components and sub-systems, and on the relationship of the system to its environment (markets, transport, government policy). The NCB define the system not as a single mine, but a complex of mines and surface activities such as coal preparation. The Barnsley West Side Complex and the Selby development are groups of mines where the coal from all the mines is processed in a single coal-preparation plant (Capstick and Newby, 1983). The next stage is to determine the sub-systems and components that make up the overall system; these items may be defined as logical, physical or functional entities. Face activity and face machinery have been identified as distinct sub-systems, although both sub-systems may in fact be descriptions of the same physical activities but chosen to answer different questions. The NCB's definition of sub-systems is largely functional as is shown in fig. 11.2. Lastly, when the systems and components have been identified, their interactions have to be considered, that is, it is necessary to identify the inputs and outputs of each sub-system, and the way in which outputs from one sub-system will become inputs to another sub-system. The NCB engineers have identified information as a major output of all their sub-systems; coal, of course, is another output. The main input is the production plan for a mine or face; the secondary inputs are capital and labour.

The MINOS system

Systems engineering is concerned with attempting to alter the observed behaviour of the system by introducing a new factor, a control element. The NCB used this approach to design MINOS (mine operating system) in the mid-1970s (Chandler, 1978), a *highly centralized, hierarchically organised* system of *remote control and monitoring* in mines. Control engineering and computerised information systems are the main technical factors on which MINOS is based; both of these are information technologies which depend on the availability of cheap and reliable micro-electronics devices. Because systems engineering requires that the

Coal in context

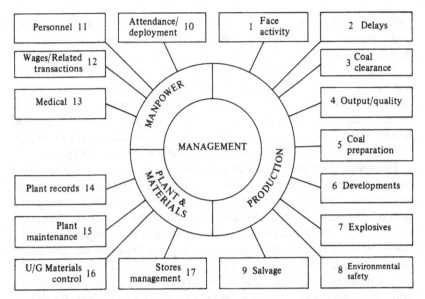

Fig. 11.2 Overview of remote control and monitoring applications.

objectives of the proposed system be clearly defined, the design of MINOS reflects the NCB's objectives, and other sets of objectives would have led to different designs. Where technical changes appear to be inappropriate, then it is not the technical features as such that should be challenged, but the objectives themselves. The objectives of the Board are, in detail:

  reduction in manpower
  acceleration of operations
  increase in machine availability
  reduction of repair and maintenance costs
  improvement in output quality
  improvement in monitoring and information
  control of processes that are difficult to monitor
  elimination of human error
  increase in safety levels and improvement of working conditions

Although MINOS does not significantly affect the way in which coal is mined, its effect on the industry and work organisation within the industry is as significant as any of the earlier changes in mining. MINOS consists of a number of sub-systems, each of which can be treated as a system in its own right (see fig. 11.3). Each of the sub-systems given in fig. 11.3 has been implemented independently of the overall MINOS system in many pits throughout the areas. The Barnsley West Side Complex is the first mine complex which will have the full MINOS

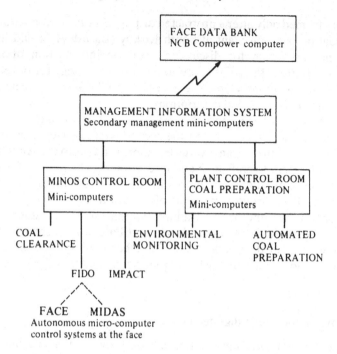

Fig. 11.3 MINOS hierarchy (Burns *et al.*, 1983, p. 13).

system, and the new Selby complex has been designed to use MINOS from the start.

The systems approach has had three effects on the structure of MINOS. First, the priority of increased output per shift has concentrated attention on coal transport and coal clearance and on coal preparation, just as in the earlier phases of development. Secondly, the overall system has been defined in terms of sub-systems with strict standards for data communication so that they can communicate with each other; this means that the sub-systems can be implemented in a modular, stand-alone fashion without requiring the whole system for their functioning. Lastly, the system is hierarchical and highly centralised, designed to remove control and decision-making from the lowest level of activity by bringing information to the highest levels of management.

The modular approach to the introduction of MINOS sub-systems has served to obscure the overall systems philosophy from the miners and the NUM. Throughout the piecemeal introduction of MINOS, the NCB has at no time involved the NUM or informed the union of its automation programme. Only where disputes over downgrading arise are cases taken to the Joint Committee on Grading and Technology. This committee, which was formed only after a protracted dispute over the introduction of a new coal preparation plant at South Kirkby (Barnsley), would have been a natural forum for discussion over the introduction of new technology. Rather, the NCB chose to conceal its strategy for development (Public Relations Department, 1983), while allowing technical publications to give detailed descriptions.

The confrontational approach is new to the NCB, where a tradition of consultation is more the norm. In the second phase of mechanisation, over 50 per cent of the design awards for improvements to the Anderton shearer loader went to craftsmen and face workers. The reasons for this apparent change of attitude are more difficult to assess, but the effect of the 1972 and 1974 disputes, the shift of control to the workers during mechanisation, and the need to adopt external practices rather than adapt internal methods, may each have contributed to the change. The sub-systems described in detail below have been chosen because they demonstrate most clearly the MINOS philosophy and the effects on the industry.

FIDO – face information digested online

It has already been noted that the Board had discovered that one-third of the available cutting-time in a shift was what it considered 'lost time'. FIDO is designed to remove this 'lost time'. If FIDO is successful then production per shift will be doubled and in a static market this implies that the number of working faces will be reduced. The reduction in the number of working faces is not the only consequence.

FIDO does not control any plant or machinery. Its purpose is to gather information about the activities at the face and report them to the control room, the control computer, and hence to the secondary management computer (see fig. 11.3). The sub-system consists of what the NCB engineers call 'general purpose monitoring outstations', which are standardised electronic interfaces allowing many kinds of information to be collected from transducers. In addition, the control-room operators can enter information into the FIDO sub-system when they recognise a delay and determine its nature by telephoning the face. The function of FIDO is to identify delays in coal-cutting, to note the delay, its cause and its duration. FIDO's primary purpose is thus one of *supervision* in order to reduce the 'lost time'; its effect is to increase machine-running time and managerial control, and to intensify work. Its nature is summed up by a Board engineer: 'The controller knows immediately the face is stopped; he does not have to rely on a message from underground ... People underground are aware of the resources that are available to the controller. They realise that he will not be fobbed off with imprecise information' (Cleary, 1981).

Technical developments and changes in work organisation are also related to alterations in the systems of payment. The area incentive schemes (AIS) have eased the introduction of automation just as the power-loading agreements eased the introduction of mechanisation (Winterton, 1981). FIDO's ability to identify delays and to record their duration is linked directly to the incentive scheme. Under the AIS, 'short delays', that is, delays of less than 20 minutes, are paid for by the men through loss of bonus, while 'long delays', unavoidable delays of more than 20 minutes, are paid for by the NCB at an average bonus rate, or contingency rate. FIDO is specifically designed to analyse delays and their causes so that where a 'long delay' is recorded it can be determined whether it is a 'split delay' made up of two delays of less than 20 minutes following each other (Cleary, 1981). Thus the face workers either accept the rate of work determined by management or suffer a loss of earnings for controlling the pace of work by creating breaks themselves. The AIS has incorporated the miners into the process of automation and has enabled the NCB through FIDO to achieve a level of supervision that it has never previously had over underground work; supervision and control have increased the intensity of work, removed the autonomy of the face team, and threatened jobs through increasing productivity.

IMPACT – in-built machine performance and condition testing

The full mechanisation of mining through power-loading increased the technical complexity of mining and created the need for an adequate number of skilled craftsmen to maintain and install the machinery used. By the 1970s 20 per cent of the work force were craftsmen. The NCB now wishes to reduce the number of craftsmen and to simplify the task of maintenance in line with the recommendations of the Monopolies and Mergers Commission Report (1983).

The objectives of the IMPACT sub-system derive from the overall objectives of the NCB. The primary objective is to increase machine running time. Just as FIDO, by imposing close supervision of men, increases management control and attempts to recover 'lost time', IMPACT monitors machines with the aim of reducing 'operational and ancillary time' (Cooper, 1982). A secondary objective of IMPACT is a reduction in the number of skilled electricians and fitters required to carry out installation, repair and maintenance (Horton, 1983). The installation of many of the MINOS sub-systems is carried out by the manufacturers with the use of sub-contract labour, thus denying NCB fitters and electricians the opportunity to gain knowledge of the systems or to obtain the skills necessary to maintain them.

The Board is setting out to achieve its objectives by introducing new and sophisticated testing equipment for use by fitters in diagnostic work and in standard inspections of machinery; the longer-term plan is to install the measuring equipment (transducers) in the machines themselves. By using this approach the NCB is able to evaluate the equipment before it is committed to a particular design. The information gathered is stored at present in desk-top computers, but will be fed directly into the MINOS system when the full IMPACT system is implemented (see fig. 11.3). This information is used to plan maintenance, to predict breakdowns, and to record and diagnose faults as they occur. The overall effect is one of deskilling, although a few craftsmen will receive training to upgrade their skills through the creation of specialist teams to implement and control IMPACT installations: 'Another recommendation made . . . was that work at a pit should be the responsibility of a specialist craftsmen team, totalling perhaps 1% to 2% of the available craftsmen, led by a Test Engineer' (Fennelly, 1982).

The IMPACT system is thus being designed within the overall framework of MINOS to meet the objectives of increased machine running time while at the same time reducing manning levels and deskilling for the majority of craftsmen. IMPACT not only reflects MINOS objectives, but also the MINOS philosophy in that it consists of an *information gathering system* and a *decision* and *control* system. The information will be passed upwards from the MINOS control computer to the secondary management computer. Further, in line with MINOS philosophy, many decisions are to be made automatically by the computer system rather than by human beings.

The information-gathering side has already been outlined. It now remains to draw out the implications of the decision and control elements. With existing work organisation, the installation and maintenance of machinery is carried out by colliery craftsmen who also carry out regular planned maintenance procedures and repairs when necessary. Because IMPACT records information about the state of machinery, and has available standard times for maintenance tasks, the planning of maintenance by management is simplified, allowing for a reduction of the number of craftsmen involved in planned maintenance. IMPACT has the ability to predict breakdowns, for example by noting temperature rises or excessive vibration, thereby eliminating some of the regular inspections and tests, while still avoiding breakdowns during cutting time. There are statutory requirements for the regular testing of many pieces of plant and equipment, but the use of sophisticated equipment simplifies this: a technique known as 'shock pulse measurement' has reduced the time for testing a main conveyor system from two full shifts to ten minutes. When breakdowns do occur, IMPACT can give a diagnosis and refer to the parts and personnel required to effect a repair. Thus IMPACT removes the central element of the fitter's skill, and all that is then required is manual dexterity.

The ability to forecast breakdowns and to diagnose faults when they occur also removes the need to have fitters and electricians on standby with each face team and throughout the pit; instead a smaller number can be on standby, being directed to deal with breakdowns from the MINOS control room. The IMPACT system not only performs the technical function of monitoring the condition of plant and machinery, but also increases the level of management control over the whole maintenance operation. The easy availability of information and increased control allow management to change the organisation of fitters' work by reducing the numbers required and by exercising more direct control over their activities.

The effects on skilled craftsmen are: a reduction in the numbers required; a deskilling and intensification of the remaining work for those outside the specialist teams; a loss of autonomy and scope for decision-making; and lastly, a move towards a homogeneous, or undifferentiated work force where repairs and maintenance are undertaken by whoever is available. 'The philosophy will bring about a change in the composition and deployment of colliery maintenance staff, with the need for a nucleus of technical craftsmen trained in condition monitoring techniques, supported by the face operative trained to carry out the small "nuisance breakdown" maintenance' (Horton, 1983).

MIDAS – machine information display and automation system

MIDAS again reflects the MINOS philosophy, in that it has both a monitoring and a control function. The control function is concerned with the vertical guidance of the shearer, that is, it ensures that the shearer drum is correctly positioned so that it does not cut into the roof or the floor. The monitoring function is very similar to that of IMPACT, and is identical in terms of the transducers used and the information gathered, but is logically different in terms of the system design. MIDAS monitors the condition of the shearer and feeds the information into a micro-processor in the machine for display locally; eventually the information will be passed to the MINOS control computer and from there into the management information system, thus shifting control to the surface.

The immediate effect of MIDAS is on the level of output: prototype systems have doubled output per shift (MRDE, 1983a). One such system recovered its £175,000 cost in 40 working days, or 92 shifts, with additional revenue of more than £800,000 attributable to that face. The significance of these remarkable increases in output is that the number of working faces is likely to be reduced given static demand for coal and the capacity limitations of coal-clearance systems.

Because MIDAS is part of the overall MINOS philosophy, it not only controls the vertical position of the machine but reports to the control room, and hence management, the distance travelled by the shearer, the rate of extraction, and many other details of conditions at the face. All of the information gathered is available at the touch of a button in management offices. Management thus not only remove skill and discretion through automation, but extend their knowledge of underground operations, and increase the level of supervision and control through the information-gathering capabilities of the system.

MIS – management information system

One of the main objectives of MINOS is to provide management with information on all aspects of the mining operation. Systems which provide such a comprehensive picture are found in many organisations and are usually referred to as MIS. The purpose of MIS is to provide managers with as much information as possible in the belief that this in itself will lead to increased management control and better decision-making (Burns, 1984).

Figure 11.3 shows a number of important MINOS sub-systems; these sub-systems are linked by a unidirectional information flow from the lowest level to the highest levels. The information is collated in the secondary management computer for colliery management and in the Face Data Bank for use at national level, as shown in fig. 11.4. The lowest levels of MINOS perform many monitoring functions through the general-purpose monitoring outstations, microcomputers in machines and through a whole range of transducers. The information collected at this lowest level is passed into a standard telecommunications network and thence to the central control computer in the control room. The control computer acts directly on many of these inputs and also passes summary information to the secondary management computer for permanent storage.

The MIS consists of a number of programs and software packages designed to allow managers to analyse summary data, to produce reports of productivity, absenteeism, shift performance and machine perform-

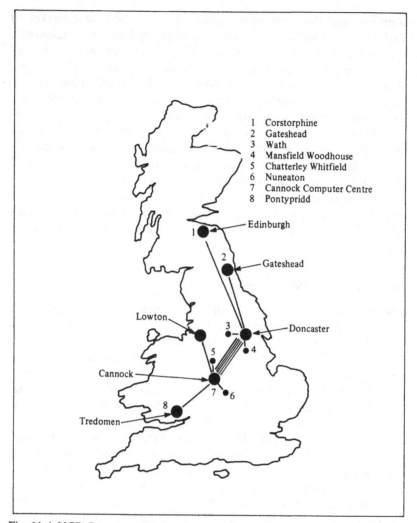

Fig. 11.4 NCB Compower National network, showing wide-band connections and distributed processing installations at Regional and Area laboratories for scientific control.

ance, as well as to make comparisons of these over time and between shift teams. The systematic collection of information is used to reduce the miners' job control and to increase management control. The traditional skills of the work force are incorporated into the computer system as a direct consequence of its design objectives. The use of closed-loop automatic control and computer-based fault diagnosis dramatically change the work organisation underground, and this,

267

combined with the effects of work intensification and a static market for coal, imply that MINOS will lead to enormous reductions in manpower.

It is the MIS that links the sub-systems together into the overall system, and therefore it is the key element in the NCB's strategy. However, the colliery level of the MIS is not the top of the hierarchy: it feeds its information into a national computer network that allows the NCB, and by implication government, to compare performance over time, between collieries, and between shifts, between faces, and between areas. Planning and control can thus be exercised rapidly and directly from the highest levels of management. The information collected is used by the CPU in its strategic model to construct scenarios based on the policy choices before management. So-called 'uneconomic pits' can be identified according to the criteria in force at any particular time, and the list can be revised at a moment's notice should different criteria be applied.

Implications of MINOS for jobs

The first major structural change in the nationalised industry came with the competition from cheap oil after Suez. Slum clearance, the 1956 Clean Air Act, the move to diesel and electric-rail traction, the contraction of the steel industry, and the increased thermal efficiency of steam-raising plant all contributed to the collapse of coal demand from 1958 to 1970. The shearer loader and longwall working were developed in order to reduce the price of coal relative to oil. The technical choice of the shearer loader as the main piece of coal-getting machinery meant that even at that stage the coalfields of Wales and Scotland were put at risk, because the shearer is best suited to the conditions of the Nottinghamshire and Yorkshire coalfields. The changes from nationalisation through the sixties were accompanied by the loss of 500,000 jobs, about 66 per cent of the work force, and the migration of miners from Scotland and the North-East to the pits of Nottinghamshire and Yorkshire (Allen, 1981). About half of the job loss can be attributed to declining demand and about half to technical changes (Burns *et al.*, 1982; MMC, 1983). Production was concentrated on the best faces at the biggest pits.

The present restructuring threatens the closure of entire *areas* as the NCB sees the need to contract its operations into large pit complexes with high labour productivity and to discard what it terms 'peripheral' areas. Since the Coal Industry Act was passed in 1980, requiring the NCB to become profitable by the end of the financial year 1983/4, estimates of the number of pits on the 'hit list' have increased and 40 pits have already closed. The Monopolies and Mergers Commission Report, published

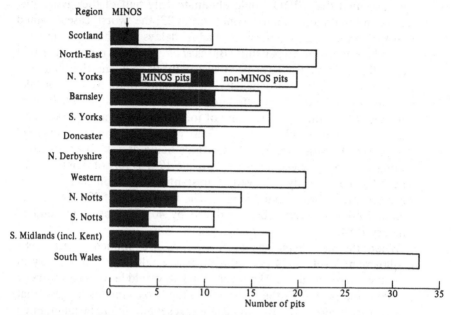

Fig. 11.5 Area differences in MINOS applications (Burns *et al.*, 1984b).

shortly after the Conservatives' 1983 election victory, defined 141 of the 198 pits then operating as unprofitable. The present exercise is aimed at eliminating 'high-cost' pits and concentrating production on the 'super pits'. As more pit complexes are created with their enormous productive capacity, more pits are defined as uneconomic and as surplus capacity. The MMC Report recommendation of independent accounting for NCB areas and CEGB demands for coal at pit-head prices are the first steps in preparing the industry for privatisation. This continued attempt to drive down costs may result in profitability while the industry is state owned and effectively in a monopoly position. However, if the CEGB is allowed to import coal, then the excess capacity in the world and the cheapness of open-cast coal are likely to make even the Selby Complex uncompetitive in price.

The plans for the coal industry, if carried through, will entail a massive job loss. The NCB has achieved a rate of implementation of new technology unparalleled in any other industry. There are currently about 80 instances of MINOS sub-systems in operation, only 5 of which are concerned with environmental monitoring. The majority of applications are aimed at increasing productivity. In the interim report we estimated that between 55 and 74 per cent of mining jobs were at risk. The 'best' case assumed that FIDO would eliminate only half of the 'avoidable' delays and that face manning would stay at 22; the 'worst' case assumed that FIDO would eliminate all 'avoidable' delays and that face manning would be reduced to 16 per shift (Burns *et al.*, 1982). It is now clear that MIDAS and IMPACT have been successful in reducing the 'unavoidable', or 'operational and ancillary' delays, something we did not take into account in our earlier estimates. If half of *both* types of delay is eliminated then the 'best' estimate of jobs at risk becomes 74 per cent, while the complete elimination of all 'avoidable' and 'unavoidable' delays would result in 83 per cent of jobs being at risk. It needs to be emphasised that the estimates refer to the 1981 levels of employment. The NCB has already achieved a substantial reduction in manpower since this project was begun in 1979. The base figure of 224,800 jobs in March 1981 had already been reduced by 40,496 jobs at the end of January 1984.

When the new estimates of job losses are applied to the 1981 employment levels, a 74 per cent job loss would leave an industry of 59,000 workers, while an 83 per cent job loss would leave an industry of 38,000 workers. Taking the mid-point of the two estimates suggests that the restructuring programme will enable present output to be maintained with 49,000 jobs.

The 'worst' case forecasts of our interim report were supported by the manning levels quoted at Selby. Further supporting evidence has emerged recently. In 1983 it was reported that because of MINOS coal clearance in North Derbyshire, 'the Area objective of halving the 874 men deployed to conveying systems is now well on the way toward being achieved' (Mining Department, 1983). The NCB has taken one worker off every face in the country over the last year. The advanced technology mining (ATM) programme, established in 1984, has raised average face OMS at Rawdon Colliery to 24.9 tonnes, with peak OMS at the face of 41.47 tonnes. The ATM programme was recently reviewed with the intention of bringing together separate developments: shield supports, electro-hydraulic support control, face alignment, and MIDAS, with the overall 'objective of a two-man faceline in 1987' (Mining Department, 1984).

In addition to job losses, the jobs that remain will be subject to greater managerial control, leading to work intensification and the attendant risk of increased occupational stress. Deskilling will arise from the incorporation of elements of the work of craftsmen and face workers into the MINOS software. Moreover, the physical working environment, particularly at the coal face, will deteriorate as increased machine-cutting time will expose miners to higher dust levels for longer.

Shortcomings of MINOS and alternatives

There are two major technical weaknesses of the concentration of production into pit complexes. The first is that all highly centralised operations are more vulnerable to any kind of disruption than decentralised ones. The second stems from the nature of the industry itself. The greatest single asset of the coal industry is the skill and knowledge of its workers. Automated manufacturing systems require a consistency and uniformity of inputs, particularly raw materials, because the machinery cannot cope with large variations in conditions. The working conditions in mines are notoriously unpredictable and it is only through the skill and experience of the work force that production continues unhindered. An industry with a reduced and unskilled work force and automated machinery is likely to run into serious problems in maintaining production.

The concentration of production in the 'central' coalfield not only brings technical problems, but has important strategic implications for future industrial development. There are currently reserves of about 300 years' supply of coal spread through all of the coalfields. Once mining operations have ceased and pits have closed the reserves have effectively been 'sterilised' (Schumacher, 1960), because it is impossible to return to areas where the geology has been affected by the collapse of workings. Thus the reserves of coal available to the nation may be reduced by giving precedence to short-term profitability. In a market with fluctuating demand the suppliers must have excess production capacity to cope with upward variations in demand. The NCB has decided to use the coal available on the world market as its buffer to cope with short-term increases in demand.

The NCB's present policy of concentrating production on the best seams was condemned by Schumacher (1960) when economic adviser to the NCB. Schumacher argued that the nation would be forced at some point to return to the sterilised reserves and sink new shafts or drifts at enormous expense. Thorne Colliery, closed in 1956 and now being reopened at a cost of over £200m, will not be producing coal until 1990. The present cost of energy may, as has been claimed, be reduced, but the future cost of energy will soar. Schumacher compared the closure of 'uneconomic' reserves with 'the spiteful burglar who does not merely pinch the valuables but in addition destroys everything he cannot take' (Schumacher, 1960). The cost of this strategy could be even higher if in the process of closing uneconomic pits supplies of higher-grade coal were later found to have distinct markets not served by the power-station coal that is the main product of the central coalfield.

271

Coal in context

Within the systems approach there are a large number of choices available; these could lead to alternative designs that would be far more advantageous to the miner. The structure adopted could be far less hierarchical, leaving more control with the people who are actually doing the work. In such a situation FIDO would act merely to co-ordinate the face activity with the rest of the mine. Only global information, for example, quantity of coal cut and total delay time, need leave the face and there would be no question of individuals being monitored. Another possibility is to use open-loop control systems wherever possible rather than the closed-loop systems described earlier. Open-loop control places the computer close to the work where it is used as an aid for the worker still controlling the process and making the key decisions.

The union response

Strategies and tactics of resistance have been slow to develop within the NUM compared with the rate at which the NCB have been able to install MINOS. The piecemeal introduction of MINOS sub-systems facilitated by its modular design has concealed the overall system design and the scale of automation from the union. A new automated coal preparation plant at South Kirkby (Barnsley), serving four neighbouring collieries, was blacked for two years by the NUM lodge, who succeeded in obtaining increased manning levels and upgrading of the jobs. The NCB rated the work on the lowest surface grade because of the improvement in physical conditions, and explicitly because the work demanded fewer skills. However, a single control-room operator on each shift is responsible for four TV monitors, four VDUs, the control console and 12 micro-computers running the plant (Clarke and Winterton, 1983). For a time the union was diverted from confronting the technology issue at national level by striving to maintain socially constructed skill labels for work that has been intentionally deskilled, rather than questioning the design objectives. In September 1982 the Working Environment Research Group presented its assessment of new technology in coalmining to the union side of the Grading and Technology Committee, and in December an interim report (Burns et al., 1982) was presented to the full executive committee. An educational programme was launched nationally and in several NUM areas throughout 1983.

Pressure for a new technology agreement grew out of a motion from South Kirkby, which was passed at Yorkshire Area Council and accepted at national conference last year. The union's policy on new technology now centres on a draft new technology agreement, which the NCB have so far refused to discuss. Mr R. Dunn, NCB Director General of Mining, described the technology agreement as 'not appropriate' (*Newsnight*, 16 February 1984). The agreement seeks to substitute shorter working time and earlier retirement for the job losses that will otherwise result from increased labour productivity. The agreement also seeks to prevent worker surveillance, maintain autonomy and improve working conditions. While little progress was made towards a technology agreement in formal negotiations, pressure built up as rank-and-file miners experienced the adverse effects of the new systems. During the overtime ban, begun in October in response to the Board's rejection of the 1983 pay claim, the miners' attention had shifted from the pay issue to the question of pit closures, in which the role of technology was acknowledged (Winterton and Rentoul, 1984). The recent strike, however, has diverted attention away from the *cause* of the dispute, increased productivity from restructuring and automation, to its *effect*, the closure of excess capacity.

At pits in the Doncaster area an agreement was secured that FIDO would not be used to resolve bonus disputes; this is only a temporary victory, since the information obtained from face monitoring is invaluable to management in establishing future standard tasks. One pit in Nottinghamshire is reported to have persuaded management to switch the FIDO system off entirely, which may also be a transient situation, while at another Nottinghamshire pit the NCB apparently investigated sabotage of the FIDO information network. Once the strike began in March, however, attention was diverted to the immediate issue of pit closures and the issues of control became obscured. Trade-unionism is by definition reactive or responsive so the control issues only emerge once management are implementing changes. While the NCB has been *determining* changes in the labour process at a higher level, these changes can only be perceived at the work-place and the tactics of resistance formulated by the union at branch level. A non-reactive alternative strategy for the industry has to be formulated at a higher level by the union.

There are important issues at stake for all trades-unionists. The rate of technical change is now so great that simply responding to management actions is doomed to failure. Unions must direct their attention to the strategic issues and managerial objectives in order to formulate their own set of objectives and plans. The NUM learned this lesson just in time. Such behaviour makes trade-union activity more political and more unacceptable to management and governments because it challenges their 'prerogative'. The response to union attempts to change a company's objectives are well illustrated by the struggles in Lucas Industries (Wainwright and Elliott, 1982). The NUM needs the support of trades-unionists in this struggle because, although the immediate dispute is

Coal in context

about job losses, the real fight is about the right of workers to play a part in determining their own future.

The union's alternative strategy, outlined in *Campaign for Coal*, was launched at the special delegate conference of October 1983 which decided upon the overtime ban. The strategy addresses political issues, like the recession, coal imports and nuclear energy, as well as issues more susceptible to collective bargaining within the industry. The internal issues concern pay, hours of work and technology. Central to the issue of technology is the definition of objectives that are distinct from those of the NCB.

The outcome of the miners' strike should have determined whether the coal industry is restructured for short-term financial objectives or long-term economic ones; whether the productivity gains resulting from the application of new technology are used to create unemployment and intensify work or to fund shorter working time and improved working conditions; and whether suitable alternative technologies are developed for the 'peripheral' areas.

Postscript

This chapter originated in research undertaken for the NUM into the application of new technology in the coal industry (Burns *et al.*, 1982, 1984). Criticisms of Braverman's (1974) notion of management omniscience (Wood, 1982) led us to investigate the ways in which managerial objectives become embodied in technical designs. We were particularly concerned to contrast the approaches to meeting similar objectives under mechanisation in the 1960s and automation in the 1980s.

Before the strike, the NUM accepted the implications of the interim report and incorporated material from this into the *Campaign for Coal* and the draft new technology agreement. The NCB responded to the publication of the interim report by denying the existence of an overall automation programme; public relations and industrial relations personnel contradicted articles in technical journals written by NCB engineers. During the strike the NCB succeeded in limiting the media agenda to picket violence and the back-to-work movement by refusing to engage in debate on technology, even in response to three documentary programmes to which members of the Working Environment Research Group made a substantial contribution.

In April 1985, after the publication of the original version of this chapter, one such documentary made by a *Newsnight* team uncovered the existence of the Miron Report (Bradshaw, 1985). The Miron Report mapped out a strategy for the NCB, based on the use of an area incentive scheme and new technology, that would weaken the power of the NUM, and in particular the power of the younger, emergent leadership of Peter Heathfield, Arthur Scargill, Michael McGahey and Lawrence Daly.

Further analysis has narrowed the earlier range of estimated job losses and assessed the contraction likely in each area (Winterton, 1985a). The restructuring process in Yorkshire has been studied in detail (Winterton, 1985b), and the future of individual collieries in West Yorkshire has been predicted (Winterton and Winterton, 1985). Events since the strike, including the closure by the end of 1985 of 46 collieries and workshops, have confirmed the scale of the restructuring and the processes involved. Our views on the application of systems engineering to attain NCB objectives have been reinforced.

REFERENCES

Allen, R.G.D. (1973), *Mathematical Economics*, 2nd ed., London: Macmillan.

Allen, V. L. (1981), *The Militancy of British Miners*, Shipley: Moor Press.

Babbage, C. (1832), *On The Economy of Machinery and Manufactures*, London: Kelly (Reprints of Economic Classics).

Bates, J. J. (1981), 'Inbuilt Machine Performance and Condition Testing – IMPACT', *Mining Engineer*, July, pp. 31–7.

Beer, S. (1974), *Designing Freedom*, London: Wiley.

(1975), *Platform for Change*, London: Wiley.

Beishon, J. and G. Peters (1972), *Systems Behaviour*, London: Harper and Row for the Open University Press.

Bradshaw, S. (1985), 'The Impact of High Technology on the Politics of Mining', *The Listener*, 25 April.

Braverman, H. (1974), *Labor and Monopoly Capital*, New York: Monthly Review Press.

Burns, A. (1981), *The Microchip: An Appropriate or Inappropriate Technology?* Chichester: Ellis Horwood.

(1984), *New Information Technology*, Chichester: Ellis Horwood.

Burns, A., D. Feickert, M. Newby and J. Winterton (1982), *An Interim Assessment of MINOS*, WERG Report no. 4, Working Environment Research Group, University of Bradford.

(1983), 'The Miners and New Technology', *Industrial Relations Journal*, vol. 14, no. 4, 7–20.

Burns, A., M. Newby and J. Winterton (1984a), 'New Technology and the Restructuring of Work in British Coal Mining', British Sociological Association Conference, 2–5 April, University of Bradford.

(1984b), *Second Report on MINOS*, WERG Report no. 6, Working Environment Research Group, University of Bradford.

Coal in context

Capstick, K., and M. Newby (1983), 'Dangers Behind the Showcase of Modern Technology', *Yorkshire Miner*, Christmas.

Chandler, K. W. (1978), 'MINOS – A Computer System for Control at Collieries', 2nd International Conference on Centralized Control Systems, London, March.

Clarke, F. and J. Winterton (1983), 'Coal Prep Test Case Shows MINOS Threat to Jobs', *Yorkshire Miner*, October.

Cleary, J. (1981), 'FIDO (Face Information Digested On-line) at Bold Colliery', *The Mining Engineer*, November, pp. 281–9.

Cooper, C. C. (1982), 'Improving Machine Utilization and Reliability', COMMIT 82, Computer-based Mine Management Information Technology Exhibition and Symposium, Harrogate, 8–10 December.

Dunn, R. B. (1984), 'Colliery Organization in the Future', *Mining Engineer*, May, pp. 551–5.

Feickert, D. (1979), 'Of Men and MINOS', *Computing Europe*, 22 November.

Fennelly, F. (1982), 'Coalface Machine Health', COMMIT 82, Computer-based Mine Management Information Technology Exhibition and Symposium, Harrogate, 8–10 December.

Goodrich, C. (1920), *The Frontier of Control*, London: Bell.

Hartley, D. (1979), 'The Development of Remote Monitoring and Control for Mining Systems', London: NCB.

Heath, R. H. (1969), 'The National Power Loading Agreement in the Coal Industry and Some Aspects of Workers' Control', *Trade Union Register*, pp. 185–200.

Heising, F. (1977), 'The Haus Aden Project', International Conference on Remote Control and Monitoring in Mining, vol. I, London: NCB.

Horton, E. (1983), 'Mining Techniques in the 1980s', *Mining Engineer*, February, pp. 451–5.

Lange, O. (1969), *Theory of Reproduction and Accumulation*, Oxford: Pergamon.

(1970), *Introduction to Economic Cybernetics*, Oxford: Pergamon.

Lefevre, A. (1977), 'Remote Control of Mine Machinery', International Conference on Remote Control and Monitoring in Mining, vol. 1, London: NCB.

Marx, K. (1887), *Capital*, vol. 1, London: Lawrence and Wishart.

Mining Department (1983), *Production and Productivity Bulletin*, no. 15, September, London: NCB.

(1984), *Production and Productivity Bulletin*, no. 16, March, London: NCB.

Mining Research and Development Establishment (1981), *Annual Report*, London: NCB.

(1983a), *Annual Report*, London: NCB.

(1983b), *Coalface Automation*, London: NCB.

Monopolies and Mergers Commission (1983), *National Coal Board: A Report on Efficiency and Costs in the Development, Production and Supply of Coal by the NCB*, 2 vols., Cmnd. 8920, London: HMSO.

Morris, I. H. and G. W. Gray (1977), 'Environmental Monitoring in the United Kingdom', International Conference on Remote Control and Monitoring in Mining, vol. 1, London: NCB.

Olaf, J. (1977), 'Automation in Coal Mining', International Conference on Remote Control and Monitoring in Mining, vol. I, London: NCB.

Ormerod, R. (1983), 'Corporate Planning and its Use of O.R. in the N.C.B.: A Personal View', *Journal of the Operational Research Society*, vol. 34, no. 6, pp. 461–7.

Phillips, A. W. (1954), 'Stabilization Policy in a Closed Economy', *Economic Journal*, vol. 64.

Plackett, M. W., R. J. Ormerod and F. J. Toft (1982), 'The National Coal Board Strategic Model', *European Journal of Operational Research*, vol. 10, pp. 351–60.

Public Relations Department (1983), 'University Report on Coal Mining Technology Attacked', Press Release, 21 May, NCB.

Schumacher, E. F. (1960), 'Coal – the Next Fifty Years', in *Britain's Coal*, NUM Study Conference, March 25–26.

Steiner, D. X. and J. H. Hvidsten (1978), 'A Digital Control Strategy Applied to Conveyor-mounted Shearers', London: NCB.

Thring, M. (1979), quoted in 'Making the Pitman an Electronic Engineer', *Guardian*, 11 October.

Tregelles, P. and D. K. Barham (1979), 'Progress with the Guidance of Anderton Shearer Loaders in the UK', 108th AIME Annual Meeting, New Orleans.

Trist, E. L. and K. W. Bamforth (1951), 'Some Social and Psychological Consequences of the Longwall Method of Coal Getting', *Human Relations*, vol. 4, no. 1, pp. 3–38.

Ure, A. (1835), *The Philosophy of Manufactures*, London.

Wainwright, H. and D. Elliott (1982), *The Lucas Plan*, London: Allison and Busby.

Winterton, J. (1981), 'The Trend of Strikes in British Coal Mining, 1949–79', *Industrial Relations Journal*, vol. 12, no. 6, pp. 10–20.

 (1984a), 'Security Blankets', *New Statesman*, 6 April.

 (1984b), 'How the Incentive Scheme has Cheated the Miners', *Tribune*, 6 April.

 (1985a), 'The Source of the Crisis', Coalfield Communities Campaign, Working Paper no. 1.

 (1985b), 'Investment and Jobs in Coal: The Implications of NCB Restructuring Policies for Yorkshire', Town and Country Planning Association Conference, 'Economic Prospects for the Coalfields: A Case Study of the Yorkshire Coalfield, Sheffield', 22 November.

Winterton, J. and J. Rentoul (1984), 'Confronting the New Technology', *New Statesman*, 20 January.

Winterton, J. and R. Winterton (1985), *The Implications of NCB Restructuring Policies for West Yorkshire*, West Yorkshire Metropolitan County Council Report.

Wolfenden, J. R. and D. Hartley (1977), 'Horizon Control System Designs for Longwall Face Machines', International Conference on Remote Control and Monitoring in Mining, vol. I, London: NCB.

Wood, S. (ed.) (1982), *The Degradation of Work*, London: Hutchinson.

Contributors

Berry, Tony – Lecturer in Management Control at Manchester Business School. He began a career in the aircraft industry working with both the British Aircraft Corporation and then the Boeing Company before joining MBS as a member of a research team investigating management control. He was Director of the Operational Management Course for four years and was Director of the ITP, an 8-week international management teacher development programme, in 1980 and 1981. He was Director of Studies of the MBA programme for 1982–5. He is an ex-editor of *Management Education and Development*, and has published papers and articles on management control and on management development.

Burns, Alan – Lecturer in Computer Science at the University of Bradford. He graduated from the University of Sheffield with a BSc. (Hons) in Pure Mathematics and Computer Science in 1974, and obtained a D.Phil. in Computer Science from the University of York in 1978. He has an active interest in the design of energy efficiency systems, community education programmes, general-purpose software, and decision support systems. He is the author of *The Microchip: Appropriate or Inappropriate Technology?* and edited *New Information Technology*.

Capps, Teresa – From 1980 to 1985 she taught and pursued research at Sheffield Polytechnic and the University of Sheffield. Prior to 1980 she worked as a management accountant in the brewing industry. In 1985 she returned to that industry to take up a senior financial position.

Cooper, David – Price Waterhouse Professor of Accounting and Finance in the Department of Management Sciences at UMIST. He has held appointments at the Universities of Manchester, East Anglia, British Columbia, California (Berkeley), Copenhagen and Uppsala. In 1985 he chaired the independent Inquiry on the Proposed Closure of Polkemmet Colliery. As well as his interests in the coal industry, he is currently involved in an international research project on accounting regulation as corporatist control.

Cutler, Tony – Senior Lecturer in Sociology at Middlesex Polytechnic. Joint author of *Marx's Capital and Capitalism Today* with B. Hindness, P. Hirst and A. Hussain (2 vols., RKP, 1977 and 1978) and of *Justice and Predictability* with D. Nye (Macmillan, 1983).

Davies, Gavyn – Chief UK Economist, Goldman Sachs. When the original paper was written he was Chief UK Economist, Simon and Coates.

Fothergill, Stephen – Lecturer in Economics at the University of Reading. Formerly Research Associate in the Department of Land Economy, University of Cambridge. He has extensive research experience in the field of urban and regional development, and was co-author of the NUM's evidence to the Sizewell B nuclear power station inquiry.

Glyn, Andrew – Fellow and Tutor in Economics, Corpus Christi College, Oxford and associate member, Oxford University Institute of Economics and Statistics.

Haslam, Colin – Lecturer in the Business Studies Department at North East London Polytechnic. He has recently been jointly involved in a number of projects on the coal, steel and car industries. He has published articles in *Account Magazine* and *Economy and Society*.

Hopper, Trevor – Lecturer in Accounting at the University of Manchester. He graduated in Business Administration from the University of Bradford and obtained an M.Phil. from the University of Aston. After a short period working as a management accountant he lectured at Wolverhampton Polytechnic and the University of Sheffield. He was secretary of the Management Control Workshop Group for five years.

Contributors

Kerevan, George – Senior Lecturer in Economics at Napier College, Edinburgh. He has written and broadcast widely on the Scottish economy and the management of nationalised industries. He is Convenor of the Economic Development Committee of Edinburgh District Council and a member of the Council of the Edinburgh International Festival.

Kung, Peter W. T. – After graduating in Economics from the Department of Economics and Business Studies of the University of Liverpool in 1984, he worked as a research assistant in the same department. He is currently pursuing a career in accounting.

Lowe, Tony – Retired from the Professorship of Accounting and Financial Management at the University of Sheffield in October 1986. He is currently the Research Associate to an ESRC-sponsored project on 'Accounting Regulation as Corporatist Control'. He intends maintaining his research interests in accounting and related aspects upon which he has published prolifically over three decades.

Metcalf, David – Professor of Industrial Relations, London School of Economics. When the original paper was written he was Professor of Economics, University of Kent.

Minford, Patrick – Edward Gonner Professor of Applied Economics, University of Liverpool. Prior to this he held various economic advisory positions within the Treasury, to industry and to overseas governments. He has written widely on trade and the economy and has contributed actively to the macroeconomic policy debate within the UK. In 1979, he started the Liverpool Research Group in Macroeconomics, which publishes quarterly forecasts of the UK economy and commentaries on domestic and international policy issues.

Newby, Martin – Lecturer in Operational Research and Statistics in the Schools of Industrial Technology and Mathematical Sciences at the University of Bradford. He gained a BSc. and MSc. in mathematics at the University of Sussex and a Ph.D. in reliability theory from Bradford

University. After working as an operational research scientist for Rowntree Mackintosh he joined Bradford University in 1974. His research interests are in reliability, statistics and systems theory; he is involved in adult and continuing education.

Robinson, Bill – Educated at Oxford, and did his postgraduate training at Sussex University and the London School of Economics. After a brief stint with IBM he worked as a professional economist in Whitehall (Cabinet Office and HM Treasury) and in Brussels (European Commission). He joined the London Business School in 1978 and has been editor of *Economic Outlook* and *Exchange Rate Outlook* since 1979. He is an advisor to the Treasury and Civil Service Committee of the House of Commons and is a regular speaker, both in the UK and overseas, on UK economic prospects and on exchange rates.

Saville, Richard – Lecturer in Economic History at St Andrew's University in Scotland. He is the author of numerous works on economic themes and edited *The Economic Development of Modern Scotland 1950–80* (John Donald, 1985). In 1985 he wrote, with George Kerevan and Debra Percival, *The Case for Retaining a European Coal Industry*, commissioned by the British Labour Group and the Socialist Group of the European Parliament in response to the EEC Coal Directorate's plans announced in 1985.

Williams, John – Head of the Department of Economic and Social History and Sociology at the University College of Wales, Aberystwyth. He has written widely on Welsh industrial and social history, and on the economic history of modern Britain. He recently published *A Digest of Welsh Historical Statistics* (2 vols., 1985, Welsh Office).

Williams, Karel – Teaches economics and social history at the University College of Wales, Aberystwyth. He has written on nineteenth-century social history and on the current British economic crisis. Publications include *From Pauperism to Poverty* (RKP, 1981) and with John Williams, *Why Are the British Bad at Manufacturing?* (RKP, 1983).

Contributors

Winterton, Jonathan – Lecturer in Industrial Technology in the School of Industrial Technology and Management at Bradford University. He graduated in Industrial Technology after an engineering apprenticeship and took a Master's degree in industrial relations. He teaches industrial relations at the Universities of Bradford and Leeds and has been involved in NUM education since 1979.

Index

academics' interventions into the dispute, 17–19
acid rain; see ecological issues
advanced gas-cooled reactors (AGRs), 180–4, 229–30, 237, 242, 243, 245, 249
advanced technology mining (ATM), 270
alternative energy sources, 239
area incentive schemes (AIS), 263
Ashfordsby Colliery, 166
Australian deep-mining; output, 207; costs, 133, 195
automation of coal operations, 13, 73, 123, 132, 253–74

Babbage, C., 256
Bain, A. D., 121
balance of payments; effect of miners' strike, 91; and future coal imports, 176
Bamforth, K. W., 255
Barnsley West Side Complex, 259, 260
Barony Colliery, 127, 134, 151
Bates Colliery, 76
Beer, S., 255, 256
Benn, Tony, 225
Berry, A. J., 5, 6, 15, 16, 18, 79, 104–5, 113, 119, 124, 127, 129, 137, 167
Bilston Glen Colliery, 126, 129
Bird, J., 76
Blyth Valley Borough Council, 76
Blyth Valley Colliery, 76
Bougen, P., 19
boundaries of organisations, 3, 16, 255
Braverman, H., 274
British Leyland, 165, 167
British Rail; cost of strike, 48–9, 89–90; effect of reduced coal output, 128
British Steel Corporation; coal demand, 150, 155, 164; contraction strategy, 167–8; cost of coal strike, 50; see also Ravenscraig Steel Works

bureaucratisation of NCB, 254
Burns, A., 13, 14, 18, 256, 272

Campaign for Coal, 274
Capps, T., 5, 6, 15, 16, 18, 79, 104–5, 113, 119, 124, 127, 129, 137, 167
Capstick, K., 259
Cardowan Colliery, 120, 132, 134, 136–43, 156
cash limits, on NCB by government, 29–31, 124, 166, 171, 196, 212, 224
Central Electricity Generating Board (CEGB); cost of miners' strike, 46–7, 89–90; evidence to Sizewell B Inquiry, 13, 226, 230–1, 235–7; future demand for coal, 172, 240–1, 244–6; *Medium Term Development Plan*, 231, 238, 243; 'merit order' supply scheme, 178, 245; see also transfer price of coal, electricity generating costs
Central Planning Unit (CPU) of NCB, 254–5, 258, 268
Central Region of Scotland, effect of Polmaise Colliery closure, 148
Chandler, K. W., 257, 258
channel link for electricity; see France
Chapelcross 'power station', 234–5
Cleary, J., 262–3
Coalfield Communities Campaign, 249
coal-fired power stations; future openings and closures, 238, 245; see also electricity generating costs
Coal Industry Act (1980), 268; (1983), 122
colliery closures; criteria of NCB, 25, 26, 36, 167; public justification, 95–6, 107, 158, 167; rate of closure, 26, 29, 31, 41–2, 72, 148–50, 162, 164, 204–6, 214, 222; see also exhaustion of collieries, strategy of NCB

283

Index

284

Index

285

Index

marginal costs of coal production, 51–2, 100, 113–15, 196, 206, 208, 210–15, 218–22

market price of coal, 6, 8, 10–11, 32, 69–71, 98, 109–12, 223–4, 231; *see also* transfer price of coal

Mason, N., 232–3, 249

Massey Ferguson, 121

media, treatment of economic issues, 16, 105–6, 115, 274–5

Medium Term Development Plan of CEGB, 231, 238, 243

Medium Term Financial Strategy of UK government, 216

Metcalf, D., 7, 10, 11, 17, 53, 62, 66–7, 78, 139, 161, 210

MIDAS, machine information display and automation system, 265–6, 270

Midlands coalfield, 168, 253

Minford, P., 7, 10, 17, 67–9

Mining Research and Development Establishment (MRDE), 257, 258, 264

MINOS, mine operating system, 259–62, 264–74

Miron Report, 274–5

Monktonhall Colliery, 126, 129, 134, 151

Monopolies and Mergers Commission; report on CEGB (1981), 177–8, 179, 226–7; report on coal (1983), 12, 28, 37, 43, 52, 63, 96, 100, 108, 109, 110, 113, 119, 120–4, 127, 128, 130, 132, 138, 143, 154, 161, 162, 163, 165–6, 175, 204, 206, 208, 213, 257, 263, 268–9

Morgan, Rev. J. I., 76

Morpeth, D., 6, 15, 105

Mouritsen, J., 104–5

multiplier effect of mining redundancies; *see* employment projections

National Coal Board *Report* for 1983/4, 165, 166, 172

National Coal Board Strategic Model, 254–5

National Economic Development Council, 153

National Union of Mineworkers (NUM); involvement in planning, 19–20, 253–4, 261–2; pit-closure criteria, 25, 30, 36, 44, 76, 107–9, 162, 164, 274; response to automation, 272–5; use of accounting information, 106, 107, 249

nationalised industries; capital charges, 30, 44, 124–5; contraction patterns, 167; relationship to government, 122–4, 158, 165; reorganisations, 120–1

net present value (NPV); *see* discounted

cash flows, social cost benefit analysis of coal mines

Newby, M., 13, 14, 18, 256, 259, 272

North Sea gas, effect on coal demand, 198–203

North Sea oil revenues; use by government, 74; effects of future decline, 176

Nottingham coalfield, 168, 253, 268

Nuclear Engineering International, 184

nuclear power stations, 177–87; construction time, 179–81, 231; costs, *see* electricity generating costs; decommissioning costs, 177; demotion in 'merit order', 245–6; estimated lives, 232, 237, 244–5; performance rating, 179–84, 230–1

objectives of organisations, 255–6

O'Donnell, K., 9

Ogden, S., 19

oil prices, 32, 239; relation to coal prices, 196–203, 214–24

oil-fired power stations; replacement and conversion to coal, 244–5; *see also* electricity generating costs

Operational Research Executive (ORE) of NCB, 254–5

opportunity costs of coal mining, 7–11, 29–30, 32, 37–8, 44–5, 53–5, 61–3, 73–4, 123, 211–12

organisation structure of NCB, 120–1

Ormerod, R. J., 254

output per manshift (OMS); *see* productivity of UK coal-getting

pensioners, cheap coal, 155

Philips and Drew, 91

Plackett, M. W., 254

Plan for Coal, 12, 26, 41–2, 112, 119, 123, 143, 149, 150, 162–5, 170, 195, 200, 203

plutonium production and nuclear policy, 234–5

Poland, supplies of coal, 98, 208

policing, costs due to miners' strike, 49, 90

Polkemmet Colliery, 14, 20, 76, 127, 129, 134, 156, 158

Polmaise Colliery, 64, 65, 120, 127, 134, 143–8, 156, 159

port facilities for coal imports, 98, 176

pressurised water reactors (PWRs), 180–4, 230–4, 238–9

price elasticity of demand for energy; long run, 200–1, 217; UK pricing policy, *see* energy policy of UK government

price of coal, *see* demand for coal, market

Index

Index